Crime and Society

Much of a society's resources are devoted to dealing with, or preparing for the possibility of, crime. The dominance of concerns about crime also hint at the broader implications that offending has for many different facets of society. They suggest that rather than being an outlawed subset of social activity, crime is an integrated aspect of societal processes. This book reviews some of the direct and indirect social impacts of criminality, proposing that this is worthwhile, not just in terms of understanding crime, but also because of how it elucidates more general social considerations. A range of studies that examine the interactions between crime and society are brought together, drawing on a wide range of countries and cultures including India, Israel, Nigeria, Turkey, and the USA, as well as the UK and Ireland. They include contributions from many different social science disciplines, which, taken together, demonstrate that the implicit and direct impact of crime is very widespread indeed.

The chapters in this book were originally published as a special issue of *Contemporary Social Science*.

Donna Youngs is a Reader in Psychology at the University of Huddersfield, UK, where she directs the doctoral program in Investigative Psychology. She has published on many aspects of criminality and criminal psychology. Her particular interests are in criminals' personal narratives and their experiences of crime.

Contemporary Issues in Social Science
Series editor: David Canter, University of Huddersfield, UK

Contemporary Social Science, the journal of the **Academy of Social Sciences**, is an interdisciplinary, cross-national journal which provides a forum for disseminating and enhancing theoretical, empirical and/or pragmatic research across the social sciences and related disciplines. Reflecting the objectives of the Academy of Social Sciences, it emphasises the publication of work that engages with issues of major public interest and concern across the world, and highlights the implications of that work for policy and professional practice.

The *Contemporary Issues in Social Science* book series contains the journal's most cutting-edge special issues. Leading scholars compile thematic collections of articles that are linked to the broad intellectual concerns of *Contemporary Social Science,* and as such these special issues are an important contribution to the work of the journal. The series editor works closely with the guest editor(s) of each special issue to ensure they meet the journal's high standards. The main aim of publishing these special issues as a series of books is to allow a wider audience of both scholars and students from across multiple disciplines to engage with the work of *Contemporary Social Science* and the Academy of Social Sciences.

Most recent titles in the series:

Social Death
Questioning the life-death boundary
Edited by Jana Králová and Tony Walter

International and Interdisciplinary Insights into Evidence and Policy
Edited by Linda Hantrais, Ashley Thomas Leniham and Susanne MacGregor

The People and the State
Twenty-First Century Protest Movement
Edited by Thomas O'Brien

Civic Engagement
Edited by Robin G. Milne

Exploring Social Inequality in the 21st Century
New Approaches, New Tools, and Policy Opportunities
Edited by Jennifer Jarman and Paul Lambert

Political Activism across the Life Course
Edited by Sevasti-Melissa Nolas, Christos Varvantakis and Vinnarasan Aruldoss

Crime and Society
Edited by Sevasti-Melissa Nolas, Christos Varvantakis and Vinnarasan Aruldoss

Crime and Society

Edited by
Donna Youngs

LONDON AND NEW YORK

First published 2018
by Routledge
2 Park Square, Milton Park, Abingdon, Oxon, OX14 4RN, UK

and by Routledge
711 Third Avenue, New York, NY 10017, USA

Routledge is an imprint of the Taylor & Francis Group, an informa business

© 2018 Academy of Social Sciences

All rights reserved. No part of this book may be reprinted or reproduced or utilised in any form or by any electronic, mechanical, or other means, now known or hereafter invented, including photocopying and recording, or in any information storage or retrieval system, without permission in writing from the publishers.

Trademark notice: Product or corporate names may be trademarks or registered trademarks, and are used only for identification and explanation without intent to infringe.

British Library Cataloguing in Publication Data
A catalogue record for this book is available from the British Library

ISBN 13: 978-0-8153-8288-1

Typeset in Times New Roman
by RefineCatch Limited, Bungay, Suffolk

Publisher's Note
The publisher accepts responsibility for any inconsistencies that may have arisen during the conversion of this book from journal articles to book chapters, namely the possible inclusion of journal terminology.

Disclaimer
Every effort has been made to contact copyright holders for their permission to reprint material in this book. The publishers would be grateful to hear from any copyright holder who is not here acknowledged and will undertake to rectify any errors or omissions in future editions of this book.

Contents

Citation Information vii
Notes on Contributors ix

Introduction: Crime and society 1
David Canter and Donna Youngs

1. Fragile masculinity: social inequalities in the narrative frame and discursive construction of a mass shooter's autobiography/manifesto 7
 Chrystie Myketiak

2. Pride and prejudice: the context of reception for Muslims in the United States 22
 Elif Bulut

3. Does Islam deter crime in a secular Islamic country? The case of Turkey 33
 Ozden Ozbay

4. Is there a natural rate of crime in India? 52
 Jagadish Prasad Sahu and Chandan Kumar Mohanty

5. Use of drugs and criminal behaviour among female adolescent prostitutes in Lagos metropolis, Nigeria 65
 Sogo Angel Olofinbiyi, Babatunde Ajayi Olofinbiyi and John Lekan Oyefara

6. A reason for reasonable doubt in social justice: the weight of poverty, race and gender in lopsided homicide case clearances outcomes 80
 Alonzo DeCarlo

7. A consideration of the social impact of cybercrime: examples from hacking, piracy, and child abuse material online 91
 Mary Aiken, Ciaran Mc Mahon, Ciaran Haughton, Laura O'Neill and Edward O'Carroll

8. The impacts of organised crime in the EU: some preliminary thoughts on measurement difficulties 110
 Michael Levi

9. Homelessness among formerly incarcerated African American men: contributors and consequences 121
 Myia C. Egleton, Diari Marcus Banigo, Branden A. McLeod and Halaevalu F.O. Vakalahi

CONTENTS

10. An inside look at Israeli police critical incident first responders 132
    Brenda Geiger

11. Tackling sexual violence at UK universities: a case study 150
    Graham Towl

    Index 157

Citation Information

The chapters in this book were originally published in *Contemporary Social Science*, volume 11, issue 4 (December 2016). When citing this material, please use the original page numbering for each article, as follows:

Introduction
Crime and society
David Canter and Donna Youngs
Contemporary Social Science, volume 11, issue 4 (December 2016) pp. 283–288

Chapter 1
Fragile masculinity: social inequalities in the narrative frame and discursive construction of a mass shooter's autobiography/manifesto
Chrystie Myketiak
Contemporary Social Science, volume 11, issue 4 (December 2016) pp. 289–303

Chapter 2
Pride and prejudice: the context of reception for Muslims in the United States
Elif Bulut
Contemporary Social Science, volume 11, issue 4 (December 2016) pp. 304–314

Chapter 3
Does Islam deter crime in a secular Islamic country? The case of Turkey
Ozden Ozbay
Contemporary Social Science, volume 11, issue 4 (December 2016) pp.315–333

Chapter 4
Is there a natural rate of crime in India?
Jagadish Prasad Sahu and Chandan Kumar Mohanty
Contemporary Social Science, volume 11, issue 4 (December 2016) pp. 334–346

Chapter 5
Use of drugs and criminal behaviour among female adolescent prostitutes in Lagos metropolis, Nigeria
Sogo Angel Olofinbiyi, Babatunde Ajayi Olofinbiyi and John Lekan Oyefara
Contemporary Social Science, volume 11, issue 4 (December 2016) pp. 347–361

CITATION INFORMATION

Chapter 6
A reason for reasonable doubt in social justice: the weight of poverty, race and gender in lopsided homicide case clearances outcomes
Alonzo DeCarlo
Contemporary Social Science, volume 11, issue 4 (December 2016) pp. 362–372

Chapter 7
A consideration of the social impact of cybercrime: examples from hacking, piracy, and child abuse material online
Mary Aiken, Ciaran Mc Mahon, Ciaran Haughton, Laura O'Neill and Edward O'Carroll
Contemporary Social Science, volume 11, issue 4 (December 2016) pp. 373–391

Chapter 8
The impacts of organised crime in the EU: some preliminary thoughts on measurement difficulties
Michael Levi
Contemporary Social Science, volume 11, issue 4 (December 2016) pp. 392–402

Chapter 9
Homelessness among formerly incarcerated African American men: contributors and consequences
Myia C. Egleton, Diari Marcus Banigo, Branden A. McLeod and Halaevalu F.O. Vakalahi
Contemporary Social Science, volume 11, issue 4 (December 2016) pp. 403–413

Chapter 10
An inside look at Israeli police critical incident first responders
Brenda Geiger
Contemporary Social Science, volume 11, issue 4 (December 2016) pp. 414–431

Chapter 11
Tackling sexual violence at UK universities: a case study
Graham Towl
Contemporary Social Science, volume 11, issue 4 (December 2016) pp. 432–437

For any permission-related enquiries please visit:
http://www.tandfonline.com/page/help/permissions

Notes on Contributors

Mary Aiken is an Adjunct Associate Professor at University College Dublin, Ireland, and Academic Advisor (Psychology) to the European Cyber Crime Centre (EC3) at Europol. She is a Lecturer in Criminology and Research Fellow at the School of Law, Middlesex University, UK, a Fellow of the Society for Chartered IT Professionals, and a Sensemaking Fellow at the IBM Network Science Research Centre. She is also a member of the Hague Justice Portal advisory board and Director of the Cyberpsychology Research Network.

Diari Marcus Banigo is a Clinical Supervisor with Baltimore County Department of Social Services and Director of Claribel Hart Associates Inc. Her scholarship interests are issues related to veterans of war and homelessness.

Elif Bulut earned her PhD in Sociology from Georgia State University, USA. Her principal research interests are in the areas of immigrant integration, racial, ethnic, and gender inequalities. She was based at Ipek University, Turkey.

David Canter is Editor in Chief of *Contemporary Social Science*, Director of the International Research Centre for Investigative Psychology at the University of Huddersfield, UK, and Emeritus Professor at the University of Liverpool, UK. He has published widely on many aspects of applied and social psychology over the last 45 years.

Alonzo DeCarlo is the Division Chair of Social and Behavioral Sciences at Benedictine University at Springfield, USA. He is also Associate Vice Chancellor for Academic Affairs at Elizabeth State University, USA. His research interest involves studying maladaptive aggressive behaviour with African-American adolescents, policy collaboration models for mental health and juvenile justice stakeholders, and inter-racial social justice dynamics in judicial, policy, and criminal justice affairs.

Myia C. Egleton, PhD, is an Enforcement Analyst at the Department of Housing and Urban Development, USA. Her areas of scholarship are the well-being of women and children living in poverty, housing and health disparities, and homelessness.

Brenda Geiger is currently a Full Professor in Criminal Justice at the Western Galilee College, Israel. She earned two PhDs in Educational Psychology and Legal Philosophy from SUNYA, USA. Her research interest focuses on violence (physical, emotional/verbal and sexual) against women, and children (verbal abuse) and resistance. More recently Geiger has been focusing on immigration, cultural conflict, crime, and terrorism.

Ciaran Haughton is a Research Psychologist at the Centre for Abuse & Trauma Studies (CATS) at Middlesex University, UK.

NOTES ON CONTRIBUTORS

Michael Levi is Professor of Criminology at the School of Social Sciences, Cardiff University, UK. He is an advisor to Europol, the European Commission, and the UK government, and has published a study of the policing of economic cybercrimes and the uninintended consequences of anti-money laundering measures. He is currently researching insider cybercrime, fraud against vulnerable adults by family and friends, and other aspects of economic crime

Branden A. McLeod, PhD, is an Assistant Professor at Jane Addams College of Social Work at University of Illinois at Chicago, USA. His areas of scholarship are: fatherhood among Black fathers and families, reentry into society from incarceration, and criminal justice reform.

Ciaran McMahon is an Information Security Consultant and award-winning academic psychologist from Ireland. He is primarily interested in the psychology of technology, from ancient methods of writing to modern social media.

Chandan Kumar Mohanty is a PhD candidate at the Centre for Economic Studies and Planning, School of Social Sciences, Jawaharlal Nehru University, India. He is also working as a Senior Research Analyst at the Institute of Economic Growth, Delhi. His research interests include economics of crime, political economics, and labour economics.

Chrystie Myketiak is Senior Lecturer in English Language at the University of Brighton, UK, where she researches the relationship between language, power and inequalities, specifically discourses of gender and sexualities in text. She holds a PhD in Linguistics and Computer Science from the University of London and was previously an EPSRC postdoctoral researcher at Queen Mary University of London.

Edward O'Carroll was a Research Assistant at the RCSI CyberPsychology Research Centre, Ireland.

Laura O'Neill was a Research Assistant at the RCSI CyberPsychology Research Centre, Ireland.

Babatunde Ajayi Olofinbiyi is a Senior Lecturer/consultant obstetrician, gynaecologist and minimal access surgeon at Ekiti State University College of Medicine, Nigeria. He is a life member of World Laparoscopic Surgeons. His main field of study is materno-fetal medicine with special interest in adolescent reproductive health and risk factors.

Sogo Angel Olofinbiyi is a Lecturer and PhD candidate in the Department of Criminology and Forensic Studies at the University of Kwazulu-Natal, South Africa. He is an active member of Canadian Criminal Justice association, with research interests focused on terrorism, counter-terrorism, radicalization, peace and conflict studies, forensic investigation (Crime and Intelligence Analysis), victim studies, political crimes and related offenses.

John Lekan Oyefara teaches demography, social statistics and social research methods at the University of Lagos, Nigeria. He is an erudite scholar and a recipient of various research grants and fellowships within and outside Nigeria. Rooted and grounded in ontological, epistemological and other philosophical ideologies that guide pedagogical discourses and debates in the behavioural sciences globally, he is one of the leading social scientists in the African continent.

Ozden Ozbay works in the Faculty of Communication at Cumhuriyet University-Sivas, Turkey. His areas of interest are causes of crime and criminological theories. His recent articles appeared in *International Journal of Offender Therapy & Comparative Criminology, Journal of Criminal Justice* as well as some Turkish journals.

NOTES ON CONTRIBUTORS

Jagadish Prasad Sahu is a PhD candidate at the Centre for Economic Studies and Planning, School of Social Sciences, Jawaharlal Nehru University, India. His research interests include macroeconomics, development economics and economics of crime.

Graham Towl is a Professor of Forensic Psychology at the Psychology Department, Durham University, UK. He Chaired the Durham University Sexual Violence Task Force as PVC. He is an expert on prisoner suicide and risk assessment. He is an experienced Senior Civil Servant, academic, and practitioner, and he is currently on a research sabbatical.

Halaevalu F.O. Vakalahi, PhD, is a Professor and the Associate Dean in the School of Social Work at Morgan State University, USA. Her areas of scholarship are: Pacific Islander culture and community, and Women of Color in academia.

Donna Youngs is a Reader in Psychology at the University of Huddersfield, UK, where she directs the doctoral program in Investigative Psychology. She has published on many aspects of criminality and criminal psychology. Her particular interests are in criminals' personal narratives and their experiences of crime.

Crime and society

David Canter and Donna Youngs

Much of society's resources are devoted to dealing with, or preparing for the possibility of, crime. The dominance of concerns about crime also hints at the broader implications that offending has for many different facets of society. They suggest that rather than being an outlawed subset of social activity crime is an integrated aspect of societal processes. As an introduction to this themed issue of *Contemporary Social Science,* a brief review is undertaken of some of the direct and indirect social impacts of criminality, proposing that this is worthwhile, not just in terms of understanding crime but also because of how it elucidates more general social considerations. A range of studies that examine the interactions between crime and society are brought together drawing on a wide range of countries and cultures, India, Israel, Nigeria, Turkey and the USA, as well as Britain and Ireland. They include contributions from many different social science disciplines, which complement each other. Taken together the 11 papers reviewed do demonstrate that the implicit and direct impact of crime is very widespread indeed.

Introduction

Although most citizens in developed Western societies have relatively little direct contact with crime as victims and even fewer as offenders, criminality reaches out to influence most aspects of people's daily lives. Criminology and related social science disciplines rarely examine these broader aspects, yet a moments consideration reveals how much of societal processes are geared to dealing with crime. Would large-scale police forces be necessary if they only had to deal with crowd and traffic control? Would a vast judiciary and all their related employees in support be necessary if they just needed to deal with family disputes and civil proceedings? Then there is the insurance industry and the financial activity which builds on it. Would it be so commercially successful if its clients felt no need to insure against crime? Television drama, of course, would be impoverished if it could not upload a nightly diet of murder and mayhem. Factual broadcasting also has a prominent stream reporting on criminality.

These considerations show how much of society's resources are devoted to dealing with, or preparing for the possibility of, crime. But they also hint at the broader implications that crime has for many different facets of society. They suggest that rather than being an outlawed subset of social activity crime is an integrated aspect of societal processes. Therefore consideration of all the direct and indirect social impacts of criminality is worthwhile, not just in terms of understanding crime but also because of how it elucidates more general social considerations.

A range of studies that examine the interactions between crime and society are brought together in this current issue of *Contemporary Social Science*. The studies draw on a wide range of countries and cultures, India, Israel, Nigeria, Turkey and the USA, as well as Britain and Ireland. They include contributions from many different social science disciplines, which complement each other building a holistic picture to illustrate:

- The crucial social and social psychological aspects of crime, which include personal attitudes as well as the broader societal context.
- The investigation and management of crime. This increasingly includes careful consideration of the forms that crime is taking in contemporary society.
- The aftermath of crime, both for those who are convicted as well as those who have to deal directly with the consequences, is an important but too rarely examined area.
- Approaches to tackling all of these issues can be informed by social science perspectives that complement the often limited approaches of law enforcement.

Crime as a reflection of society

At the heart of criminal activity is an individual carrying out illegal activity. Understanding the processes that move and shape that activity are therefore crucial to any consideration of crime and society. When the crimes considered are of the most heinous kind, such as the mass shootings examined by Myketiak (2016), then it is tempting to assume that there are unique individual aspects of the culprit that are the cause. Yet as Myketiak demonstrates, the views of the perpetrator she studied are deeply embedded in his reactions to social and societal processes. His extremely low self-esteem is related to the multiple social inequalities he believes he has experienced.

A recent issue of *Contemporary Social Science* is devoted to the many different inequalities that abound and their wide-ranging consequences. But Myketiak's in-depth study of a mass shooter demonstrates how these inequalities are internalised by an individual to influence his feelings of low-self worth. Society cannot be blamed for his violent actions, but the social inequalities he perceives go some way to explain his developing anger and frustration.

The other side of this experience are public attitudes to minorities that influence their experiences. Bulut's (2016) review of prejudice towards Muslims shines an interesting light on the basis for such attitudes. She reveals that, contrary to commonly held views, widespread negative attitudes towards Muslims are not based on fear of violence in the wake of terrorist attacks, notably those of 9/11, but rather the view that the American way of life is the best and any sub-culture that is different from that is a threat to the traditional American values. It is therefore a lack of contact with Muslims and a belief that they are fundamentally 'un-American' that gives rise to prejudice against them. Thus, the well-established finding in relation to attitudes to other ethnic minorities, that lack of contact and ignorance are usually on the basis of prejudice, is shown to be relevant today in attitudes to Moslems.

Islam is, of course, a powerful religion that provides rules that cover every aspect of daily life. These rules typically include strictures on a wide range of criminal activities. It may therefore be assumed that adherence to conventional Islamic requirements, far from leading to anti-social activity, should actually deter from crime. To study this directly Ozbay (2016) surveyed a large number of people in various locations in Turkey. Because Turkey is constitutionally a secular country although the great majority of its population is Moslem, this enables Ozbay to explore correlations between crime and religiosity. He found that there was no strong direct relationship at all. But interestingly the Islamic prohibition on alcohol did tend to relate to lower crime levels. This is no surprise in many other countries where alcohol abuse is known to fuel many aspects of criminality.

The role of a religious component in influencing criminality is one aspect of many cultural forces that shape the amount of crime in any country. It is therefore of value to explore the possibility that a country may have a 'natural' crime rate as this lends support to the view that there are many currents in any social context that support offending. This issue is explored in a statistically sophisticated manner by Jagadish Sahu (2016), looking at crime rates in India. He shows that although there are small discontinuities from time to time, there is a general trend for the crime rate to remain stable. Even examining different types of crime this stability remains, but importantly that is more likely to be the case for instrumental crimes that have a financial incentive. This raises the possibility that violent crimes may be a stronger reflection of short-term changes in society than property-related crimes.

As Sahu makes clear, the existence of a natural crime rate in India over an extended period of time raises questions about how powerful conventional deterrents, such as policing and legal processes, are likely to be. Structural forces within society appear to maintain crime levels, whether it is education, inequality, employment or other ingrained processes. It is these that must be tackled if natural crime rates are to be influenced.

The social processes that support criminal activity can be complex. This is clearly illustrated by the remarkable study by Sogo Olofinbiyi (2016) in Nigeria. Through discussions with and surveys of sex workers and those associated with them, including brothel keepers, he revealed that sex workers become involved in criminality for many of the same reasons that led them into prostitution, mainly financial gain. Many of the young women he surveyed were also drug users, but his important finding is that their use of drugs did not generate their criminal activity. Rather it was the network of contacts that sex work brought them into contact with that opened the way for a variety of criminality, even murder of clients, and these actions were typically to enhance their meagre income for prostitution.

Olofinbiyi's unusually deep study of adolescent, female sex workers in Lagos shows that once individuals drift outside of the prevailing cultural norms in order to survive that a way is opened to further illegal activity. The survival of the sub-cultures that foster sex work contributes to general patterns of criminality, being an important component of the natural crime rate. Drug use amongst these young women cannot be blamed for the criminality they drift into. They make choices that relate to their understanding of the limited opportunities available to them.

The societal challenges of investigating and managing crime

Social processes not only influence the prevalence of crime but also how it is investigated. In a salutary study of homicide clear-up rates Alonzo DeCarlo (2016) concludes 'The investigation of patterns over 10 years reveal that homicide victims who live in cities with high poverty and who happen to be young, black and male are less likely to have their case solved or cleared.' His figures show that in a city with a high poverty level the murder of an African-American is solved in a little over half the cases. This contrasts with a clear-up rate of close to 90% for Caucasian victims in small, affluent towns.

The reasons for this disparity in identifying the killer are many. They relate to the resources available to law enforcement and the relationship of the police with their communities as well as the investigative challenges that come from high levels of homicide. But these variations in clear-up rate also feed back into suspicions of the police in some communities creating a vicious loop that makes investigation even more difficult. Society thus creates a self-sustaining process that maintains challenges to the fundamental right of equal treatment before the law.

The challenges of investigations in disenfranchised communities have parallels in the rapidly growing area of cybercrime. But as Mary Aiken and her colleagues (2016) argue there are also problems of determining what is criminal and locating it. There is an important question of whether cybercrime is in effect 'old wine in new bottles', requiring updated methods for dealing with offences similar to those that have always occurred. Or is it a range of new forms of criminality that requires a radically different approach to law enforcement and detection? The extensive exploration by Aiken of what cybercrime can be indicates that it covers both established forms of offending and some novel developments.

However, central to a majority of cybercrime crime is the paradox that individuals using the internet often think of themselves as operating in a private domain, unaware that they are opening themselves up to the World Wide Web at large. This suggests that one of the challenges of dealing with many forms of cybercrime is the requirement of changing people's understanding of their place in internet society and the way that society functions. For the moment many criminals have become alert to the new opportunities for crime this novel society offers. Their victims have yet to catch up with them.

The internet with all its private, secret and 'dark' aspects provides increased opportunity for clandestine contact between criminals, but this is just one aspect of increasing globalisation of all aspects of criminality. Levi (2016) puts this into context by reviewing what is known about criminals working together in many different ways, broadly characterised as 'organised crime'. The broader social consequences of these activities are encapsulated in the estimate that these forms of crime cost the EU well over a hundred billion pounds a year of which a very large proportion is various forms of fraud. However, as Levi makes clear there are very different forms of exposure to organised crime in different countries across Europe. Therefore considerable effort is needed to clarify the varying social contexts of criminal gangs, teams and networks in order to have a co-ordinated response to the challenges they pose.

The destructive impact on society of criminality

The social processes that maintain crime and its investigation also leave their mark on the consequences of criminality. A noteworthy example of this is revealed in Egleton's (2016) study of homelessness in African-Americans who have been in prison. She shows that in addition to, and probably as a consequence of, the lack of employment and related debilitating effects of incarceration these men are very likely to find themselves without anywhere to live on leaving prison. Being homeless makes integration back into society much more difficult and increases the likelihood that these men will drift back into a crimogenic context. This is another example of the recursive societal processes that maintains levels of offending in any population.

It is not only offenders who suffer the consequences of their actions; many others are touched by them. One group that is rarely considered are those who deal directly with the immediate aftermath, especially of violent terrorist atrocities. These first responders are often assumed to be stoic heroes who have little reaction to the tragedies they deal with. However as Geiger (2016) shows in her unusual study in Israel, where sadly the experience of terrorist acts is not unusual, these first responders are indeed affected by their experiences and have to find ways of coping with them. Geiger's interviews reveal that a dominant coping mechanism is to engage with the belief that they are serving a higher power, whether this draws directly on religious beliefs or secular identification with the mission of the state.

Once again, Geiger's study shows that internalisation of cultural perspectives provides individuals with psychological resources that influence their actions. Just as the mass shooter studied by Myketiak interpreted his social context to provide a personal narrative which shaped his actions, so Geiger's first responders' view of themselves as part a greater whole helped them to cope with the tragedies they faced.

The systemic challenge of crime

The central message that emerges from all these studies is that criminality is an integral part of how society, and its culture, is constructed. Thinking of crime as generated by abnormal individuals that is the responsibility of law enforcement and the judicial system is to ignore the endemic processes that sustain it and those who deal with it on a daily basis. Therefore the innovative approach to reducing sexual abuse and violence on university campuses presented by Graham Towl (2016) is instructive in demonstrating a holistic, socially oriented approach to tackling a growing problem.

Towl's starting point is that the institution should unashamedly recognise the existence of a problem. This means addressing the unwarranted fear that such recognition will damage the institutions reputation. He shows that once the issue is out in the open prevention procedures can be put in place. These can change the overarching culture that sustains sexual violence in a university with such initiatives as bystander intervention and consent workshops. Crucially this process changes the relationship between the authorities and the students, generating a virtuous cycle that gives rise to a very different culture.

Conclusions

The extensive international coverage of the papers brought together here, from the USA to Turkey and the UK to Nigeria and India, is testament to the growing understanding across the world of the social psychological and societal process that maintain criminality and its consequences. They also demonstrate the combined value of contributions from many different social science disciplines. For example, the econometric analyses of Sahu that provide quantitative evidence of the stable levels of crime complement the sociological surveys of DeCarlo and Egleton which demonstrate the cycles that maintain offending. Despite the fact that Sahu's data are from India and DeCarlo and Egleton Carried out surveys in the USA it is not difficult to see how they relate to similar processes.

The range of studies demonstrates that crime is an aspect of society, not just the activities of a subset of individuals. This is true whether it is levels of crime associated with prostitution or variations in opportunities emerging in cyberspace. The fascination with crime is therefore an understandable exploration of how society works and the conditions under which it breaks down. To paraphrase Sigmund Freud's claim that dreams are the royal road to the unconscious, the study of crime is a main avenue to understanding what makes society function.

Disclosure statement

No potential conflict of interest was reported by the authors.

ORCID

David Canter http://orcid.org/0000-0003-899b-8250

References

Aiken, M., Mc Mahon, C., Haughton, C., O'Neill, L., & O'Carro, E. (2016). A consideration of the social impact of cybercrime: Examples from hacking, piracy, and child abuse material online. *Contemporary Social Science*. doi:10.1080/21582041.2015.1117648

Bulut, E. (2016). Pride and prejudice: The context of reception for Muslims in the United States. *Contemporary Social Science*. doi:10.1080/21582041.2016.1176243

DeCarlo, A. (2016). A reason for reasonable doubt in social justice: The weight of poverty, race and gender in lopsided homicide case clearances outcomes. *Contemporary Social Science*. doi:10.1080/21582041.2014.997275

Egleton, M. (2016). Homelessness among formerly incarcerated African-American Men: Contributors and consequences. *Contemporary Social Science*. doi:10.1080/21582041.2016.1258590

Geiger, B. (2016). An inside look at Israeli police critical incident first responders. *Contemporary Social Science*. doi:10.1080/21582041.2016.1228012

Levi, M. (2016). The impacts of organised crime in the EU: Some preliminary thoughts on measurement difficulties. *Contemporary Social Science*. doi:10.1080/21582041.2015.1090802

Myketiak, C. (2016). Fragile masculinity: Social inequalities in the narrative frame and discursive construction of a mass shooter's autobiography/manifesto. *Contemporary Social Science*. doi:10.1080/21582041.2016.1213414

Olofinbiyi, S. A., Olofinbiyi, B. A., Oyefara, J. L. (2016). Use of drugs and criminal behaviour among female adolescent prostitutes in Lagos metropolis, Nigeria. *Contemporary Social Science*. doi:10.1080/21582041.2016.1243255

Ozbay, O. (2016). Does Islam deter crime in a secular Islamic Country? The case of Turkey. *Contemporary Social Science*. doi:10.1080/21582041.2015.1008562

Sahu, J. P., Mohanty, C. K. (2016). Is there a natural rate of crime in India? *Contemporary Social Science*. doi:10.1080/21582041.2016.1249937

Towl, G. (2016). Tackling sexual violence at UK universities: A case study. *Contemporary Social Science*. doi:10.1080/21582041.2016.1260764

Fragile masculinity: social inequalities in the narrative frame and discursive construction of a mass shooter's autobiography/manifesto

Chrystie Myketiak

> Mass shootings, where four or more people are injured or killed, are widely constructed as a contemporary American social problem. This article uses critical discourse analysis guided by thematic analysis to examine the text written and distributed by a mass shooter in California in 2014. Analysis of the narrative frame and discursive construction shows that the author is motivated by a precarious or 'fragile' relationship to masculinity that involves positioning himself against both women and other minority ethnic men in a way that underscores multiple social inequalities. This work contributes to the social science of narrative by building on the connections between positioning theory and framing, which are applied to a text that contributes to debates in feminist linguistics and broader discussions of mass shootings. The findings contribute to feminist linguistics by demonstrating how a mass shooter uses language to rationalise his actions through a frame of hegemonic masculinity based on social inequalities, namely gender, race/ethnicity, sexuality and social class. Finally, this work contributes to broader discussions of mass shooters by demonstrating how this mass shooter does not construct or position himself in a way that is exceptional or extraordinary but rather hinges on a fragile form of contemporary masculinity that uses violence as a way to prove self-worth, dominance and superiority.

Introduction

On 23 May 2014, in Isla Vista, California, a young man stabbed three men to death in his apartment, shot three women at a sorority house (killing two), shot and killed one man in a deli, and then drove through the city's streets shooting and injuring several pedestrians while striking others with his car. Police found the perpetrator, Elliot Rodger, in his car, dead from a self-inflicted gunshot. In the autobiography or manifesto called *My twisted world: The story of Elliot Rodger* that he circulated on the day of the murders he alternates between referring to himself as a weak, invisible, good guy and a magnificent, superior god who posits that a beautiful, blonde girlfriend will provide him with recognition from others. As the text progresses, he gives up on the idea of a girlfriend, believing that women have persecuted him, and plans a 'Day of Retribution' to be enacted primarily towards women, whom he blames for rejecting him, and secondarily towards the men he believes that women prefer.

This article uses critical discourse analysis (CDA) grounded by thematic analysis to investigate framing and positioning within the text. While the shooter may have had mental health issues, as some newspaper articles have underscored (e.g. Nagourney, Cieply, Feuer, & Lovett, 2014; Parker, 2014), he does not emphasise his mental health in the text.[1] The research question in this data-driven analysis is how this mass shooter discursively constructs his narrative frame with respect to women and minority ethnic men, given that he refers to himself as 'half white' (Rodger, 2014, p. 17, 84), 'half-Asian' (Rodger, 2014, p. 17, 121) and 'Eurasian' (Rodger, 2014, p. 121). This question is addressed because women/sexuality are a key theme in the text, and how this theme intersects with race/ethnicity contributes to the understanding of social inequalities and cultural codes, particularly as they concern mass shootings and masculinity.

Mass shootings

Mass shootings are a serious social issue in the United States, and the Federal Bureau of Investigation (FBI) reports that the number of active shootings doubled between 2000–2006 and 2007–2013 (FBI, 2013).[2] Statistics on the number of mass shootings vary greatly: from a low of 64 between 2000 and 2013 (FBI, 2013) and a high of approximately 1000 occurring between November 2012 and October 2015, as calculated by the website www.shootingtracker.com, which crowd-sourced information before joining the non-profit organisation Gun Violence Archive in 2016. While the statistics from a crowd-sourced website/non-profit organisation may appear to lack legitimacy, they are worth mentioning because broadsheet news organisations have repeatedly used them, making the statistics appear both prominent and credible to the general public, while mass shootings are constructed as newsworthy.[3]

The variation in the data can be attributed to different definitions of 'mass shooting'. The statistics on the lower end reflect the FBI's precise definition, which is currently defined as 'three or more killings in a single incident' (FBI, 2013, p. 9), and excludes shootings that can be attributed to gang- or drug-related violence (FBI, 2013, p. 5). The federal explanation of a 'single incident' is dependent upon the event occurring within a 'confined and populated area' (FBI, 2013, p. 5). 'Confined' operates as a linguistic marker that requires the caveat that incidents occurring outside, albeit in a confined space, are included (FBI, 2013). The Gun Violence Archive uses the more flexible criteria of an incident in which at least four people are *injured* or killed, which includes the intent to kill, and the possibility that the actions are carried out over a general space. The mass shooting discussed in this article fits within the more open definition: three individuals were shot, with two killed, in one location; another was shot and killed shortly after; then more individuals were shot and injured as the perpetrator drove through the city's streets.[4] In addition to the gun violence, three people were stabbed to death and others were struck by the offender's automobile.[5]

While there is disparity in mass shooting definitions, demographics about shooters are consistent. Men commit the vast majority of these crimes, and findings show minimal variation: 95.8% from 1976 to 2011 (Fox & DeLateur, 2014), 96.2% from 2000 to 2013 (FBI, 2013) and 97.7% from 1966 to 2015 (Bridges & Tober, 2016). Although women are extremely unlikely to perpetrate mass shootings, they represent 43.4% of mass shooting victims but only 23.4% of all murder victims (Fox & Levin, 2015). As well as the over-representation men as perpetrators and of women as victims in this murder subtype, there is an obstinate association of whiteness with both mass murderers and mass shooters (Lankford, 2016); however, approximately 62% of American mass shooters are considered white (Fox & DeLateur, 2014), while 2010 Census data indicates that 74.8% of the American population identifies as white (Humes, Jones, & Ramirez, 2011).[6]

Masculinity discourses

Studies of masculinity have stressed that masculinity is a social and cultural construct that is variable across space, time and practice (e.g. Bridges, 2014; Connell, 1995; Coston & Kimmel, 2012), although not all versions are valued equally (Connell, 1995). Hegemonic masculinity derives meaning from its relationship to both femininities and non-hegemonic masculinities, and serves an orienting function, which 'require[s] all other men to position themselves in relation to it' (Connell & Messerschmidt, 2005, p. 832). With these two elements working in tandem, hegemonic masculinity supports the dominance of men and the subordination of others, particularly women.

Although hegemonic masculinity is related to issues of privilege and oppression, it is not a binary in which people are either privileged or marginalised. Individuals have multiple identities, some of which may accord them with privilege (e.g. masculinity and whiteness) and others that may not (e.g. queerness and poverty), and not all those who benefit from inequality may feel privileged (Kimmel, 2013). One reason why this may be the case is that gender can be considered 'done' (West & Zimmerman, 1987) or constituted in everyday life. If we consider hegemonic masculinity as comprised in practices, it can be gained or lost. This means that it is possible to reconceptualise 'attributes', which tend to be seen as fixed or inherent, as values that are demonstrated. If thought this way, masculinity is associated with: bravery, strength, dependability, emotional stability, rationality and economic security (Coston & Kimmel, 2012, p. 98). People can exhibit various aspects of masculinity in one interaction, or even in a conversational turn, as sociolinguists have shown (e.g. Coates, 2003; Kiesling, 2007). Masculinity can also be demonstrated through symbols as Stroud's (2012) work shows, which investigates the reasons that men carry concealed handguns, finding that they often do so out of fantasies of violence. For these men, the gun symbolises bravery, strength and the ability to protect others – grounding the wearer's ideas (and ideals) of hegemonic masculinity. As well as the physical gun, Mechling (2014) discusses how 'marksmanship' was constructed by American rifle organisations as an activity for developing characteristics associated with masculinity, such as mental alertness, competitiveness and physical fitness. The argument here is that masculinity can be understood as *practices* enacted into being that realise and constitute gender, individually and socio-culturally.

Related to hegemonic masculinity is the notion that there are a number of ways in which its 'fragility' or contestability can be exhibited in everyday life. This is heightened by what Kimmel (2013, p. xiii) describes as 'the end of the era of men's entitlement, the era in which a young man could assume, without question, it was not only "a man's world", but a straight man's world'. Examples where this can be seen include: symbols (e.g. carrying a concealed handgun to demonstrate bravery on demand, because the value [i.e. bravery] requires a prop); consumer products (e.g. tissues marketed as 'mansize' or satchels as 'manbags', implying that gender-neutral products are insufficiently masculine); communicative practices (e.g. saying 'no homo' after demonstrating affection or complimenting another man in order to stress heterosexuality, implying that compliments and affection are not hetero-masculine practices).

In other words, the fragility of masculinity is the sticky space of enacting masculinity within narrow confines, and the fear of being caught failing at demonstrating dominance and superiority, given that hegemonic masculinity is privileged and rewarded (Kimmel, 2013). Because of the relationship between the practice and its acceptance, Connell and Messerschmidt (2005) assert that hegemonic masculinity is *proved*, which is echoed by Coston and Kimmel (2012, p. 99) who state, 'masculinity often includes a preoccupation with proving gender to others'. Critical to the notion of proving masculinity is the idea that individuals' actions (e.g. the interactional level) are understood and interpreted as symbolic performances (e.g. placed within social and cultural contexts).

Theorising masculinity in a way that takes its delicacy into consideration links to 'positioning' (cf. Harré & van Lagenhove, 1999), which serves as an alternative view to the more traditional and fixed 'role' (Harré, Moghaddam, Cairnie, Rothbart, & Sabat, 2009). Positioning works as a metaphor on multiple levels when used to understand social and linguistic dynamics. Starting from the spatial metaphor that people occupy positions, and that these change (e.g. sitting/standing; professor/partner), at the socio-interactional level people communicate ideas about themselves (self-positioning) and attempt to place others. To understand masculinity within positioning theory emphasises how masculinity is constructed, flexible and dependent upon the axes of time and space.

> 'Hegemonic masculinity' is not a fixed character type, always and everywhere the same. It is, rather, the masculinity that occupies the hegemonic position in a given pattern of gender relations, a position that is always contestable ... It is the successful claim to authority, more than direct violence, that is the mark of hegemony. (Connell, 1995, p. 77)

Here Connell (1995) posits that hegemonic masculinity rests in successful claims to authority that are negotiated in social acts. Discursive research on masculinity has shown that these social practices include interaction (e.g. Andersson, 2008; Cameron, 1997; Myketiak, 2015). While Connell (1995) states that successful declarations of 'authority' characterise hegemonic masculinity more than direct violence, violence represents the most toxic claim to dominance. When a claim to hegemonic masculinity is made through violence, a co-interlocator cannot contest it in the same way that might be possible in a conversation. This is most pronounced if the person claiming hegemonic masculinity through violence murders those who could potentially challenge a claim to authority. Murder is literally, rather than figuratively, a toxic form of silencing potential dissent to masculine claims of supremacy.

Exceptionality, masculinity and mass shootings

Mass shootings represent a specific type of extraordinary violence, and there may be a tendency to frame perpetrators as extraordinary for committing these acts. Cameron and Frazer (1987) explain this process as constructing murderers as either heroes or monsters. The focus on framing murderers as exceptional has been critiqued by Downing (2013), who suggests that it allows society to see murders as anti-social subjects rather than as social products. Within mass shooter research, there is often a focus on what makes mass shooters 'different' or 'deviant' that emphasises potential cognitive distortions of mass shooters (e.g. Dutton, White, & Fogarty, 2013; Knoll, 2010a, 2010b; Meloy, Hempel, Mohandie, Shiva, & Gray, 2001; Sandberg, Oksanen, Berntzen, & Killakoski, 2014). This stress has the potential to absolve sociocultural discourses, perpetrators' interpretations of those discourses, as well as other salient information. For example, when connecting mental health concerns and mass shootings Metzl and MacLeish (2015, p. 240) focus on the information that 'up to 60% of perpetrators of mass shootings in the United States since 1970 displayed symptoms including acute paranoia, delusions, and depression before committing their crimes'. However, if the focus is on commonalities amongst offenders, there is no aspect more significant than gender, and rape is the only crime similarly gender segregated.[7] Mass shootings may be a psychological issue, but they are also a community, societal, cultural and discursive issue – and key to understanding this multi-faceted subject is recognising that shootings are overwhelmingly perpetrated by men (Kimmel, 2013).

Prioritising mental illness or cognitive distortions among mass shooters raises a number of concerns. The context leading to this emphasis must be acknowledged:

> Only when white boys began to open fire in schools did psychologists and journalists rush to [a] diagnosis of mental illness. Apparently, urban black youth who open fire in their schools are being 'rational', while suburban white boys require significant psychological analysis. (Kalish & Kimmel, 2010, p. 452)

While Kalish and Kimmel (2010) attribute this to assuming that African-American youth were considered culpable for their actions, it is possible to understand this within the context of American race relations that perpetuates racist discourses that do not treat African-American men as rational but, as Morgan (1999) notes, hyperphysical and violent. This evident in Fox and Levin (2001, pp. 73–89), who have a chapter titled 'The coming and goings of the young superpredators [sic]', which hinges on a dehumanising animalistic metaphor that evokes both hyperphysicality and violence, and is applied to primarily urban, disadvantaged, African-American youth. While the African-American shooter could be othered through a racist discourse, the 'suburban, white boy', as described by Kalish and Kimmel (2010), is universalised as 'anyone's son' (though with implied class, race and family structure bias) within the same problematic race relations.[8] To envisage 'anyone's son' as someone who commits an extraordinary act of violence elicits fear; emphasising difference through cognitive distortion allows a separation based on presumed pathology. Arguably, the emphasis on cognitive distortion further stigmatises mental illnesses by linking psychological disturbance with rage and extraordinary violence, although people with mental illnesses commit just 4% of violent crimes (Fazel & Grann, 2006). Furthermore, there is evidence that severe cognitive disturbances, such as schizophrenia, reduce the risk of violent behaviour (Brekke, Prindle, Bae, & Long, 2001; Nestor, 2002). Rather than focusing on offenders' cognitive disturbance to analyse the text to uncover psychological motives for the incident, the text in this analysis is approached as a 'cultural code' that connects discourse, crime and society.

Researchers have linked mass shooters and masculinity in various ways (e.g. Consalvo, 2003; Kalish & Kimmel, 2010; Kellner, 2008; Tonso, 2009), although there is often a linking of media and cultural studies. Consalvo (2003) examines news coverage of the Columbine shooting determining that the focus is on what could be called their exceptionality: the press constructed them as subordinated 'geeks' or as 'monsters'. Kellner (2008) links masculinity and the media spectacle produced by maximising casualties. Tonso (2009) suggests that some shooters borrow from sociocultural images and tropes of violent masculinities. Kennedy-Kollar and Charles (2013) argue that the majority of mass murderers, in their sample of 28, experienced stressors (financial, social, romantic and/or psychological) that can be linked to hegemonic masculine ideals. What draws this body of work together is the focus on masculinity for understanding mass shootings, and what is missing is a discursive analysis of mass shooter texts.

Narrative frames

There is a tradition within sociolinguistics that examines how people position themselves and their social worlds in narratives (e.g. de Fina & Georgakopoulou, 2008; Grimshaw, 2003; Thornborrow & Coates, 2005). Labov's (1972) classic model for understanding narrative focuses on the structural components of narratives, and he later asserts that the most important aspects of a narrative are the 'complicating action', or explanation of what happened, followed by the resolution (Labov, 1997). An alternative framework provided by Blum-Kulka (1993), drawing from Schiffrin (1987), focuses on the potential of narratives for constructing identity within a rubric that includes the story, the narrator and the act of delivery. However, neither of these perspectives considers how positioning and framing within narratives might not be consistent with *discursive construction*. How people tell stories, and the ways that they situate themselves in those stories, link to their understanding of and relationship to social and cultural contexts. As de Fina and Georgakopoulou explain:

> Tellers perform numerous social actions while telling a story and do rhetorical work through stories: they put forth arguments, challenge their interlocutors' views and generally attune their stories to

various local, interpersonal purposes, sequentially orienting them to prior and upcoming talk. It is important to place any representations of self and any questions of story's content in the context of this type of relational and essentially discursive activity as opposed to reading them only referentially. (2008, p. 382)

The discursive approach for examining narratives proposed by de Fina and Georgakopoulou (2008) is socio-interactional and links speakers with social practices and semiotics. Recognising these 'sociocultural ways of telling' (cf. Hymes, 1996) allows for understanding self-positioning and self-representations within a broader contextual framework. This approach makes it possible to emphasise the complexities between speakers' self-positioning, narrative frames and discursive activities allowing for more possibilities than the rigidity of identity alone.

Framing in discourse is generally associated with Tannen (1993) who understands it as the metamessages that occur in all interaction, spoken and written, and affects how utterances or messages are interpreted. This perspective draws on Bateson's (1972) work on play, which finds that monkeys use interactional metamessages to decode 'hostile' moves as 'playful' in appropriate circumstances. This perspective of framing is also indebted to Goffman (1974), who argues that there is a complicated and precise system with varying types of metamessages in everyday interaction. While Goffman (1974) was more focused on framing within the interaction, framing may emphasise social and cultural codes (Tannen, 1993).

Methodology

This work applies feminist linguistics in its analysis of discourse in social and cultural contexts, which is an interpretative endeavour (Lincoln, 1995). Discourse usually refers to the study of language above and beyond the sentence (Schiffrin 1996); however, there are two other widely used definitions, 'language "in use"', and a 'social practice in which language plays a central role' (Cameron & Panovic, 2014, p. 3). In all cases, discourse analysts study the structure of text or talk in terms of form and function, but how this transpires depends on the operationalisation of 'discourse'. The subfield of CDA is a method indebted to the Frankfurt School of critical social theory that underlines both the social and linguistic dimensions of analysing text/talk. van Dijk (2003, p. 352) explains it as 'a type of discourse analytical research that primarily studies the way social power, abuse, dominance, and inequality are enacted, reproduced and resisted by text and talk in the social and political context'. In practice this requires examining data to find covert patterns of *language use* that can be linked to social inequalities in their broader social contexts.

The CDA presented here is complemented by prior thematic analysis. Thematic analysis is a natural fit with CDA and can be applied to narrative study (Kohler Riessman 2005/1993; Marshall & Rossman, 2015). The thematic analysis uses a staged approach to identify prominent themes in the text, while the CDA fosters the analysis and discussion of those themes in relation to inequality and the social and cultural contexts.

My twisted world: The story of Elliot Rodger (MTW) is 137 pages of text, consists of approximately 107,000 words, and is divided into an introduction, followed by six sections and an epilogue. The text covers Rodger's life in spatiotemporal order, with each part dedicated to specific years of his life, although approximately 100 pages are devoted to his last 10 years of life. The document can be considered an autobiography in that it chronicles his life and a manifesto in that it is ideological.

In order to critically analyse social inequality in the text, it is necessary to briefly contextualise it. Rodger completed the document in Isla Vista, California, at 22 years of age. He was born in London, England, to a white English father and a Malaysian mother of Chinese descent (Rodger, 2014, p. 1). He expresses anger that his parents divorced when he was seven, which was also the age when he was introduced to his future stepmother (Rodger, 2014, p. 11). His parents were able to provide for him financially via: private school education (e.g. Rodger, 2014, pp. 2, 5, 27, 43); vacations to see extended family in England, Malaysia and Morocco, usually involving first- or business-class flights (Rodger, 2014, pp. 26, 36, 96); rent, monthly stipend and luxury sports car, the latter he believes should attract women (Rodger, 2014, pp. 128, 129).

The process of thematic coding and analysis was iterative, and directed by two matters: first, exacting and recording the patterns of themes in the data; and second, the link between the themes and masculinity. Both high-level themes and low-level subthemes were generated, with the highest level as follows: (1) women/sex, (2) wealth/money, (3) prestige, (4) popularity/invisibility, (5) race/ethnicity, (6) war/retribution and (7) media consumption. The analysis and discussion focus on the intersection of two themes (1 and 5) but draw from the others. As will become evident, women and sex are collapsed together as a single category because the two are conflated in the text.

Using this text raises ethical issues, the first of which is whether the document is 'public'. Rodger wrote the text for readers and shared it with more than two-dozen people on the day of the incident (Brown, 2014; Winton, Xia, & Lin II, 2014). California news station KEYT was one of the first news organisations to make the text available after reporting that they received a copy from one of Rodger's friends (Buttitta 2014).[9] While the text can be considered part of the public domain, I have removed any given names, except the author's, from all extracted text in an attempt to minimise any potential harm to the individuals mentioned in it.

Some researchers might raise objections to my use of the shooter's name on the grounds that this feeds into the 'media spectacle' (Kellner, 2008) or his desire for recognition, even posthumously. I acknowledge this and have attempted to use his name sparingly. However, complete refusal to name individuals is usually done either protectively or to change the emphasis in a narrative, as Canadian feminists have done with the 1989 mass shooting at the École Polytechnique de Montréal.[10] Neither of those rationales fit here. My analysis is based on a first-person narrative that the author distributed, and it is *his* use of language that is key to the positioning and frame in the text. Finally, the analysis centres upon a mass shooter who attempted to legitimise the 'annihilation' (Rodger, 2014, p. 131) and 'eradication' (Rodger, 2014, p. 136) of women, and there is a deep schism under those circumstances by choosing not use his name and actively making this intersectional feminist study less accessible.

Heterosexual success and a racial hierarchy: analysis

Key to analysing the narrative in relation to the frame and discursive construction of the intersection of gender and race/ethnicity in this text are situating masculine 'claims of authority' that Connell (1995) asserts are part of hegemonic masculinity. One of Rodger's methods for claiming power is through the construction of a racial hierarchy in which he places his objects of desire and those whom he perceives to be his competitors. He positions himself as more deserving of heterosexual success than other minority ethnic men and he privileges white, blonde women, describing himself at one point as 'obsessed with blondes' (Rodger, 2014, p. 66). For example,

> How could an inferior, ugly black boy be able to get a white girl and not me? I am beautiful, and I am half white myself. I am descended from British aristocracy. He is descended from slaves. I deserve it more. I tried not to believe his foul words [that this other man lost his virginity at a young age to a 'blonde white girl'], but they were already said, and it was hard to erase them from my mind. If this is actually true, it this ugly black filth was able to have sex with a blonde white girl at the age of thirteen while I've had to suffer virginity all of my life, then this proves how ridiculous the female gender is. They would give themselves to this filthy scum, but they reject ME? The injustice! (Rodger, 2014, p. 84)

His failed heterosexuality, desire for white, blonde women, and racist ideologies coalesce here. Immediately the author attempts to establish his dominance by describing the other man as 'inferior' on the basis that he is an 'ugly black boy', which is slightly modified two further times (*ugly black filth, filthy scum*). In each iteration of this at least one term is repeated for emphasis, 'ugly' and 'black' from the initial phrasing are recycled for the second, and in the third the noun 'filth' from the second is used as an adjective. Rodger uses figurative language, and metaphor and repetition more specifically, to make a direct link between worthlessness and Black masculinity. The grounding of the metaphor is further illustrated by the shooter's frustration at women for failing to conceptualise Black masculinity in the same way.

Though the author is 19 years old at this point in the narrative, and the man he is describing is also an adult, he uses the term 'boy'. This noun can be understood within the context of slavery and colonialism in which many African-American men, and other colonised men throughout Africa and Southeast Asia, were reduced or denied masculinity through the diminutive (e.g. 'boy', 'field boy' and 'houseboy') (Leong-Salobir, 2015). Even if Rodger was not conscious of implications of his word choice, three sentences later he evokes slavery outright, '[h]e is descended from slaves'. This statement stands in contrast to Rodger's claim to be a descendent of 'British aristocracy', which is also important in a colonial context. The two together are part of Rodger's racist claim to dominance. In addition to stressing 'British' aristocracy, he marks his whiteness directly (i.e. referring to himself as *half white*) as a reason why he believes he should be able to attract a white woman. It is crucial to note that it is a specific social class of whiteness that he associates himself with, especially when contrasted with the man he others. Rodger believes that he is inherently of more worth than the man he discusses on the basis of his race and lineage, not because of his personality, behaviour or practices.

He conflates women and sex in this same paragraph when saying that he 'deserves it more'. It is possible to read a lack of discourse cohesion here. In the case of nouns and pronouns, generally, the pronoun that follows a noun should be congruous. Instead, he writes that the other man was able to 'get a white girl' and then states, 'I deserve it more'. This is an example of linguistic slippage where women and sex are amalgamated. To Rodger women are sex and sex is women because they serve the same function. He views women as something to be 'got' or 'had', and himself as entitled to both – women and (hetero)sex. Additionally, he frames women as proving men's masculinity and worth through providing sex.

Rodger privileges whiteness and blondeness in both men and women throughout the text. The words that appear one word before 'blonde' in the document are not merely positive but erotically charged. These are most significant word collocates: beautiful, hot, tall, pretty, handsome, silky, luscious, bright and golden. Therefore, when his co-interlocutor confides that he has had sex with an attractive, blonde white woman Rodger experiences envy but attempts to position himself with strength (e.g. superiority) rather than envy (e.g. weakness). Although he is mixed race, he emphasises being 'half white'; the association of whiteness with beauty and desire is reconfirmed throughout the text. For example, when explaining why he dyed his hair blonde at the age of nine he states, 'I always envied and admired blonde-haired people, they always seemed so much more beautiful' (Rodger, 2014, p. 17). In contrast to the linking of whiteness with beauty and supremacy, which is evident in the self-positioning of his white British identity, when he prioritises his Asian identity, it is in negative terms.

> I came across this Asian guy who was talking to a white girl. The sight of that filled me with rage. I always felt as if white girls thought less of me because I was half-Asian, but then I see this white girl at the party talking to a full-blooded Asian. I never had that kind of attention from a white girl! And white girls are the only girls I'm attracted to, especially the blondes. *How could an ugly Asian*

attract the attention of a white girl, while a beautiful Eurasian like myself never had any attention from them? (Rodger, 2014, p. 121; emphasis in original)

This extract shows the complexities in how he chooses to linguistically frame his Asian ethnicity. While he initially frames his mixed ethnicity as a reason that white women might not desire or recognise him, he describes himself as full of 'rage' when realising that this rejection was not based on his ethnicity. When attempting to position himself as dominant he uses the adjective 'beautiful' and switches from 'half-Asian' to 'Eurasian'. While the adjective 'beautiful' marks an obvious difference, the choice of 'Eurasian', encompasses both ethnicities while evoking British colonialism, including the exclusionary responses of mixed-race people in European colonial communities that were provoked during imperialism (Pomfret, 2009). Rodger dismisses this man, using the same adjective that he used in the previous extract (i.e. *ugly*), indicating a tendency to draw connotations between multiple minority ethnic groups and 'ugliness'. This is supported by his statement 'white girls are the only girls I'm attracted to, especially the blondes', which he presents as social fact. This further use of the adjective 'ugly' supports the argument that the term is used in a racist hierarchy that diminishes the worth of individuals who are ethnically othered by the author rather than as a reference to attractiveness. Given that his racial hierarchy privileges whiteness, and a specific subtype (i.e. blondeness), above all else, his masculinity is threatened because these minority ethnic men have been desired by women that Rodger bestows with the most social value.

Rodger's envy and hostility is not reserved for African-American and Asian men who have relationships or conversations with Rodger's ideal type. He relays another experience where seeing a man he assumed to be 'Mexican' with a 'hot blonde white girl' made him angry.

> When we [Rodger and his father] sat down at our table, I saw a young couple sitting down a few tables down the row. The sight of them enraged me to no end, especially because it was a dark-skinned Mexican guy dating a hot blonde white girl. I regarded it as a great insult to my dignity. How could an inferior Mexican guy be able to date a white blonde girl, while I was still suffering as a lonely virgin? I was ashamed to be in such an inferior position in front of my father. When I saw the two of them kissing I could barely contain my rage, and my father was there to watch it all. It was so humiliating. I wasn't the son I wanted to present to my father. I should be the one with the hot blonde girlfriend, making my father proud. (Rodger, 2014, p. 87)

In the incident that Rodger describes, he does not speak to the couple or engage with them, yet he describes himself as 'barely able to contain my rage'. The occurrence that causes such 'rage' and 'humiliation' for him is seeing a 'dark-skinned Mexican guy dating a hot blonde white girl'. Again, as with the African-American man, he positions himself as superior and the man he racially others as 'inferior', using the same adjective as previously seen. In retelling this experience, he explains that being the one without the 'white blonde girl' placed him in an 'inferior position', which is offered as an explanation as to why this incident was an 'insult to [his] dignity': the author believes that he *deserves* a 'white blonde girl' more than a 'dark-skinned Mexican guy', just as he believes that he deserves to have sex with a 'blonde white girl' more than an 'ugly black boy'.

Reflecting back to Labov's scheme for understanding narrative, Rodger provides an evaluation here. While the complicating action is seeing the couple while out with his father, the 'so what' is the emotive response he has to the encounter. The evaluation comes in the form of the emotional responses (e.g. *ashamed, humiliated*) but also through the use of stylistic devices, including intensifiers (e.g. *great, so*) and explicatives (e.g. *I regarded it as a great insult to my dignity*). Because Rodger understands his masculinity as liminal and weak as a result of his lack of heterosexual success he is unable to cope with seeing a man that he believes that he is racially superior to with a woman whom he finds desirable.

There are differences in these vignettes, notably in terms of the adjectives he applies to the other men, the amount of detail provided, and in the circumstances (one is based on a conversation he took participated in, while the other was a couple that he observed while with his father). Yet despite these differences, the use of descriptive language is similarly emotive, though applied to different subjects. The emotive adjectives were applied to the other man in the former example, while here Rodger uses them in reference to himself. In his idealised version of masculinity he should have the good (i.e. a 'hot white blonde girl') that would elicit pride from his father because he sees himself as more entitled and worthy than a 'dark-skinned Mexican boy'.

In these examples, he racially others the men he describes, particularly in relation to women and sex, and race/ethnicity is the central tenet he uses to underscore his envy that these men were able to obtain the type of white, blonde woman that he could not. This occurs in other places in the text where Rodger underscores the race/ethnicity of men in his discussions of heterosexual desire and failure. For example,

> [My counsellor] was half Hawaiian and half Mexican, and he wasn't that good looking. How on earth could he have managed to sleep with four girls in Isla Vista, while I had been there for two years and had none? It seemed absolutely preposterous. I didn't want to see him after I found this out. (Rodger, 2014, p. 120)

While the author does not use the term 'inferior' here as in other examples, the message is similar in that he is jealous, positions himself as superior and makes ethnicity salient. He constructs himself as superior through references to the man's ethnicity and appearance, writing that it is 'absolutely preposterous' that a man he constructs as lesser than is more successful with women. As noted in other examples, Rodger provides no other details about this man beyond his ethnicity and a subjective comment about his appearance. What is striking is that even for his counsellor, someone whom he knows, Rodger is unable to offer any deeper assessment of what might make a person attractive, and his masculinity is fragile enough that he does not want to see his counsellor again after this, which is perceived as an attack on his masculinity.

Insight into Rodger's racist hierarchy in which he believes that he is more entitled and deserving of a blonde girlfriend can be read early in the text:

> Everything my father taught me was proven wrong. He raised me to be a polite, kind gentleman. In a decent world that would be ideal. But the polite, kind gentleman doesn't win in the real world. Girls don't flock to the gentleman. They flock to the alpha male. They flock to the boys who appear to have the most power and status. (Rodger, 2014, p. 28)

He privileges whiteness because that is what he believes has the most power and status. Along with that, a 'beautiful blonde girlfriend' (Rodger, 2014, pp. 111, 112, 115) works as a material good that he believes he is more entitled to than those men whom he constructs as less deserving on account of their race/ethnicity. He frames women as capable of raising men's power and authority, but also as serving the means to for men to demonstrate masculinity. He claims to have first learned this when he was seven:

> Because of my father's acquisition of a new girlfriend, my little mind got the impression that my father was a man that women found attractive, as he was able to find a new girlfriend in such a short period of time after divorcing my mother. I subconsciously held him higher regard because of this. It is very

interesting how this phenomenon works ... that males who can easily find female mates garner more respect from their fellow men, even children. (Rodger, 2014, p. 11)

Here Rodger provides a context for understanding his anger and rage towards minority ethnic men for dating women that he covets. He explicitly connects heterosexual success with hegemonic masculinity, seeing it as a way to command respect from others, especially men, and prove masculine entitlement. Beyond that, he also sees his father, a white British man, as successful with women, which feeds into larger social and cultural discourses about inequality, particularly as they pertain to masculinity.

Throughout the analysis Rodger has described himself as full of rage (e.g. Rodger, 2014, pp. 84, 87, 121) towards men he has ethnically othered for dating white, blonde women because they have upset his understanding of who is entitled to enact hegemonic masculinity. Therefore, he places the blame both on these men for having a good (i.e. access to particular women) that he desires and on women as a group because they 'are incapable of having morals or thinking rationally' (Rodger, 2014, p. 136). For Rodger, women's 'rational' choice would be choosing him over these other men, because he identifies as a half-white (Rodger, 2014, pp. 17, 84, 121), 'beautiful, magnificent gentleman' (Rodger, 2014, p. 90).

Discussion and conclusions

Both Rodger's narrative frame and discursive construction emphasise hegemonic masculinity through inequality. These play out on different levels simultaneously and often in complex ways. The instability of his masculinity is at the core of the narrative, which is first fragile then toxic. He understands masculinity as something that is proved to others, confirming Coston and Kimmel (2012), and he attaches his self-worth to how he thinks others perceive his masculinity, which is confirmed in the final sentences of the text when he writes: 'I will punish *everyone*. And it will be beautiful. Finally, at long last, I can show the world my true worth' (Rodger, 2014, p. 137; emphasis in original). He constructs a version of masculinity that is based on social inequality across axes of gender, race/ethnicity, social class/status and sexuality, which demonstrates the importance of the 'claim to authority' to hegemonic masculinity (Connell, 1995). This is complicated, however, by Rodger's mixed-race identity. His version of masculinity derives its worth from the recognition and validation of others, which he views through a racial hierarchy of white supremacy that is based in British colonialism. He sees hegemonic masculinity as enacted through possessing the ideal girlfriend. To him, she is a beautiful blonde white woman who serves a specific function: her visibility proves his worth to others. Women in general, and beautiful, blonde women, more specifically, represent both his failure in and his method for claiming masculine power and authority through non-violent means.

Rodger uses language, including figurative language, to demonstrate masculine-oriented entitlement of women and to position himself as dominant. Linked to this is his rage when he believes women reject him, while other men are 'chosen', as he sees it as a statement about his value. His racial hierarchy that privileges white blonde women leads him to denigrate minority ethnic men who date women that he desires. The reasoning behind this is twofold: firstly, in Rodger's construction of masculinity, women operate as high-status material goods who exist only as objects, with the primary purpose of raising men's status. It is quite revealing that early in the text Rodger refers to his stepmother as 'my father's acquisition' (Rodger, 2014, p. 11), as this cements the idea that he believes women can be bought or purchased at will, and that they serve a symbolic function. Secondly, he believes that he is more entitled to date the women he covets (i.e. blonde, white women) because he identifies as 'half white', which he equates with prestige and power.

Throughout the text he attempts to claim authority over women and other minority ethnic women, which he eventually plans to act out through a violent 'Day of Retribution'. He believes that a girlfriend will provide him with recognition and status. When he is unsuccessful in 'acquiring' a girlfriend, it is not simply that his sexuality is under threat but his masculine identity is rendered invisible *because* he sees the social acknowledgement of heterosexuality as confirmation of masculinity. He positions himself as a 'good guy', similar to Stroud's (2012) concealed handgun carriers, but one who is victimised and persecuted by women, and uses grandiose and excessive terms to position himself as dominant, such as 'magnificent, beautiful' and 'descended from British aristocracy'. Although these two sides may appear to be in conflict they show the toxicity of his feebleness: he is caught fumbling at proving hegemonic masculine authority and being unable imagine it, let alone seize it, without gender, racial or class-based inequality or mass violence. When he gives up on the idea of achieving masculinity through possessing a girlfriend, turns to violence as a technique for claiming masculine authority and exerting dominance over both women and other men because he sees no other way to gain the power that he believes he has been denied as a result of heterosexual failure. While Kennedy-Kollar and Charles (2013, p. 70) stress that 'subordination and control of women are crucial aspects of the hegemonic masculinity identity' of 25% of mass murderers in their sample, and that is obviously key here, what is imperative to note is that it is not misogyny acting alone.

Analysis of the narrative frame and discursive construction of this text demonstrates that misogyny, racism, colonialism and a heteropatriarchial discourse whereby women are commodified as sexual goods for masculine subjects operate in tandem. Furthermore, this is not an 'exceptional' discourse or an 'exceptional' man, this is a man whose perspectives are represented in the sticky spaces of hegemonic masculinity. The toxicity of his ideologies is represented in how violence becomes a way to demonstrate the worth that he feels he has been unjustly denied. The conclusions of this work demonstrate how the framing and discursive construction of this incident are based on a complex and fragile relationship to masculinity that cannot be separated from social inequalities and the desire for domination, providing insight into this specific case as well as the metamessages of a mass shooter text, especially as they relate to contemporary masculinities more generally, and how mass shootings might be understood as grounded in social and cultural discourses that are characterised by inequality.

Disclosure statement

No potential conflict of interest was reported by the author.

Notes

1. While Rodger refers to appointments with psychiatrists and counselors, he glosses over his health when discussing his counselors, both men and women. He frames them in relation to dynamics of heterosexuality, race and materialism that he uses in the text more generally. Health providers who are women are treated as potential (sexual) material goods that can improve his status. Meanwhile, health providers who are men are seen as competition for women and their perceived heterosexual success is contrasted with his failure.
2. The FBI considers mass shootings as a sub-type of active shootings. The definition of active shooter used by American government agencies is 'an individual actively engaged in killing or attempting to kill people in a confined or populated area' (FBI, 2013, p. 5).
3. *The Guardian* and *The Washington Post*, for example, have published multiple news stories that use these data (e.g., Ingraham, 2015a, 2015b; Teague, 2015; Woolf, 2015).
4. When www.shootingtracker.com joined the Gun Violence Archive, the Gun Violence Archive's methodology was adopted, which means that the shooter is not counted among the dead/injured. The Gun Violence Archive defines a single event as an incident occurring 'at the same general time and location' (www.gunviolencearchive.org/methodology, Retrieved July 1, 2016).

5. Combining a mass shooting with other violence is not unusual. For example, Eric Harris and Dylan Klebold set two bombs that failed to detonate at the Columbine shootings (Kellner, 2008; Tonso, 2009), while Anders Breivik was successful with his bomb, which killed eight people, before shooting 69 teenagers at a youth summer camp in Norway (Seierstad, 2016).
6. It is not clear how Fox and DeLateur (2014) define 'white'. The US Census uses the definition of people who identify their 'origins in any of the original peoples of Europe, the Middle East or North Africa' (Humes et al., 2011, p. 3).
7. The FBI (2013) reports that 96.2% of mass shooters are men. The statistics for rape arrests are only slightly higher at 97.2%; the next most segregated crimes are other sex offenses (excluding prostitution) at 92.3% and weapons crimes (including carrying and possessing) at 91.2% (FBI, 2014).
8. This argument is an inversion of Caputi (1989, p. 447), who discusses how American serial killer Ted Bundy's white, young, middle class victims were universalised as 'anyone's daughters'.
9. Evidence that Rodger wrote the text with readers in mind includes a statement on the first page of MTW proclaiming, '[t]his is the story of how I, Elliot Rodger came to be' (Rodger, 2014, p. 1) and in the text's penultimate paragraph he addresses readers directly with the use of a second-person pronoun: '[w]hy was I condemned to live a life of misery and worthlessness while other men are able to experience the pleasures of sex and love women? Why do things have to be this way? I ask all of you' (Rodger, 2014, p. 137). Other news organisations, including the *New York Times* and the *Mirror*, followed; as of July 2016 the text remains available at both websites.
10. Since the second anniversary of the École Polytechnique de Montréal shooting, 6 December has been recognised as the National Day of Remembrance and Action of Violence Against Women in Canada, thus formalising an emphasis on the victims.

References

Andersson, K. (2008). Constructing young masculinity: A case study of heroic discourse on violence. *Discourse & Society, 19*(2), 139–161.
Bateson, G. (1972). *Steps to an ecology of mind: Collected essays in anthropology, psychiatry, evolution and epistemology*. Chicago: University of Chicago Press.
Blum-Kulka, S. (1993). 'You gotta know how to tell a story': Telling, tales, and tellers in American and Israeli narrative events at dinner. *Language in Society, 22*(3), 361–402.
Brekke, J. S., Prindle, C., Bae, S. W., & Long, J. D. (2001). Risks for individuals with schizophrenia who are living in the community. *Psychiatry Services, 52*(10), 1358–1366.
Bridges, T. (2014). A very 'gay' straight? Hybrid masculinities, sexual aesthetics and the changing relationship between masculinity and homophobia. *Gender & Society, 28*(1), 58–82.
Bridges, T., & Tober, T. L. (2016). Mass shootings and masculinity. In M. Stombler & A. Jungels (Eds.), *Focus on social problems: A contemporary reader* (pp. 507–512). Oxford: Oxford University Press.
Brown, P. (2014, 28 May). California killer's parents frantically searched for son during shooting. *CNN.com*. Retrieved July 1, 2016, from http://edition.cnn.com/2014/05/25/justice/santa-barbara-shooter-parents/
Buttitta, J. (2014, 24 May). Elliot Rodger manifesto: A look inside. *KEYT.com*. Retrieved July 1, 2016, from http://www.keyt.com/news/elliot-rodger-manifesto-sneak-peekinside/26162212
Cameron, D. (1997). Performing gender: Young men's talk and the construction of heterosexual masculinity. In S. Johnson & U. H. Meinhof (Eds.), *Language and masculinity* (pp. 47–64). Oxford: Blackwell.
Cameron, D., & Frazer, E. (1987). *The lust to kill: A feminist perspective on sexual murder*. Cambridge: Polity.
Cameron, D., & Panovic, I. (2014). *Working with written discourse*. London: Sage.
Caputi, J. (1989). The sexual politics of murder. *Gender & Society, 3*(4), 437–456.
Coates, J. (2003). *Men talk*. Oxford: Blackwell.
Connell, R. W. (1995). *Masculinities*. Berkeley: University of California Press.

Connell, R. W., & Messerschmidt, J. W. (2005). Hegemonic masculinity: Rethinking the concept. *Gender & Society, 19*(6), 829–859.

Consalvo, M. (2003). The monsters next door: Media constructions of boys and masculinity. *Feminist Media Studies, 3*(1), 27–45.

Coston, B. M., & Kimmel, M. (2012). Seeing privilege where it isn't: Marginalized masculinities and intersectionality of privilege. *Journal of Social Issues, 68*(1), 97–111.

de Fina, A., & Georgakopoulou, A. (2008). Analysing narratives as practices. *Qualitative Research, 8*(3), 379–387.

Downing, L. (2013). *The subject of murder: Gender, exceptionality, and the modern killer.* Chicago: University of Chicago Press.

Dutton, D. G., White, K. R., & Fogarty, D. (2013). Paranoid thinking in mass shooters. *Aggression and Violent Behavior, 18*(5), 548–553.

Fazel, D., & Grann, M. (2006). The population impact of severe mental illness on violent crime. *American Journal of Psychiatry, 163*(8), 1397–1403.

Federal Bureau of Investigation (FBI). (2013). *A study of active shooter incidents between 2000 and 2013.* Washington, DC: US Department of Justice.

Federal Bureau of Investigation (FBI). (2014). Table 42: Arrests by sex, 2014. Retrieved July 1, 2016, from https://www.fbi.gov/about-us/cjis/ucr/crime-in-the.u.s/2014/crime-in-the-u.s.-2014/tables/table-42

Fox, J. A., & DeLateur, M. J. (2014). Mass shootings in America: Moving beyond Newtown. *Homicide Studies, 18*(1), 125–145.

Fox, J. A., & Levin, J. (2001). *The will to kill: Making sense of senseless murder.* London: Allyn & Bacon.

Fox, J. A., & Levin, J. (2015). *Extreme killing: Understanding serial and mass murder* (3rd ed.). London: Sage.

Goffman, E. (1974). *Frame analysis.* New York, NY: Harper & Row.

Grimshaw, A. (2003). Discourse and sociology: Sociology and discourse. In D. Schiffrin, D. Tannen, & H. E. Hamilton (Eds.), *The handbook of discourse analysis* (pp. 750–771). Oxford: Blackwell.

Harré, R., Moghaddam, F. M., Cairnie, T. P., Rothbart, D., & Sabat, S. R. (2009). Recent advances in positioning theory. *Theory & Psychology, 19*(1), 5–31.

Harré, R., & van Lagenhove, L. (1999). *Positioning theory.* Cambridge: Blackwell.

Humes, K. R., Jones, N. A., & Ramirez, R. R. (2011). Overview of race and Hispanic origin: 2010 census briefs. *US Census Bureau.* Retrieved July 1, 2016, from http://www.census.gov/prod/cen2010/briefs/c2010br-02.pdf

Hymes, D. (1996). *Ethnography, linguistics, narrative inequality.* London: Taylor and Francis.

Ingraham, C. (2015a, 1 October). Shooting in Oregon: So far in 2015, we've had 274 days and 294 mass shootings. *The Washington Post.* Retrieved July 1, 2016, from https://www.washingtonpost.com/news/wonk/wp/2015/10/01/2015-274-days-294-mass-shootings-hundreds-dead/

Ingraham, C. (2015b, 12 October). There have been 1,001 mass shootings in America since 2013. *The Washington Post.* Retrieved July 1, 2016, from https://www.washingtonpost.com/news/wonk/wp/2015/10/12/there-have-been-1001-mass-shootings-in-america-since-2013/

Kalish, R., & Kimmel, M. (2010). Suicide by mass murder: Masculinity, aggrieved entitlement, and rampage school shootings. *Health Sociology Review, 19*(4), 451–464.

Kellner, D. (2008). *Guys and guns amok: Domestic terrorism and school shootings from the oklahoma bombing to the Virginia tech massacre.* Boulder, CO: Paradigm.

Kennedy-Kollar, D., & Charles, C. A. D. (2013). Hegemonic masculinity and mass murderers in the United States. *Southwest Journal of Criminal Justice, 8*(2), 46–58.

Kiesling, S. (2007). Men, masculinities, and language. *Language and Linguistics Compass, 1*(6), 653–673.

Kimmel, M. (2013). *Angry white men: American masculinity at the end of an era.* New York: Nation Books.

Knoll, J. L. (2010a). The "pseudocommando" mass murderer: Part I, the psychology of revenge and obliteration. *Journal of the American Academy of Psychiatry and the Law Online, 38*(1), 87–94.

Knoll, J. L. (2010b). The "pseudocommando" mass murderer: Part II, the language of revenge. *Journal of the American Academy of Psychiatry and the Law Online, 38*(2), 263–272.

Kohler Riessman, C. (2005/1993). *Narrative analysis.* Thousand Oaks, CA: Sage.

Labov, W. (1972). *Sociolinguistic patterns.* Philadelphia: University of Pennsylvania Press.

Labov, W. (1997). Some further steps in narrative analysis. *Journal of Narrative and Life History, 7*(1–4), 395–415.

Lankford, A. (2016). Race and mass murder in the United States: A social and behavioural analysis. *Current Sociology, 64*(3), 470–490.

Leong-Salobir, C. (2015). "Cookie" and "Jungle Boy": A historical sketch of the different cooks for different folks in British colonial Southeast Asia, ca. 1850–1960. *Global Food History, 1*(1), 59–79.

Lincoln, Y. S. (1995). Emerging criteria for quality in qualitative and interpretive research. *Qualitative inquiry, 1*(3), 275–289.

Marshall, C., & Rossman, G. B. (2015). *Designing qualitative research* (6th ed.). London: Sage.

Mechling, J. (2014). Boy Scouts, the National Rifle Organisation, and the domestication of rifle shooting. *American Studies, 53*(1), 5–25.

Meloy, J. R., Hempel, A. G., Mohandie, K., Shiva, A. A., & Gray, B. T. (2001). Offender and offense characteristics of a nonrandom sample of adolescent mass murderers. *Journal of the American Academy of Child & Adolescent Psychiatry, 40*(6), 719–728.

Metzl, J. M., & MacLeish, K. T. (2015). Mental illness, mass shootings, and the politics of American firearms. *American journal of public health, 105*(2), 240–249.

Morgan, M. (1999). No woman no cry: Claiming African American women's place. In M. Bucholtz, A. C. Liang, & L. A. Sutton (Eds.), *Reinventing identities: The gendered self in discourse* (pp. 27–45). Oxford: Oxford University Press.

Myketiak, C. (2015). The co-construction of cybersex narratives. *Discourse & Society, 26*(4), 464–479.

Nagourney, A., Cieply, M., Feuer, A., & Lovett, I. (2014, 1 June). Before brief, deadly spree, trouble since age 8. *New York Times*. Retrieved July 1, 2016, from http://www.nytimes.com/2014/06/02/us/elliot-rodger-killings-in-california-followed-years-of-withdrawal.html

Nestor, P. G. (2002). Mental disorder and violence: Personality dimensions and clinical features. *American Journal of Psychiatry, 159*(12), 1973–1978.

Parker, R. (2014, 27 June). Peter Rodger: Elliot Rodger was not evil, but he was mentally ill. *Los Angeles Times*. Retrieved July 1, 2016, from http://www.latimes.com/local/lanow/la-me-peter-rodger-son-20140627-story.html

Pomfret, D. (2009). Raising Eurasia: Race, class, and age in French and British colonies. *Comparative Studies in Society and History, 51*(2), 314–343.

Rodger, E. (2014). *My twisted world: The story of Elliot Rodger*. Retrieved May 27, 2014 and July 1, 2016, from http://www.nytimes.com/interactive/2014/05/25/us/shooting-document.html?_r=0 [Unpublished Manifesto].

Sandberg, S., Oksanen, A., Berntzen, L. E., & Killakoski, T. (2014). Stories in action: The cultural influences of school shootings on the terrorist attacks in Norway. *Critical Studies on Terrorism, 7*(2), 277–296.

Schiffrin, D. (1987). *Discourse markers*. Cambridge: Cambridge University Press.

Schiffrin, D. (1996). Narrative as self-portrait: Sociolinguistic constructions of identity. *Language in Society, 25*(2), 167–203.

Seierstad, A. (2016). *One of us: The story of a massacre and its aftermath*. London: Virago.

Stroud, A. (2012). Good guys with guns: Hegemonic masculinity and concealed handguns. *Gender & Society, 26*(2), 216–238.

Tannen, D. (1993). *Framing in discourse*. Oxford: Oxford University Press.

Teague, M. (2015, 11 October). Inglis, Florida: Home to the 1000th US mass shooting since Sandy Hook. *The Guardian*. Retrieved July 1, 2016, from https://www.theguardian.com/world/2015/oct/11/mass-shooting-florida-1000th-sandy-hook

Thornborrow, J., & Coates, J. (2005). *The sociolinguistics of narrative*. Amsterdam: John Benjamins.

Tonso, K. L. (2009). Violent masculinities as tropes for school shooters: The Montreal massacre, the Columbine attack and rethinking schools. *American Behavioral Scientist, 52*(9), 1266–1285.

van Dijk, T. (2003). Critical discourse analysis. In D. Schiffrin, D. Tannen, & H. E. Hamilton (Eds.), *The handbook of discourse analysis* (pp. 352–371). Oxford: Blackwell.

West, C., & Zimmerman, D. H. (1987). Doing gender. *Gender & Society, 1*(2), 125–151.

Winton, R., Xia, R., & Lin II, R. G. (2014, 25 May). Isla Vista shooting: Read Elliot Rodger's graphic, elaborate attack plan. *Los Angeles Times*. Retrieved July 1, 2016, from http://www.latimes.com/local/lanow/la-me-ln-isla-vista-document-20140524-story.html#page=1

Woolf, N. (2015, 2 October). Oregon college shooting is 994th mass gun attack in US in three years. *The Guardian*. Retrieved July 1, 2016, from http://www.theguardian.com/us-news/2015/oct/01/obama-oregon-college-shooting-routine

Pride and prejudice: the context of reception for Muslims in the United States

Elif Bulut

Public opinion surveys suggest that Americans increasingly have negative perceptions of Muslims especially following the tragic attacks on World Trade Center and Pentagon on 9/11. The widespread negative attitudes towards Muslims suggest potential challenges for Muslim immigrants' integration into American society. Drawing from theory and prior research on prejudice and using data from the nationally representative Religion and Diversity Survey, this study uncovers variation in prejudice towards Muslims in the United States. Specifically, this study investigates whether nativist attitudes towards immigrants – such as beliefs that nothing in other countries can beat the American way of life, immigrants are a threat to traditional American values and immigrants should give up their foreign ways and learn to be like other Americans – fear of terrorism and contact with Muslims can account for the prejudice against Muslims in the United States. The findings suggest that strongest predictor of prejudice towards Muslims is not the fear of terrorism, but nativist attitudes towards immigrants and lack of contact with Muslims.

Introduction

The United States has experienced a dramatic influx of immigrants in the twentieth century. In particular, the passage of the 1965 Immigration Act has given rise to an unprecedented diversification of the American population over the subsequent 50 years. One of these new immigrant groups is Muslim immigrants in the United States. Although they constitute a growing and increasingly important segment of American society and according to many accounts, Islam is the third largest and fastest growing religion in America (Haddad, Smith, & Esposito, 2003), there is little research about the attitudes and opinions of Americans regarding Muslims in this country.

Public opinion surveys suggest that Americans increasingly have a negative view of Muslims after 9/11 terrorist attacks on World Trade Center and Pentagon (Pew Research Center for the People and the Press, 2006). After the attacks, public opinion towards Muslims reached a level such that, in the public mind, Muslim and terrorist became almost synonymous (Wuthnow, 2005). Along with increasing reports of violence towards Muslims, these negative perceptions suggest potential challenges for Muslim immigrants' succesful integration into the American society. Identifying obstacles to integration of Muslims remains an important task for researchers

(Merino, 2010). Thus, this study is concerned with identifying and analysing factors affecting Americans' prejudice towards Muslims in the United States. Drawing from theory and prior research on prejudice, I investigate variation in prejudiced attitudes towards Muslim immigrants in the United States. Specifically, I examine whether nativist attitudes towards immigrants, contact with Muslims and fear of terrorism can account for prejudice towards Muslims. The link between these factors and prejudice toward Muslims will be studied using data from 2002–2003 Religion and Diversity Survey, a nationally representative survey that includes questions about immigrants, perceptions of Muslims, religious beliefs and practices, and opinions regarding national identity (Gibbon, 2005).

Background and research hypotheses

Research suggests that there is a positive correlation between the extent to which a group is perceived to pose a threat and the extent of negative feelings towards that group (Stephan, Ybarra, & Bachman, 1999). In this regard, Muslims in the United States, especially after the tragic attacks on 9//11 by violent Muslim extremists, have increasingly been perceived as a threat to the security in the United States and suspected to commit acts of terrorism. After the attacks, public hostility towards Islam and Muslims reached a level such that, in the public mind, Muslim and terrorist became almost tantamount (Bulut & Ebaugh, 2014; Wuthnow, 2005). Based upon insights from previous research, I anticipate to find the following:

H1: Prejudice towards Muslims is positively associated with fear of another terrorist attack.

Although people migrating from place to place often adopt the culture of the societies they enter, at the same time, they carry with them their own practices, ideas and traditions to places they move to, and create new cultural spheres in the dominant culture of a particular state or a city to express their differences (Appadurai, 1996). Research suggests that differences of Muslims in the United States are intensified and became more visible to the American society following the tragic events of September 11, 2001 (Kaya, 2007). The negative portrayals of Muslims in the media and the tendency to equate Islam with extremism and terrorism found its way through general American public and led to pervasive stereotypes. In a survey conducted about a year after the attacks, negative perceptions of Muslims were significantly more common than any other non-Western group. Almost half (47%) of the public said that *fanatical* applied to Muslims, also they were more likely to perceive Muslims as *violent* (40%) and *backward* (34%) and *close minded* (57%) and *strange* (44%) as opposed to perceiving *tolerant* (32%) (Wuthnow, 2005).

In this context, Muslim practices became symbols that challenge or fail to support American culture and way of life. That is, Muslims, simply by maintaining different religious and cultural practices that are believed to be at odds with American culture (e.g. women wearing headscarves, men wearing a beard or turban, practice of sex-segregated worship) are perceived to pose a symbolic threat to a uniquely American culture and way of life (Kaya, 2007). This form of thinking represents a nativist perspective which postulates that American way of life is threatened and needs to be protected against foreign influences (Fry, 2007; Higham, 2002; Knoll, 2010; Perea, 1997). In this regard, the nativist attitudes centre around the idea of the inassimilability of 'foreigners' or immigrants – be it the Irish Catholics of the nineteenth century or Latino, Asian or Muslim immigrants of the twenty-first century – because of their 'uncivilized social customs and habits supposedly grounded in their traditional religion' (Casanova, 2008, p. 108). For instance, the increasing prevalence of Spanish language in the United States is perceived as a threat by nativists (Fry, 2007). In light of this research, in the present study, I expect to find the following regarding the relationship between nativist attitudes and prejudice towards Muslims:

> H2: Americans who perceive immigrants as a threat to traditional American values are more likely to be prejudiced towards Muslims.
> H3: Americans who believe that foreigners who come to live in America should give up their foreign ways and learn to be like other Americans are more likely to be prejudiced against Muslims.
> H4: Americans who believe that nothing in other countries can beat the American way of life are more likely to be prejudiced against Muslims.

In addition to fear of terrorism and nativist attitudes, personal contacts with Muslims may also play a role in shaping attitudes towards Muslims in the United States. Research has shown that intergroup contact is related to higher levels of tolerance and can reduce individuals' prejudice towards other groups (Allport, 1954; Dovidio, Gaertner, & Kawakami, 2003). Known also as contact hypothesis, this scholarship suggests that the more people get to know members of a minority group personally, the less likely they are to be prejudiced against that group (Allport, 1954). Thus, in this study, I expect to find the following:

> H5: Americans who have more contact with Muslims are less likely to be prejudiced against Muslims.

Data and methods

For this study, I use data from the Religion and Diversity Survey, a nationally representative telephone survey conducted between September 2002 and February 2003. The survey results are based on a nationally representative sample of 2910 adults, 18 or older. The sample was chosen using a random digit dialling procedure and the response rate was 43.6% (Wuthnow, 2005).

I have limited my sample to respondents who were born in the United States to be able to separate immigrants' attitudes from US-born citizens. This is determined by using a question that asked 'were you born in the United States or in another country?' By excluding those who answered 'no' ($N=265$), I have limited my analysis to those Americans who are born in the United States. Finally, I dropped 60 cases with missing values on dependent and independent variables, resulting in a final sample size of 2585.

Dependent variable: prejudice against Muslims in the United States

Prejudice toward Muslims in the United States is measured by a scale derived from the summed scores of seven items that ask respondents, 'please tell me if you think each of these words applies to the Muslims–fanatical, backward, violent, strange'; and three questions that ask respondents whether they favour or oppose 'the U.S government making it harder for Muslims to settle in the United States', 'collecting information about Muslims religious groups in the United States' and 'making it illegal for Muslims to meet in the United States'.[1] For all the items, if a respondent said a word applied to Muslims and responded in affirmative to above statements, she or he is coded as 2 on that item. 'Don't know' responses are coded as 1 and 'No' responses are coded as 0. To form the prejudice scale, I summed the seven items, producing a range of values from 0 to 14 (Cronbach's alpha = .74). Thus, the most prejudiced respondents scored 14 by affirming all seven negative statements.

To assess the validity of this scale, I measure prejudice using another question from the survey that asked half of the respondents whether they would (1) object strongly, (2) object somewhat,

(3) object a little, (4) not object at all if their child wanted to marry a Muslim who had a good education and came from a good family.[2] Responses are recoded such that higher values indicate greater prejudice towards Muslims. I expect the coefficients predicting prejudice against Muslims to be comparable to those predicting reaction to marrying a Muslim.

Independent variables

Fear of terrorism: Fear of another terrorist attack is measured by the following question: 'How worried are you about the threat of another terrorist attack – extremely worried, very worried, somewhat worried, not very worried, or not at all worried?' I dichotomised fear of terrorism variable to '1 = extremely/very worried' versus '0 = otherwise'.

Nativist attitudes: To measure nativist attitudes towards immigrants and the United States, I used questions that asked respondents to agree or disagree with the following statements: 'Foreigners who come to live in America should give up their foreign ways and learn to be like other Americans', 'these new groups are a threat to our traditional values' and 'nothing in other countries can beat the American way of life'. For all statements, if a respondent responded in affirmative, she or he was coded as 1 on that item. 'Don't know' responses and 'No' responses were coded as 0.

Contact with Muslims: To measure the contact with Muslims, I used the following question: 'How much personal contact have you had with Muslims? – a great deal, a fair amount, only a little, almost none, or none?' I generated a dummy variable to represent the highest levels of contact (1 = a great deal contact/ a fair amount, 0 = otherwise).

Control variables

Socioeconomic and demographic controls include: level of education (1 = some college degree or higher, 0 = otherwise), age (years), gender (1 = female, 0 = male), race (1 = white, 0 = otherwise).

Regression models

Because my dependent variable is a scale that consists of seven items, I used ordinary least squares (OLS) regression to model prejudice towards Muslims in the United States. I first modelled prejudice towards Muslims as a function of the fear of a terrorist attack, educational attainment and control variables:

Model 1: $\text{Prej\_Mus}_i = \alpha + \beta_1 \text{FEAR}_i + \beta_2 \text{EDUCTION}_i + \beta_3 \text{WHITE}_i + \beta_4 \text{FEMALE}_i$
$+ \beta_5 \text{AGE}_i + U_i.$ (1)

In the next two models, I added variables that measure nativist attitudes towards immigrants and prior contact with Muslims.

Model 2: $\text{Prej\_Mus}_i = \alpha + \beta_1 \text{FEAR}_i + \beta_2 \text{FORN\_LRN}_i + \beta_3 \text{THREAT}_i + \beta_4 \text{AMR\_LIFE}_i$
$+ \beta_5 \text{EDUCATION}_i + \beta_6 \text{WHITE}_i + \beta_7 \text{FEMALE}_i + \beta_8 \text{AGE}_i + U_i,$ (2)

Model 3: $\text{Prej\_Mus}_i = \alpha + \beta_1 \text{FEAR}_i + \beta_2 \text{FORN\_LRN}_i + \beta_3 \text{THREAT}_i$
$+ \beta_4 \text{AMR\_LIFE}_i + \beta_5 \text{CONT\_MUS}_i + \beta_6 \text{EDUCATION}_i + \beta_7 \text{WHITE}_i$
$+ \beta_8 \text{FEMALE}_i + \beta_9 \text{AGE}_i + U_i.$ (3)

In the fourth model, I used the marriage variable as the dependent variable to compare the results to previous models and assess the validity of my original scale.

$$\text{Model 4: MARRYMUS}_i = \alpha + \beta_1 \text{FEAR}_i + \beta_2 \text{FORN\_LRN}_i + \beta_3 \text{THREAT}_i + \beta_4 \text{AMR\_LIFE}_i$$
$$+ \beta_5 \text{CONT\_MUS}_i + \beta_6 \text{EDUCATION}_i + \beta_7 \text{WHITE}_i$$
$$+ \beta_8 \text{FEMALE}_i + \beta_9 \text{AGE}_i + U_i.$$

(4)

Results

Table 1 presents descriptive statistics for all study variables. Overall, respondents in our sample had a mean age of 45, 80% of the sample identified as white, 58% identified as female and 67% of the sample had some college degree or higher.

Table 1 also reports survey findings on the three factors that are the focus of this study: nativist attitudes towards immigrants, fear of another terrorist attack and prior contact with Muslims. Majority of the respondents (70%) appear to take pride in their native country and believe that 'nothing in other countries can beat the American way of life'. Reflective of nativist attitudes towards immigrants, nearly half of the sample (45%) believe that 'immigrants should give up their foreign ways and learn to be like other Americans when they come to live in America'. Seventy-seven per cent of the sample are worried about another terrorist attack on the United States. Finally, the results from the survey suggest that half of the respondents (50%) have had contact with Muslims.

Table 2 provides additional insight into the context of reception for Muslims in the United States by showing descriptive statistics for each item of the prejudice scale. Almost half of the sample (45%) believes that the word fanatical and strange applies to Muslims and 38% think the word violent does. In addition, 38% of the sample favour making it harder for Muslims to settle in the United States, and 59% favour collecting information about Muslim religious groups. On the other side, though, the majority of the respondents did not agree that any of the negative attributes (i.e. fanatical/violent/backward/strange) apply to Muslims, and they did not support interfering with Muslim's right to meet (74%), or making it harder for Muslims to settle in the United States (56%).

Table 1. Descriptive statistics.

Variables	Minimum	Maximum	Mean	SD
Dependent variables				
MARRY MUSLIM	0.00	1.00	0.54	0.50
PREJUDICE	0.00	14.00	6.18	4.05
Independent variables				
Nothing in other countries can beat the American way of life	0.00	1.00	70.5	0.44
Foreigners should give up their foreign ways and learn to be like other Americans	0.00	1.00	45.6	0.55
Immigrants are a threat to our traditional values	0.00	1.00	33.5	0.44
Very worried about the threat of another terrorist attack against the United States	0.00	1.00	77.1	0.42
Contact Muslim	0.00	1.00	51	0.50
AGE	18	91	45.23	17.64
SOME COLLEGE/HIGHER	0.00	1.00	0.67	0.54
FEMALE	0.00	1.00	0.58	0.49
WHITE	0.00	1.00	0.80	0.40

Table 2. Descriptive statistics of items on prejudice scale.

'Please tell me if you think each of these words applies to the Muslim religion ... '

	Yes (%)	No (%)	Don't know (%)	Observation
Fanatical	45.0	39.8	14.6	2244
Violent	38.3	49.8	11.7	2244
Backward	33.3	52.5	13.8	2244
Strange	45.1	45.2	9.7	2244
Government should:				
Collect info on Muslims	59.2	34.9	5.5	2585
Making it illegal for Muslims to meet in the United States	20.7	74.7	4.3	2585
Make it harder for Muslims to settle in the United States	38.1	56.4	5.3	2585

Multivariate analysis predicting prejudice against Muslims in the United States

Table 3 presents the results of OLS regressions predicting scores on the 14-point prejudice scale. Model 1 is designed to test hypothesis 1 and includes the control variables. In support of hypothesis 1, the results indicate that the fear of a terrorist attack significantly predicts prejudice against Muslims. However, after adjusting for differences in contact with Muslims, fear of another terrorist attack loses its significance at the .05 level. This suggests that those who fear another terrorist attack would be less prejudiced against Muslims if they were more likely to have contact with Muslims.

As for the control variables, the effect of the education is in the predicted direction, meaning that, it is significantly and negatively associated with prejudice across all models. The results reveal that having some college degree or higher reduces prejudice against Muslims by .35 points, holding all variables constant (see Model 3, Table 3). As for the other control variables, while age is statistically significant and positively related to prejudice, it loses its statistical significance when other variables are introduced into the model. Race and gender are not statistically significant measures of prejudice against Muslims and they remain so across all three models predicting prejudice.

Model 2 introduces variables that measure nativist attitudes towards immigrants. The results regarding nativist attitudes provides strong support for hypotheses 2, 3 and 4 which predicted a positive relationship between nativism and prejudice against Muslims. Thus, those who believe that immigrants are a threat to traditional American values maintain greater prejudice against Muslims, as well as those who believe that nothing in other countries can beat the American way of life, and those who think that foreigners should give up their foreign ways and learn to be like other Americans when they come to live in America. In fact, nativist and anti-immigrant attitudes emerge as *the strongest* predictor of anti-Muslim prejudice across all subsequent models.

Model 3 indicates that, as hypothesised, prior contact with Muslims is significantly associated with lower levels of prejudice against Muslims. Moreover, this variable emerges as the second strongest predictor of prejudice in the entire analysis. This finding provides evidence that contact with Muslims leads to less prejudicial attitudes towards Muslims in the United States.

Model 4 tests the effects of the same variables on the likelihood of being bothered by the idea of one's child wanting to marry a Muslim who had a good education and came from a good family. For the most part, the results are very similar to those predicting prejudice. Variables concerning a nativist orientation have similar effects on attitudes towards marrying a Muslim as they did for prejudice scores. Specifically, among three variables measuring nativist orientation,

Table 3. Ordinary least square regressions predicting prejudice.

Dependent variable	Model 1 PREJ_MUS	Model 2 PREJ_MUS	Model 3 PREJ_MUS	Model 4 MARRY_MUS	Model 5 MARRY_MUS
Variables					
FEAR	.505**	.287**	.281*	.009	.008
	(.187)	(.166)	(.166)	(.031)	(.031)
FORN_LRN		.638***	.615***	.036**	.036**
		(.076)	(.076)	(.015)	(.015)
THREAT		.565***	.567***	.140***	.140***
		(.077)	(.077)	(.015)	(.015)
AMR_LIFE		.533***	.534***	.082***	.081***
		(.081)	(.081)	(.015)	(.015)
CONTACT			−.587***	−.064**	
			(.145)	(.028)	
EDUCATION	−.667***	−.398***	−.352***	.011	.020*
	(.050)	(.046)	(.047)	(.009)	(.011)
WHITE	.346*	.209	.103	.118***	.119***
	(.196)	(.173)	(.175)	(.034)	(.034)
FEMALE	−.253	−.265*	−.216	−.088***	−.088***
	(.159)	(.060)	(.141)	(.027)	(.027)
AGE	.024***	.003	.002	.002**	.002**
	(.004)	(.004)	(.004)	(.001)	(.001)
CONT_EDUC					−.244***
					(.032)
Observation	2541	2526	2512	1222	1222
Adjusted *R*-square	.078	.284	.291	.164	.164

Note: Data shown are regression coefficients with standard errors in parentheses.
Two-tailed tests:
*$p < .10$.
**$p < .05$.
***$p < .001$.

believing that foreigners are a threat to traditional American values is the most powerful predictor. Belief that 'immigrants should give up their foreign ways and learn to be like other Americans' is the second important predictor and its effect is robust compared to the other measures as it was in the other models predicting prejudice. Overall, nativist attitudes towards immigrants are the strongest predictor in all models, which lends support to hypotheses 2, 3 and 4.

Again, similar to the prejudice scores, fear of another terrorist attack does not significantly increase the likelihood of being bothered by one's child marrying a Muslim. Similarly, contact with Muslims has the predicted effect on attitudes towards marrying a Muslim. However, there is a striking result in regard to the effect of education in this last model which suggests that, in contrast to the previous models, there is a positive relationship between educational attainment and opposing marriage to a Muslim. Yet, this relationship is insignificant at .05 level. Given this result, I tested for an interaction between education and contact with Muslims. The post-hoc interaction results revealed a significant result (see Model 5, Table 3). This suggests that for those respondents who have prior contact with Muslims, their reactions to marrying a Muslim vary with educational level; that is, people with some college degree or higher are less likely to oppose marrying a Muslim compared to those who are not college graduates.

In contrast to previous models predicting prejudice, the control variables (i.e. race, gender, age) are all significant in the last two models predicting attitudes towards marrying a Muslim. Accordingly, whites, in comparison to other racial groups, and women in comparison to men are less supportive of marriage to a Muslim. Opposition to marrying a Muslim is also associated with higher age.

Discussion and conclusions

This study addresses a significant gap in the literature on prejudice and nativism: Americans' attitudes towards the growing numbers of Muslims in the United States. The findings of the study present a consistent picture of the context of reception for Muslim immigrants in the United States. The findings of this study reveal that an important segment of the study sample is prejudiced against Muslims. Specifically, almost half of the respondents (45%) said that the word fanatical and strange applies to Muslims and more than half (59%) favoured collecting information about Muslims in the United States. On a positive note, though, this study showed that the majority of the respondents neither agreed that any of the negative attributes (i.e. fanatical/violent/backward/strange) apply to Muslims, nor did they support interfering with Muslim's right to meet (74%), or making it harder for Muslims to settle in the United States (56%). This finding suggests that respect for the fundamental rights of the Muslims prevails in the general public. This is in line with the research that found that, although many Muslim Americans (55%) report that 'it has become more difficult to be a Muslim in the United States', majority of Muslim Americans (66%) believe that 'the quality of life for Muslims in the US is better than the quality of life in most Muslim countries' (Pew Research Center for the People and the Press, 2011, p. 3).

With respect to the possible mechanisms explaining prejudice against Muslims, the findings of this study suggest that nativism in general, that is, one's taking pride in his or her native country or origins, and anti-immigrant biases in particular must be recognised as important factors. That is, respondents who believe that immigrants are a threat to traditional American values and those who maintain that foreigners should give up their foreign ways and learn to be like other Americans as well as those agreeing that nothing in other countries can beat the American way of life are the ones most likely to be highly prejudiced against Muslims and be bothered by the idea of their child wanting to marry a Muslim even though he or she had a good education and came from a good family.

These findings suggest that prejudice against Muslims is linked to nativitist attitudes, more specifically to an anti-immigrant bias. Nativist attitudes towards immigrants in this study are positively linked to higher anti-Muslim prejudice, suggesting that respondents perceive Muslims as foreign. Thus, we could infer that, Muslims in the United States suffer from prejudice mostly because they are perceived as un-American. This is in accordance with the previous literature that underlines that nativism is linked closely to exclusive attitudes toward those perceived as 'outsiders' which may contribute to prejudice against foreigners in general (Anbinder, 2006; Haslam & Pedersen, 2007; Kilty & Haymes, 2000), and Muslims in particular (Alba, 2005; Cainkar, 2007; Malik, 2009; Mir, 2011; Samhan, 1987). This finding is important in a number of ways. First, nativist attitudes are shown to be a key determinant of restrictive immigration policy preferences (Knoll, 2010), and may serve as a ground for justification of mistreatment of immigrants as 'fair' (Lippard, 2015). The nativist attitudes also reveal serious challenges to the integration of Muslim immigrants into the life in the United States.

One of the most important findings of this study underscores the significance of prior contact with Muslims. Regression results reveal a linear negative relationship between contact with Muslims and prejudice as well as opposition to marrying a Muslim. This robust finding suggests that increasing the amount of contact with Muslims as well as promoting intergroup dialogue and understanding could help reduce prejudice against Muslims in the United States considerably. This finding supports the contact hypothesis which suggests that the more people get to know members of a minority group personally, the less likely they are to be prejudiced against that group (Allport, 1954). Thus, the finding of this study that contact with Muslims is negatively associated with prejudice casts shadow on the theories of an inherent and unavoidable 'clash' (Huntington, 1997) between Muslims and Americans.

Surprisingly, this study found that being worried about another terrorist attack on the United States is not significant in the models predicting opposition to marrying a Muslim. This is an interesting finding. Given the negative connotation of Islam with terrorism – especially and increasingly after the tragic attacks on World Trade Center and Pentagon on 9/11 – one would think that a respondent who is worried about another terrorist attack would be less supportive towards marrying a Muslim. However, results of this study suggest that fear of another terrorist attack does not have a significant effect in explaining variation in the reactions regarding marriage to a Muslim.

Finally, while educational attainment emerges as a predictor of prejudice against Muslims – those who have some college degree or higher report lower levels of prejudice- it appears to be insignificant in predicting opposition to a marrying a Muslim. Only after testing for an interaction between contact with Muslims and education that the effect of education becomes significant. This finding suggests that opposition to marrying a Muslim vary with educational level, that is, for those who had prior contacts with Muslims, educational attainment is negatively associated with prejudice.

Overall, this study reveals that nativist attitudes and lack of contact with Muslims appear to be the strongest predictors of respondents' prejudice towards Muslims.

One of the limitations of this study is that majority of the sample consists of white, female and well-educated respondents. This suggests that we need to exercise caution in generalising the results of this study to the general public. Studies that use more varied samples of respondents might better reflect the public attitude towards Muslims in the United States. It is also important to note that the Religion and Diversity (2002–2003) survey was conducted in the very recent aftermath of the tragic 9/11 terrorist attacks, and thus, the results might reflect the feelings of the public at the time and caution should be exercised about the findings regarding the extent of prejudice against Muslims in the United States. Also noteworthy is the fact that the majority of the respondents neither agreed that any of the negative attributes apply to Muslims, nor did they support interfering with Muslim's right to meet, or making it harder for Muslims to settle in the United States. In addition, more recent data from the Pew Research Center show the belief that Islam is connected with violence has declined, and almost half of the American public (45%) believes that 'Islam is no more likely than other faiths to encourage violence among its believers' (2009, p. 2). Nonetheless, research also shows that that prejudice against Muslims in the United States is more than twice as prevalent as any other religious group (Gallup, 2009). Together with the findings of the present study, these findings underscore the importance of taking necessary measures to address prejudice against Muslims in the United States.Notes

Notes

1. Although factor analysis (results analysis not shown) suggested that I could group the first four items as one and the three questions as another variable, based on the Cronbach's alpha results, I decided to form a scale index of all seven items and consider them as one concept (prejudice).
2. The question regarding marriage is: 'Suppose you had a child who wanted to marry a Muslim who had a good education and came from a good family. How would you feel about this?'

References

Alba, R. (2005). Bright vs. blurred boundaries: Second-generation assimilation and exclusion in France, Germany, and the United States. *Ethnic and Racial Studies, 28*(1), 20–49.

Allport, G. W. (1954). *The nature of prejudice*. Cambridge, MA: Perseus Books.

Anbinder, T. (2006). Nativism and prejudice against immigrants: An historiographic assessment. In R. Ueda (Ed.), *A companion to American immigration* (pp. 177–201). Malden, MA: Blackwell.

Appadurai, A. (1996). *Modernity al large: Cultural dimensions of globalization* (Vol. 1). Minneapolis: University of Minnesota Press.

Bulut, E., & Ebaugh, H. R. (2014). Religion and assimilation among Turkish Muslim immigrants: Comparing practicing and non-practicing Muslims. *Journal of International Migration and Integration, 15*(3), 487–507.

Cainkar, L. (2007). Using sociological theory to defuse anti-Arab/Muslim nativism and accelerate social integration. *Journal of Applied Social Science, 1*(1), 7–15.

Casanova, J. (2008). Public religions revisited. In H. De Vries (Ed.), *Religion: Beyond a concept* (pp. 101–119). New York: Fordham Univ Press.

Dovidio, J. F., Gaertner, S. L., & Kawakami, K. (2003). Intergroup contact: The past, present, and the future. *Group Processes & Intergroup Relations, 6*(1), 5–21.

Fry, B. N. (2007). *Nativism and immigration: Regulating the American dream*. New York: LFB Scholarly Pub.

Gallup, P. (2009). *Analysis by Gallup Center for Muslim Studies*. Retrieved from http://www.gallup.com/poll/125312/religious-prejudice-stronger-against-muslims.aspx

Gibbon, J. D. (2005). *Unveiling Islamophobia in the U.S.: Muslim immigrants and their context of reception*. Paper presented at the annual meeting of the American Sociological Association, Marriott Hotel, Loews Philadelphia Hotel, Philadelphia, PA.

Haddad, Y. Y., Smith, J. I., & Esposito, J. L. (2003). Becoming American-religion, identity, and institution building in the American Mosaic. In Y. Y. Haddad, J. I. Smith, & J. L. Esposito (Eds.), *Religion and immigration* (pp. 1–19). Walnut Creek, CA: AltaMira Press.

Haslam, N., & Pedersen, A. (2007). Attitudes towards Asylum Seekers: the Psychology of Exclusion. In *Yearning to Breathe Free: Seeking Asylum in Australia* (pp. 208–218). Sydney: Federation Press.

Higham, J. (2002). *Strangers in the land: Patterns of American nativism, 1860–1925*. New Brunswick, NJ: Rutgers University Press.

Huntington, S. P. (1997). *The clash of civilizations and the remaking of world order*. New Delhi: Penguin Books India (P) Ltd.

Kaya, I. (2007). Muslim American identities and diversity. *Journal of Geography, 106*(1), 29–35.

Kilty, K. M., & Haymes, M. V. D. (2000). Racism, nativism, and exclusion: Public policy, immigration, and the Latino experience in the United States. *Journal of Poverty, 4*(1–2), 1–25.

Knoll, B. R. (2010). *Understanding the 'new nativism': Causes and consequences for immigration policy attitudes in the United States* (Doctoral dissertation). The University of Iowa.

Lippard, C. D. (2015). Playing the 'immigrant card' reflections of color-blind rhetoric within Southern attitudes on immigration. *Social Currents*. doi:10.1177/2329496515604640

Malik, M. (2009). Anti-Muslim prejudice in the West, past and present: An introduction. *Patterns of Prejudice, 43*(3–4), 207–212.

Merino, S. M. (2010). Religious diversity in a 'Christian nation': The effects of theological exclusivity and interreligious contact on the acceptance of religious diversity. *Journal for the Scientific Study of Religion, 49*(2), 231–246.

Mir, S. (2011). 'Just to make sure people know I was born here': Muslim women constructing American selves. *Discourse: Studies in the Cultural Politics of Education, 32*(4), 547–563.

Perea, J. F. (1997). Introduction. In J. F. Perea (Ed.), *Immigrants out! The new nativism and the anti-immigrant impulse in the United States* (pp. 1–13). New York, NY: New York University Press.

Pew Research Center for the People and the Press. (2006). *Prospects for inter-religious understanding: Will views toward Muslims and Islam follow historical trends?* Washington, DC: Author.

Pew Research Center for the People and the Press. (2009). *Results from the 2009 Annual Religion and Public Life Survey*. Retrieved from http://www.pewforum.org/files/2009/09/survey09091.pdf

Pew Research Center for the People and the Press. (2011). *Results from the Muslim Americans: No signs of growth in alienation or support for extremism.* Retrieved from http://www.people-press.org/files/legacy-pdf/Muslim%20American%20Report%2010-02-12%20fix.pdf

Samhan, H. H. (1987). Politics and exclusion: the Arab American experience. *Journal of Palestine Studies, 16*(2), 11–28.

Stephan, W. G., Ybarra, O., & Bachman, G. (1999). A threat model of prejudice: The case of immigrants. *Journal of Applied Social Psychology, 29,* 2221–2237.

Wuthnow, R. (2005). *American and the challenges of religious diversity.* Princeton, NJ: Princeton University Press.

Does Islam deter crime in a secular Islamic country? The case of Turkey

Ozden Ozbay

'Does Islam deter crime in a secular country like Turkey' is the research question for which the current study tries to find a tentative answer. The data came from 619 undergraduate university students, 352 academic and non-academic staff at a public university and 498 shop owners in a small city in a Central Anatolian region in Turkey in 2010. The research on the relationship between Islam and crime is almost absent in the criminology literature. The findings of the correlation analysis pointed out that the impact of Islam on crime was more pronounced regarding alcohol use, and generally weak. More importantly, the results of the multivariate statistics showed that some religious measures deterred individuals themselves engaging in deviance and alcohol use. No relationship was found between Islam and violence.

Introduction

About one-fifth of the people in the world believe in Islam (Kurtz, 2012). Religion is a fundamental aspect of any human society, besides being a reflection of human beings looking for meaning. Also, religion gives one a feeling of identity, a map to follow in one's life and a feeling of security (Yavuz, 2004). It humanises a dehumanising situation (like prison), gives meaning to one's life, provides hope for the time to come, gives peace of mind, and so on. (O'Connor & Duncan, 2011). What differentiates Islam from Christianity and Judaism is Islam's stress on obedience to God's order in every aspect of human life (Serajzadeh, 2001–2002). What differentiates Turkey from other Middle Eastern societies is its age-old secular life (Eligur, 2010; White, 1995; for more differences, see Yavuz, 2004).

Unlike other Islamic countries, Turkey has been a *unique* country in the World since its establishment as a Republic in 1923 in terms of *mixing Islam with secularism*. Against this background, it will be interesting to know to what extent religion affects deviance/crime. The present paper, therefore, explores the key question: 'Does Islam deter crime?' This research question was tested by using the data obtained from both youth and adult samples in a small central Anatolian city in Turkey in 2010.

There are very few studies that have tested the negative link between Islam and crime (e.g. Groves, Newman, & Corrado, 1987; Helal & Coston, 1991; Özbay, 2007; Serajzadeh, 2001–2002; Souryal, 1987; Stark, 2001). The present study used both young and adult samples to study the issue in question, as also several comprehensive religious measures, which were not used earlier in Islam-crime literature. The data obtained from both young and adult samples from a small central Anatolian city in Turkey in 2010 were used for testing the research question.

Religion, crime and sociological theories of control

Several theories of diverse genres have been developed to explain the relationships between religion and crime: sociological or social psychological (e.g. social control, social learning, Marxist, see O'Connor, 2004; Stark, 1984; Tittle & Welch, 1983), legal or economic (deterrence theory, see Tittle & Welch, 1983), psychological (see Tittle & Welch, 1983) and bio-social theories (arousal theory, Ellis, 1987, cited in O'Connor, 2004).

Among these, the present author considers that sociological theories, based on the notion of *social control* in a Durkheimian sense, are more relevant to the study in hand. As mentioned earlier, the Turkish society by design has been historically characterised by a secular understanding of the social world. For this reason, a 'type of community' thesis appears to be the most relevant to frame the study in question. This thesis has two opposite versions: 'the moral community theory" and "the secular social disorganisation theory'.

First, according to the moral community theory (Stark, 1984), the impact of religion on the reduction of crime will be stronger in religious communities than in non-religious communities because the religious thoughts or actions of an individual will be energised by the group with which she/he associates. In Stark's words (1984, p. 275):

> What is critical is whether the *majority* of the kid's *friends* are religious. In communities where most young people do not attend church, religion will not inhibit the behavior even of those teenagers who personally are religious. However, in communities where most kids are religious, then those who are will be less delinquent than those who aren't.

Second, according to the secular social disorganisation theory (Tittle & Welch, 1983), an individual's religiousness will deter the individual from committing crime most effectively when there exist common normative dissensus (moral wrongness of deviance), weak social integration (e.g. sense of belonging to one's area of residence, degree of personal pride to one's own country, marital status, etc.), general view of weak peer conformity (degree of committing deviance by one's social surroundings) and a great number of non-religious individuals in a community. In other words, the effect of religion on crime is high if the levels of secular or social controls are none or little.

According to the moral community theory (Stark, 1984 or see O'Connor, 2004), the impact of religion on decreasing crime is dependent on the *type* of crime. That is, while crimes such as violent behaviour (impulsive deviance), which suddenly takes place, are not affected by one's religiousness, crimes such as theft (rational deviance), which requires much thinking, will be affected by one's religiousness. According to Stark (1984, p. 279),

> Indeed, acts of impulsive deviance lie outside the scope of *any* current *sociological* theories of deviance. All sociological theories of deviance assume a self-aware actor who chooses to deviate or to conform, and who displays patterns of deviance having some duration. Sociological theories have virtually nothing to say about brief moments of uncontrolled, irrational, impulse. Indeed, it is here that a fruitful division of labor with psychology would seem to be indicated.

Likewise, according to 'anti-ascetic theory' (O'Connor, 2004), the negative impact of religion on crime tends to be greater on criminal behaviours that are continuously forbidden by religious traditions, for example, illegal sex, gambling, or use of drugs.

The current study is not particularly designed to test 'the moral community' or 'the secular social disorganisation theory', and their corollaries. Yet, they are the only available theoretical/conceptual tools that appear to be more relevant to the relationship between religion and crime in the 'secular' context of Turkey.

Islam and Turkey

Turkey is a secular country, and almost all the people in Turkey believe in Islam. Secularism has been one of the dominant features of the Turkish society since 1923, and religion is controlled in the strict sense of the word by the Turkish state (Tapper, 1994). Also, most Muslims belong to Sunni Islam sect (Öktem, 2002).

In recent years, one of the most important issues in the Western World is *the fear of Islam*. Likewise, in today's Turkey, one of the most important questions is whether revival of Islam creates a danger for the survival of the Republic of Turkey (Tapper, 1994). This is because, within Turkish history, there has been a ceaseless fight between the secular Kemalist values and Islamic values (Yavuz, 2003).

Ataturk, the founder of the Turkish Republic, was cognizant of the dual role of Islam: The first role is a private one which gives an affectual and cognitive meaning to one's life as well as salvation, the idea of the other world, and ethics. The second role is a public one, which gives identity, ideology of politics and social integration. He was not in favour of either of these two roles, especially the second one. Ataturk aimed at substituting religion with contemporary secular thought. His social changes limited Islam to an individual's private life. Furthermore, political Islamic elements such as 'tarikats' (religious orders) and local religious practices were considered illegitimate and hence pushed underground. A dualistic notion of opposition was developed between the 'Islamic' (e.g. Ottoman, primitive and decadent) and the 'Republican' (e.g. European, contemporary and secular) (Tapper, 1994).

With the beginning of plural-party politics in 1946, there were two major opposing parties: Republican People's Party founded by Ataturk (CHP) and the Democrat Party (DP, which later became the Justice Party [AP]). Whereas CHP had a social democratic political orientation, buttressed by intellectuals and workers with a strong 'conservative' secular view, DP/AP had a liberal or 'progressive' political and economic orientation supported by local people with a strong religious view. The DP came into power following the national elections in 1950. At that time, an Islamic resurgence came into existence, for example, reopening of shrines, Islamic courses and state support for the Hajj (Tapper, 1994).

By the end of 1960s and 1970s, Islam was generally seen as an issue that was dealt with by political parties as well as the resurgence of the religious order. In 1980, the religious revival became more obvious in areas such as religious journals, newspapers and such other literature. Following 1980, religious order and some religious elements became effective in domains such as bureaucracy, state, military and education (Tapper, 1994).

According to World Value Survey (Erguder, Esmer, & Kalaycioglu, 1991; Esmer, 2002, 2011), religion played a very important role among the Turks. According to one study (Esmer, 2011), the importance of religion (rate of importance 92–93%) among the Turkish individuals remained the same in the last 15 years. Moreover, those who considered themselves 'religious' constituted 81% of the population in both 2000 and 2011 (the online web-based reference for this information is not currently available). Additionally, most Turks (79%) believe that religion is important, not in this world, but in the other world. Also, two-thirds of the Turks see the essential meaning of religion as not doing favours to other people, but obeying the rules and following rituals.

Concerning the rituals of the Turkish people, it is argued that there is *a disharmony between thoughts and actions* among the Turkish Islamic individuals. According to one of the experts on Turkish Islamic politics (Yavuz, 2004, p. 227), 'Turkish Islam is essentially a ritualized Islam that has very limited impact on one's moral conduct. There is a major gap between believing and behaving in Turkish Islam'. In fact, a similar type of observation was made by some other scholars on Turkish individuals' connection with their faith (Esmer, 2002; Junger, 1989).

There is no universal way, but a wide variety of ways of being and becoming an Islamic individual (Yavuz, 2004). In Turkey, many kinds of Islamic political identities exist. Against the backdrop of the conflict between the fundamentalist Islamic groups and the secularists, there are several intermediate groups standing between the fundamentalists and the secularists (White, 1995). Although the present study included some individuals of a particular religious order (the Gulen movement), the others had a *moderate* degree of religious orientation.

Islam and crime

All major religions in the world follow a paradoxical philosophy: While killing of people is considered a necessary act during holy war (frequently in the name of God), it is mostly forbidden at other times. Religions forbid violence on the basis of the following three reasons (Kurtz, 2012): It is in opposition to the nature of human beings; it is unproductive owing to spiralling violence in the long term; and it is wrongful because the deity does not wish it. All these themes are valid in Islamic thought also. More relevant to the present study is to understand violence in ordinary daily life in the light of what is laid down in Kur'an (5:32, cited in Kurtz, 2012, p. 304): 'Whoever kills a person [unjustly] ... , it is as though he has killed all mankind'. Also, Islam forbids the use of alcohol and drugs (Serajzadeh, 2001–2002; Souryal, 1987).

It is beyond the scope of this paper to review the relationship between non-Islamic religions and crime in a comprehensive way. There are several excellent reviews on this issue (Baier & Wright, 2001; Johnson, 2011; Johnson, Li, Larson, & McCullough, 2000; Ellis, Beaver, & Wright, 2009). Johnson et al. (2000) reviewed the relationship between religiosity and delinquency by using peer-reviewed journals in the years between 1985 and 1997 in the USA. The findings mostly indicated that religion had an inverse relationship with crime. Baier and Wright (2001) examined the link between religion and crime by using 60 publications of various types published during 1969–1998 in the USA. As before, the results of their meta-analysis indicate that religion plays the role of preventing criminal behaviour. Ellis et al. (2009) scrutinised the relationship between religious factors and criminal/delinquent acts by using around 180 official and individual studies in Europe, especially in North America. Similarly, their review points out that religious people are, in general, less likely to engage themselves in crime or delinquency. Johnson (2011) analyses the most comprehensive review of 272 studies on the link between religion and crime/delinquency, which covers the period between 1944 and 2010, mostly in North America (especially the USA). Also, this review shows that religion is inversely related to criminal or delinquent offences. Nevertheless, the most recent test of the relationship between religion and crime (Antonaccio, Tittle, Botchkovar, & Kranidiotis, 2010) in Greece, Russia and Ukraine shows that the link between religion and crime is mixed. Overall, the foregoing findings highlight the pattern that a strict adherence to religion is associated with a decrease in criminal or delinquent behaviour. All these studies suffer from two major problems: First, most studies were carried out in the Western World, especially in the USA. Second, all these studies were restricted to non-Islamic societies or religions.

The foregoing observations imply that research studies on the relationship between Islam and crime in the world are very few (Groves et al., 1987; Helal & Coston, 1991; Junger & Polder, 1993; Özbay, 2007; Serajzadeh, 2001–2002; Souryal, 1987; Stark, 2001). Whereas four of these studies used aggregate data (Groves et al., 1987; Helal & Coston, 1991; Souryal, 1987), the other three used individual-level data (Junger & Polder, 1993; Özbay, 2007; Stark, 2001). The findings of the aggregate studies are mixed. In one of the three studies, no link was found between the crime rate and Islam (Groves et al., 1987), but the other two reported that Islam plays a deterrent role on crime rate (Helal & Coston, 1991; Souryal, 1987).

More relevant to the current study are some individual-level studies on the relationship between Islam and criminal acts (Junger & Polder, 1993; Özbay, 2007; Stark, 2001). Again, the results of those studies are mixed at best. For example, Stark (2001), using the 1990–1991 data of World Value Survey, finds negative correlations between the importance of God to the individual and various deviant acts (e.g. buying stolen goods, not reporting the damage done by someone to a parked car, and using marijuana or hashish), but finds no correlation between mosque attendance and deviant acts in Turkey.

To sum up, there are numerous studies on the relationship between Christianity and crime/delinquency in the Western World, especially the USA, but relatively very few on Islam and crime/delinquency in the world, especially in Islamic societies. The current paper attempts to fill this gap through testing Islamic measures on criminal acts among samples of both young and adult people in a small Anatolian city, Nigde, Turkey. In line with the literature on the link between religion and crime in the West, as well as Islamic doctrine or lifestyle, it is hypothesised that Islam acts as a deterrent to criminal behaviour. Also, in line with 'the moral community' theory, it is hypothesised that the impact of Islam is stronger on deterring alcohol use than on deterring violence. Data for the present study were taken from university students, university staff members (academic and non-academic) and local shop owners. Welch, Tittle, and Petee (1991) argue that religion is less likely to influence students in public school settings. Therefore, it is hypothesised that the impact of religion on crime is stronger on the shop owner sample than on the samples of university students and staff members.

Method

Data

The data for this study were collected in May, 2010, from 619 college students, and 352 academic and non-academic staff members of a public university, and from 498 shop owners in the province of Nigde, a city with a population of around 105,000 in the Central Anatolian part of Turkey. Depending on the type of the dependent variables used in the regression analyses (e.g. current deviance, life-time deviance, violence and alcohol use), the sample sizes were reduced between 341 and 392 for the student, between 106 and 112 for the university staff members, and between 114 and 122 for the shop owner samples. A random sampling strategy was used to obtain the necessary number of college students. But, to obtain a suitable sample size that can maintain homogeneity in the general characteristics of the students, the study was restricted to two- and four-year university students. The self-reported survey was carried out in settings such as conference halls and classrooms. Prior to commencing the survey, the respondents were assured of the anonymous and confidential nature of the survey. The respondents were given the freedom to refrain from answering any or all questions, if they so wish. They were also provided with a signed paper that explained issues such as the importance of the study, the aim and topics of the study, besides the contact information of those who were conducting the survey. Also, the signed paper underlines the anonymous and confidential nature of the study. The students' sample was composed of 51.7% males and 47.3% females. The respondents' age ranged from 18 to 38 (their median age being 21). Moreover, parental global monthly family income varied from 150 TL to 36.000 TL (median global family income was 1.250 TL, which was approximately $810.00). In May, 2010, during the time of the survey, 1,5 TL was equivalent to 1$.

The university staff members, who participated in the study, included lecturers/readers ($n = 70$) and professors ($n = 94$) besides administrative staff members ($n = 188$). The average age of the administrative staff was 37, that of the lecturers 38, and that of the professors 40. Female administrative staff members constituted 38.3%, lecturers 42.9% and professors 18.1%. The average monthly income of the administrative staff members was 895 TL, that of the lecturers 3.000 and that of professors 3.500.

The shop owner sample was obtained on the basis of availability of the shop owners in three different locations within the province of Nigde ($N = 498$). In 2009, the population of the central part of Nigde was 105,702, that of Bor 37,566 and that of Ulukisla 5,486. The sample characteristics are as follows: The shop owners are mostly from Nigde ($n = 266$ or 53.4%), followed by those from Bor ($n = 110$ or 22.1%), and from Ulukisla ($n = 53$ or 10.6%); the number of missings is 69 or 13.8%. The average age of the shop owners is 34, the percentage of the female shop owners is 13.9 and the average monthly income of the shop owners is 1.500 TL.

Measures

Dependent variables

For studying the undergraduate students' sample, four dependent variables were used: deviance in an educational year, life-time deviance, violence and use of alcohol. *Deviance in an educational year* (current deviance) includes the following 20 items: not attending classes (73.8%); not attending school (67.5%); purchasing pirated things (58.9%); cheating during exams (40.8%); giving original or pirated things, such as music and film tapes, books, and so on, to other people (36.3%); putting a friend's signature on the attendance sheet (29.4%); battling for other reasons (except for a girl friend or political cause) (22.0%); having intercourse with someone other than his flirt, fiancée, wife (14.1%); bearing guns, knives, etc. (9.3%); disputing verbally or fighting with a male individual for the same girl (7.4%); assaulting someone for the purpose of hurting or killing him (7.2%); injuring oneself through a sharp, pointed thing (5.5%); involving in computer hacking (5.0%); attempting to have fights or having fought to establish a political hegemony at the school (3.2%); leading disorders at the campus area under the control of some political people in and outside the university (2.9%); succeeding in classes or graduating from the university by social networking ('torpil' in Turkish) (2.4%); undergoing punishment at school (2.1%); trying to steal things from places such as the dormitory, small shops, stores, and so on. (1.7%); vandalising properties of family, university, or residence (1.5%); and utilising electricity in an illegal fashion (0.7%).

The undergraduate students were asked to indicate 'How many times did you do the above acts or were exposed to them since the beginning of the 2009–2010 educational year?' The responses were rated as follows: none ($=1$), one or two times ($=2$), three–five times ($=3$) and six and more ($=4$). From these 20 questions, an index of deviance (Cronbach's alpha $=.74$) was created. Some questions in the questionnaire were obtained from Elliott and Ageton's study (1980).

The second dependent variable, *life-time deviance*, refers to an engagement in six deviant acts in one's life: attempting to engage or engaging in violence, cheating in exams, undergoing a disciplinary investigation at schools/institutions, using hard drugs (heroin, cannabis, etc.), stealing money, things, and so on, and undergoing detention or having a dispute to be settled in a court. The responses were rated as follows: none ($=1$), one or two times ($=2$), three–five times ($=3$), six–nine times and ten and more ($=4$). Of these items, an index of life-time deviance was created (Cronbach's alpha $=.49$). Because the reliability coefficient of life-time deviance is below the accepted lowest level (.60), it is used for an exploratory reason.

The third dependent variable *violence* included five deviant acts: attempting to have battle or having battled to establish a political hegemony at the school; disputing verbally or battling with a male person for the same girl to flirt; battling for some other reasons (with the exception of battling for a girl friend or political cause); assaulting someone with the purpose of hurting or killing him/her; and carrying knives, guns, and so on. Although a violence index was produced, it had a skewed distribution. For this reason, it was divided into those who were not involved in any violence (coded as 0, 65.3%), and those who did at least one violent act (coded as 1, 27.9%, excluding the missing cases which were 6.8%).

The final dependent variable is *alcohol use* which was applied only to the students and shop owners. It was measured by the amount of alcohol consumed by an individual. The responses varied from 'every day' ($=1$) to 'never' ($=7$). The response categories were regrouped thus: 'never' ($=0$) and 'to some degree' ($=1$).

Independent variables
Religion. The chief aim of the current study is to show whether religion deters *youth* from engaging in crime. However, besides the youth, *adults* are also included in the study, with several religious measures, for a *more comprehensive view* of the influence of religion on deviant acts. As the sample comprises both the youth and the adults, their religious measures are, to some extent, different.

University students. Family religiosity: The students were asked to indicate how religious their families were on a 10-point scale of 10–100. The responses varied from 10 (none) to 100 (completely). The responses were divided into two sub-groups: 10–50 as 'low family religiosity' (the reference category) and 60–100 as 'high family religiosity'.

Youth's religiosity: Nine questions on various religious acts of the students were posed commencing with the 2009–2010 school term: Belief in the existence of God, ritual worship for five times a day, fasting, reading Kur'an, giving alms, daily praying, thanking God, believing that 'everything happens for a reason' and following religious media. The response options varied from 'never' ($=1$) to 'always' ($=4$). An index of the religion of the youth was created out of the nine religious items (Cronbach's alpha $= .80$).

Belief in fate: A 10-point question was asked of the students on the degree of their belief in fate (10 = 'human beings determine their fate' and 100 = 'everything is determined by one's fate').

University Staff members. Importance of religion: The university staff members were asked to evaluate, on a scale of 10–100, the importance they give to religion. The responses ranged from 10 (none) to 100 (completely important). This question was not used in the *multivariate analysis* because of the small number of cases or high missing cases. (Likewise, although the students and the shop owner were also posed with the same question, their responses were not included in the final analysis because of the extremely skewed nature of their distribution.)

Belief in fate: The belief-in-fate question was also asked of the university staff. Their response distribution was skewed and therefore, divided into three groups: low ($=1$, the reference category), medium ($=2$) and high fate ($=3$).

Ideology of the newspaper read daily: A question was asked regarding the name of the newspaper they read daily. The responses were expected to indicate the ideological orientations of the respondents. The newspapers chosen for daily reading were divided into 'religious newspapers' (e.g. Zaman, Yeni Safak, Taraf, etc.) and 'non-religious newspapers' (e.g. Milliyet, Cumhuriyet, Radikal, etc., the reference category). The reason behind using this variable is that religion, besides ethnicity, has been a very sensitive topic in Turkey since its foundation, and it was thought that measurement of some indirect measures would be beneficial. Guided by the same logic, two more variables, namely, possessing religious symbols in office and watching television, were also included in the study.

Possessing religious symbols in office: This question was limited to *the university staff*. They were asked if they had any religious symbols in their offices (e.g. the picture of Rumi, portrait of a famous leader of Sufism; some sayings from Kur'an; staphylea, etc.). If the response was 'yes', it was coded as 1 (the reference category), otherwise 0.

Political identity: With a view to comparing and contrasting the impact of religious and non-religious political identity on deviant acts, the respondents were asked to indicate their political identity. The political identities include Turkish nationalists ($=1$, like the MHP), religious ($=2$, like the AKP, etc.), apolitical ($=3$) and leftist ($=4$, the reference category, like the CHP).

Shop owners. In the same way as the university staff, the shop owners were also asked to respond to the questions on *belief-in-fate, ideology of the newspaper read daily, and political identity*. Additionally, they were asked to indicate the TV channel they watched most in the last month. The TV channels were grouped into 'religious channels' ($=1$, for example, channels that are religious or support the Islamic AKP party in power, Samanyolu, 'TRT' as a group, Atv, etc.) and 'non-religious channels' ($=2$, the reference category being such channels as CNN-TURK, Kanal D, NTV, etc.).

Control variables

Age was measured by asking the respondents about their biological age. *Gender* was measured by asking for the respondents' gender (female was coded 1, and male 2, the reference category). *Income* referred to a family's average monthly income in the year 2010. *Deviant friend* was measured by asking the students if their closest friends ever received any punishment from school or university. If a student received at least one punishment, it was coded as 1, otherwise 0 (the reference category). *GPA* (Grade Point Average) was operationalised by asking the students about their GPA scores when they were at high school. If a student had good or very good scores, it was coded as 1, otherwise 0 (the reference category). *Risk taking* (Cronbach's alpha $= .83$) was operationalised by following responses of students to questions: 'Excitement and adventure are more important to me than security'; 'sometimes I will take a risk just for the fun of it'; 'I sometimes find it exciting to do things for which I might get into trouble' and 'I like to test myself every now and then by doing something a little risky.' The responses varied from 'never' ($=1$) to 'always' ($=4$). The questions relating to risk seeking were derived from the study of Tittle, Ward, and Grasmick (2003). *Family economic dissatisfaction* was measured by the response to the following question: 'How satisfying is your family's (parental or your own) economic situation?' The response categories varied from 'never satisfied' ($=10$) to 'completely satisfied' ($=100$). *Duration of school* was operationalised depending on whether a student was a two-year student ($=1$) or a four-year student ($=0$). Being a four-year student was used as the reference category.

Furthermore, *size of household* referred to how many people lived in the house of the respondent. Unlike in the western societies, although the number of children is currently getting smaller in Turkey (around two children), family is still a very important institution in terms of functions (social, psychological and economic supports) and structure (its size, type, etc.).

Having friends from different sects: The participants were asked to report on the number of friends they had from different sects. The responses were coded as *none* ($=0$) and *at least one* ($=1$, the reference category). *Occupational position* is relevant to only the university staff, who can be categorised into administrative staff ($=1$), academic staff with at least a Ph.

D. (= 2) and lecturers (= 3, the reference category). Because income and occupational position are related to each other on their face value, they were not used for the same analysis (e.g. income was used only for the shop owner sample, and occupational position for the university staff). Finally, the shop owners in the sample came from three different locations within the province of Nigde: Nigde (= 1, the reference category), Bor (= 2) and Ulukisla (= 3).

Results

Bivariate analysis: correlations

When correlation analysis of *the sample of the student* with all the variables in the analysis (including some religious measures which were not included in the multivariate statistics) was carried out, significant correlation coefficients, ranging from a low of ±.09 to a high of .66 (Appendix, Table A1), were obtained. Correlations of religious measures, which are significantly correlated with current social deviance, life-time social deviance, violence and use of alcohol vary from a low of −.10 to a high of −.44. The highest correlation is between the youth's religiosity and alcohol use. Furthermore, none of the religion measures is correlated with violent behaviour.

When a similar type of correlation analysis was carried out for *the sample of the academic and non-academic staff members*, significant correlations, ranging from ±.11 to −.65 (Table A2), were obtained. Correlations of religious measures with life-time deviance, violence and alcohol use range between −.12 and −.26. The highest correlation is between Islamic political identity and use of alcohol. Unexpectedly, having religious symbols in one's office ($r = .16$, in comparison with not having those symbols) is positively correlated with both life-time deviance and violence. None of the other religious measures is correlated with violence.

Finally, correlation analysis of *the shop owners sample* reveals significant correlations, ranging from ±.10 to .83 (Table A3). Correlation of religious measures with alcohol use (religious measures are not correlated with both life-time deviance and violence) ranges from .14 to −.27. Correlation between Islamic political ideology and alcohol use is the highest.

To sum up, almost all significant religious measures are negatively correlated with deviance, violence and alcohol use. In comparison to the other three dependent variables, it appears that Islam plays a more deterrent role in preventing alcohol use. Also, Islam is not related to violence. Furthermore, the correlation coefficients of most religious measures are below −.30, implying that the association of religion with deviance is, in general, weak at best.

Multivariate analysis: linear and logistic regressions

The student sample

Youth's religiosity is the only significant variable that has a negative influence on current deviance ($\beta = -0.17$) (Table A4). That is, an increase in religiosity leads to a decrease in deviance. Among the control variables, average total monthly family income has a positive influence on the dependent variable ($\beta = 0.21$). Compared to female students, male students are more likely to commit current deviance ($\beta = 0.12$). In comparison to the students with no deviant peers, the students with deviant peers are more likely to engage in deviant acts ($\beta = 0.14$). The increase in risk-seeking tendency of the youth is positively related to the dependent variable ($\beta = 0.33$). Compared to four-year university students, two-year students are less likely to be involved in current deviance ($\beta = -0.17$). The findings on life-time deviance are more or less similar to the foregoing findings. While youth's religiosity has a negative impact on life-time deviance ($\beta = -0.21$), income ($\beta = 0.19$), being male ($\beta = 0.18$), having deviant peers ($\beta = 0.11$) and risk seeking ($\beta = 0.29$) have positive impacts. Concerning violence, none of the variables relating to religion is significant. The only significant control variable is risk seeking. As risk seeking increases, so does violence (Exp. $\beta = 1.202$). As for alcohol use, religiosity of the youth is related negatively to alcohol use (Exp. $\beta = 0.793$). Students who are males (Exp. $\beta = 10.990$), aged (Exp. $\beta = 3.180$), risk seeking (Exp. $\beta = 1.346$) and in two-year university course (Exp. $\beta = 3.299$) are more likely to use alcohol.

The university staff members

As expected, an increase in the importance of religion among the university staff tends to decrease the likelihood of life-time deviance (Exp. $\beta = 0.130$) (Table A5). Compared to the male staff, the female staff is less likely to engage in life-time deviance (Exp. $\beta = 0.225$). Finally, compared to the lecturers, university teachers, with at least a Ph.D., are less likely to be involved in life-time deviant acts (Exp. $\beta = 0.295$). Also, in comparison to those staff members with low belief in fate, those staff members with high belief in fate are less likely to engage in violent acts (Exp. $\beta = 0.186$). Being female (Exp. $\beta = 0.096$), having the positions of both administrative staff members (Exp. $\beta = 0.244$) and university teachers with at least a Ph.D. (Exp. $\beta = 0.149$, compared to the lecturers) are less likely to commit violence.

The shop owners

The only significant religious measure is the ideology of the newspaper read daily. Compared to shop owners who read non-religious newspapers, those who read religious newspapers are less likely to use alcohol (Exp. $\beta = 0.290$).

As the shop owner gets older, she/he is less likely to engage in life-time deviance (Exp. $\beta = 0.942$). Compared to male shop owners, female shop owners are less likely to engage in life-time deviance (Exp. $\beta = 0.094$). Compared to the shop owners with at least one friend from different sects, those with no friends from different sects are less likely to act in a life-time deviance (Exp. $\beta = 0.252$). Similarly, as regards violence, age (Exp. $\beta = 0.936$), being female (Exp. $\beta = 0.080$) and not having friends from different sects (Exp. $\beta = 0.175$) show inverse relation to violence. In comparison to the shop owners with at least one friend from different sects, those with no friends from different sects (Exp. $\beta = 0.342$), those who are females (Exp. $\beta = 0.115$), and those who lived in the city of Bor (Exp. $\beta = 0.253$, compared to a big city, Nigde) are less likely to use alcohol.

Discussion and conclusion

The research question of the present study is: 'Does Islam deter crime in a secular country, Turkey?' This question was explored by using samples of young and adult people from a small city in the central Anatolian part of Turkey. The present study is unique in terms of being one of the very few individual studies that studied the relationship between Islam and crime.

Correlation analysis indicates that Islam plays a deterrent role in the prevention of criminal acts. However, the influence of Islam on crime is small. As Yavuz (2004) points out, this weak impact could be attributed to *the discrepancy between belief and action* among the Turkish individuals (e.g. 'ritualised Islam'). Also, while Islam generally appears to have a more deterrent effect on the *use of alcohol*, it shows, more or less, no effect on *violence* in the three samples studied. This finding is in harmony with the Islamic doctrine (e.g. Serajzadeh, 2001–2002; also see Özbay [2007] for a similar finding in Turkey) and the findings relating to the 'type-of-crime thesis', originating from the 'moral community' approach to the link between religion and crime in the West (O'Connor, 2004; Stark, 1984).

Multivariate statistical analysis of *the youth sample* shows that youth's religiosity has a significant negative impact on current deviance among the religious measures, life-time deviance and alcohol use. However, it shows no significant influence on violence. Also, concerning *the sample of the university staff members,* importance of religion and high fate (compared to low fate) have negative influences on life-time deviance and violence. Finally, for *the sample of the shop owners*, reading daily religious newspapers (compared to those who read non-religious newspapers) shows negative influence on alcohol use. Overall, the findings are in line with the *negative* relationship found between religion and crime in the western criminology literature (e.g. Baier & Wright, 2001; Johnson, 2011; Johnson et al., 2000; Ellis et al., 2009).

Furthermore, according to the *type-of-crime thesis* (as well as 'anti-ascetic theory') derived from the perspective of 'the moral community thesis' (O'Connor, 2004; Stark, 1984), religion is not expected to have any impact on violence (impulsive crime) as mentioned earlier; instead, it is expected to have a negative impact on alcohol use (rational 'deviance'). The results of multivariate statistical analysis point out that while Islam-related religious measures do not play any role in the violent acts of the youth and the adult, they play an important role in preventing them from the use of alcohol, as also some general acts of deviance (for a similar finding in Turkey, see Özbay, 2007).

Also, on the basis of the present findings, it cannot be concluded with certainty that the influence of religion on deviance/crime is more pronounced or widespread in respect of the shop owners than the university students and staff members. The results do not seem to support the argument of Welch, Tittle, and Petee (1991).

Possibly, the chief reason for not finding support for some religiosity measures is that they were measured with only one indicator. For example, the measure on (religious) political identity was operationalised with only a single question (where the respondents stood in political spectrum). A second possibility is that the Turks, especially some individuals forming part of the religious order, who consider religious issues sensitive in general, might have hidden their behaviour. Third, compared to other cities in Turkey, the city of Nigde, where the present study was conducted, has a very secular social–cultural environment. To some extent, such an environment might have decreased the effect of religion on deviant acts. Fourthly, except for some sections, the samples in the study comprised generally *ordinary people* who acted in a ritualistic manner in their religious beliefs and practices.

In an 'Islamophobic' global World, after *the September 11 Event*, the fear of Islam as a threat to the Western World has increased to a great extent. However, the issue at the centre should not concern *normal* Islamic people, but the *Jihadist* groups whose ultimate aim is to change the world by using *violent* means and thus create a worldwide Islamic society. That is, the *level* of Islam matters to a great deal. The core finding of the present study is that a *modicum* of Islam, contrary to the Islamophobic views of the Western World, deters people from deviance/crime in a *secular* country such as Turkey.

However, the present study had to contend with some serious limitations that need to be elaborated. The first is that the samples used for this study were restricted to university students and staff, and to shop owners in a small city of Turkey. Therefore, the findings cannot be considered applicable to the entire country. Second, because a cross-sectional research design was used, prior criminal/deviant behaviour was not controlled. Third, except for the youth's religiosity index, the rest of the religion measures were measured with only one indicator, and this reduced the possibility of finding strong relationships, if any, between religion and crime. Fourth, religion happens to be one of the sensitive topics in Turkey since its foundation. This could have obviously deterred the respondents from responding to the survey questions relating to religion, and therefore resulted in a small number of cases or a large number of missing cases. Hence, the findings here will have to be interpreted with caution. Obviously, further studies should be conducted on the link between Islam and crime in Turkey, as well as elsewhere.

In spite of these limitations, the contribution of the present study to the extant literature is significant on three counts. First, in the literature, it is one of the very few individual-level studies on the relationship between Islamic religion and crime. Second, the findings of the present study corroborate the negative association between religion (e.g. mostly Christianity) and crime, reported in the western literature. Third, the study covers more religious measures, besides including both young and adult samples, within its scope. Future studies should test the relationship between Islam and crime in more secular and religious social environments of Turkey or elsewhere (e.g. location comparison) or compare certain holy times (e.g. Ramadan) and normal times (other than Ramadan days) in terms of individual behaviour.

Acknowledgements

The author thanks Ms Dorothy Lee (Denver, CO) and *SPI Global* company for editing of the paper.

References

Antonaccio, O., Tittle, C. R., Ekaterina, B., & Kranidiotis, M. (2010). The correlates of crime and deviance: Additional evidence. *Journal of Research in Crime and Delinquency, 47*, 297–328.
Baier, J. C., & Wright, B. R. E. (2001). If you love me, keep my commandments: A meta-analysis of the effect of religion on crime. *Journal of Research in Crime and Delinquency, 38*, 3–21.
Eligur, B. (2010). *The mobilization of political Islam in Turkey.* Cambridge: Cambridge University Press.
Ellis, L., Beaver, K., & Wright, J. (2009). *Handbook of crime correlates.* Amsterdam: Academic Press.
Erguder, U., Esmer, Y., & Kalaycioglu, E. (1991). *Turk toplumunun degerleri [Values of Turkish society].* Istanbul: Tusiad.
Esmer, Y. (2002). Ahlaki değerler ve toplumsal degisme [Ethical values and social change]. In TUBA (Ed.), *Turkiye'de bunalım ve demokratik çıkış yolları [Crisis and democratic solutions in Turkey]* (pp. 45–68). Ankara: TUBİTAK Matbaası.
Groves, W. B., Newman, G., & Corrado, C. (1987). Islam, modernization and crime: A test of the religious ecology thesis. *Journal of Criminal Justice, 15*, 495–503.
Helal, A. A., & Coston, T. M. C. (1991). Low crime rates in Bahrain: Islamic social control – Testing the theory of synnomie. *International Journal of Comparative and Applied Criminal Justice, 15*, 125–144.
Johnson, R. B. (2011). *More god, less crime: Why faith matters and how it could matter more.* West Conshohocken, PA: Templeton Press.
Johnson, R. B., De Li, S., Larson, B. D., & McCullough, M. (2000). A systematic review of the religiosity and delinquency literature. *Journal of Contemporary Criminal Justice, 16*, 32–52.
Junger, M. (1989). Discrepancies between police and self-report data for Dutch racial minorities. *British Journal of Criminology, 29*, 273–284.
Junger, M., & Polder, W. (1993). Religiosity, religious climate, and delinquency among ethnic groups in the Netherlands. *British Journal of Criminology, 33*, 416–435.
Kurtz, R. L. (2012). *God's in the global village: The world's religions in sociological perspective* (3rd ed.). Los Angeles: Sage.
O'Connor, P. T. (2004). What works, religion as a correctional intervention: Part I. *Journal of Community Corrections, 14*, 11–27.
O'Connor, P. T., & Duncan, B. J. (2011). The sociology of humanist, spiritual, and religious practice in prison: Supporting responsivity and desistance from crime. *Religions, 2*, 590–610.
Öktem, N. (2002). Religion in Turkey. *Brigham Young University Law Review, 2*, 371–403.

Özbay, Ö. (2007). Universite ogrencileri arasında din ve sosyal sapma (religion and social deviance among university students). *Cumhuriyet Universitesi Sosyal Bilimler Dergisi, 3*, 1–24.

Serajzadeh, H. S. (2001–2002). Islam and crime: The moral community of Muslims. *Journal of Arabic and Islamic Studies, 4*, 111–131.

Souryal, S. S. (1987). The religionization of a society: The continuing application of Shariah law in Saudi Arabia. *Journal for the Scientific Study of Religion, 26*, 429–449.

Stark, R. (1984). Religion and conformity: Reaffirming a sociology of religion. *Sociological Analysis, 45*, 273–283.

Stark, R. (2001). Gods, rituals, and the moral order. *Journal for the Scientific Study of Religion, 40*, 619–636.

Tapper, R. (Ed.). (1994). *Islam in modern Turkey: Religion, politics and literature in a secular state*. London: I. B. Tauris & Co Ltd.

Tittle, R. C., Ward, A. D., & Grasmick, G. H. (2003). Gender, age, and crime/deviance: A challenge to self-control theory. *Journal of Research in Crime and Delinquency, 40*, 426–453.

Tittle, R. C., & Welch, R. M. (1983). Religiosity and deviance: Toward a contingency theory of constraining effects. *Social Forces, 61*, 653–682.

Welch, R. M., Tittle, R. C., & Petee, T. (1991). Religion and deviance among adult catholics: A test of the "moral communities" hypothesis. *Journal for the Scientific Study of Religion, 30*, 159–172.

White, B. J. (1995). Islam and democracy: The Turkish experience. *Current History, 94*, 7–12.

Yavuz, M. H. (2003). *Islamic political identity in Turkey*. Oxford: Oxford University Press.

Yavuz, M. H. (2004). Is there a Turkish Islam? The emergence of convergence and consensus. *Journal of Muslim Minority Affairs, 24*, 213–232.

Appendix

Table A1. Correlation analysis (student sample).[a]

	1	2	3	4	5	6	7	8	9	10	11	12	13	14	15	16	17	18
1. Current social deviance index																		
2. Life-time social deviance index	.66*																	
3. Violence (=yes)[b]	.49*	.35*																
4. Alcohol use (=yes)	.36*	.41*	.14*															
5. High family religiosity	−.18*	−.06	−.03	−.17*														
6. Youth's religiosity index	−.27*	−.28	−.05	−.44*	.26*													
7. Youth's fate	−.13*	−.10*	−.01	−.16*	.09*	.29*												
8. Not read any newspaper	.00	−.03	−.03	−.02	.03	−.02	.05											
9. Read AKP-related newspapers	−.07	−.08	−.05	−.10*	.02	.07	.02	−.14*										
10. Read Gulen-related newspapers	−.01	−.03	−.02	−.23*	.04	.24*	.07	−.20*	−.21*									
11. Religious and nationalist identity	−.13*	−.07	.02	−.28*	.28*	.36*	.17*	.04	−.06	.21*								
12. Casting votes to religious and nationalist parties	−.04	−.05	−.09	−.27*	.14*	.26*	.10	.04	−.06	.46*	.39*							
13. Age	.05	.10*	−.02	.04	−.01	−.07	.02	−.03	.02	−.05	−.11*	−.01						
14. Average family total income	.21*	.21*	.08	.15*	−.04	−.08	−.01	.00	−.01	−.04	−.02	−.07	.01					
15. Gender (=male)	.22*	.30*	.15*	.29*	−.04	−.26*	−.02	−.06	−.08	−.06	−.07	.03	.17*	−.03				
16. Deviant friends (=at least one)	.13*	.14*	.07	.05	.00	.01	.02	−.02	.03	−.04	.04	.01	.02	.02	.05			
17. GPA (good and very good)	−.09	−.16*	−.08	−.17*	−.02	.14*	−.05	−.06	.01	.03	.03	−.01	−.17*	.01	−.24*	−.09*		
18. Risk taking index	.37*	.35*	.19*	.31*	−.10*	−.16*	−.10*	.04	−.01	−.07	−.02	−.09	−.09*	.06	.09*	.16*	−.10*	
19. Economic dissatisfaction	−.010	−.01	−.01	.02	−.11*	−.07	−.01	−.01	.05	−.01	−.13*	.01	.11*	−.44*	.06	.00	−.08	−.02
20. Two-year university	−.14*	−.09*	−.09*	.16*	.02	−.09*	−.05	.00	−.03	−.04	.00	−.08	.07	−.11*	.04	.09*	−.16*	.00	.03

*Significant at the .05 level (two tailed).
[a]Some religious measures here were not used in the multivariate statistical analyses due to a small number of cases or high missing cases. These variables were: reading newspapers, political identity, and casting votes in general elections.
[b]Reference categories were not engaged in violence, not using alcohol, low religious family, reading moderate left and right newspapers, leftist political ideology, leftist party, being female, having non-deviant peer, low grade and four-year college.

Table A2. Correlation analysis (academic and non-academic staff sample).[a]

	1	2	3	4	5	6	7	8	9	10	11	12	13	14	15	16	17	18
1. Life-time deviance (= at least one)																		
2. Violence (= at least one)	.45*																	
3. Alcohol (= yes)	.15*	.14*																
4. Importance of religion	−.02	.04	−.25*															
5. Medium fate	−.03	−.03	−.02	.00														
6. High fate	.05	.01	−.12*	.23*	−.64*													
7. Read AKP and Gulen-related newspapers	.04	.00	−.21*	.12	.04	.06												
8. Religious symbols (= yes)	.16*	.16*	−.05	.09	−.05	.14*	.10											
9. Nationalist political identity	.11	.14*	.15*	.02	.05	−.07	−.14	.00										
10. Islamic political identity	.05	.02	−.26*	.23*	−.11*	.19*	.28*	.15*	−.45*									
11. Apolitical identity	−.21*	−.14*	−.08	−.04	.09	.00	.00	−.10	−.39*	−.32*								
12. Age	.02	.01	.06	−.03	−.11*	.02	.00	−.01	.06	−.08	−.06							
13. Gender (= women)	−.20*	−.28*	−.20*	−.14*	.14*	−.11*	−.19*	−.12	−.13*	−.12	.16*	−.18*						
14. Average family total income	−.09	.02	.16*	−.14*	.16*	−.15*	−.20*	.02	.10	−.16*	.07	−.07	.18*					
15. Marital status (= married)	.03	.04	.03	.02	.00	−.03	−.16*	.03	.00	.07	.00	−.41*	.15*	−.02				
16. Size of household	.00	−.05	−.06	.16*	−.03	.13*	.15*	.02	−.05	.10	.01	.19*	−.16*	−.12	−.47*			
17. At least one friend from different sects	.03	−.02	.10	−.08	−.03	−.03	−.15*	.11	−.05	−.07	.07	−.02	−.08	−.01	.09	.00		
18. Administrative staff	.14*	.10	−.10	.13*	−.09	.16*	.05	−.18*	.01	.10	−.14*	−.16*	.11*	−.28*	.11*	.03	−.26*	
19. Academic staff	−.02	−.05	.08	−.09	−.04	−.14*	−.06	.12*	.06	−.17*	.12	.19*	−.20*	.12	−.14*	.03	.24*	−.65*

*Significant at the .05 level (two tailed).
[a]Some religious measures here were not used in the multivariate statistical analyses due to a small number of cases or high missing cases. These variables were alcohol use and leftist political ideology.
[b]Reference categories were not involved in any deviant acts, not involved in violence, not used alcohol, low fate, reading 'non-religious' (more secular) newspapers, not having any friends from different sects, not possessing religious symbols in one's office, having leftist political identity, being men, never married, working in the positions of lecturers or research assistants.

Table A3. Correlation analysis (shop owners sample).[a]

	1	2	3	4	5	6	7	8	9	10	11	12	13	14	15	16	17	18
1. Life-time deviance (= at least one)																		
2. Violence (= at least one)	**.83***																	
3. Alcohol (= yes)	**.24***	**.20***																
4. Medium fate	.06	.02	.00															
5. High fate	−.04	−.01	**−.17***	**−.66***														
6. Read AKP and Gulen-related newspapers	.00	−.01	**−.19***	−.10	.06													
7. Not read any newspapers	−.05	−.02	−.03	.02	.01	**−.29***												
8. Nationalist political identity	.03	.01	**.18***	.00	−.05	**−.16***	−.01											
9. Islamic political identity	−.03	−.03	**−.27***	−.07	**.13***	**.31***	**.13***	**−.51***										
10. Apolitical identity	.00	.07	−.05	**.14***	.00	−.04	−.01	**−.25***	**−.40***									
11. Watching Islamic TV channels	−.05	−.05	**−.16***	−.01	**.11***	**.31***	.07	**−.15***	**.29***	−.03								
12. Age	**−.14***	**−.17***	.02	.00	−.06	.01	.04	−.05	.08	**−.18***	.01							
13. Gender (= women)	**−.24***	**−.19***	**.23***	.04	−.02	**−.12***	.08	−.06	−.07	.10	.02	**−.14***						
14. Average family total income	.07	.09	**.14***	**.10***	−.08	.01	**−.11***	.06	−.05	−.09	−.07	.01	−.02					
15. Marital status (= married)	−.03	−.06	−.04	−.01	.05	.02	.07	−.05	**.18***	**−.12***	**.12***	**.52***	**−.19***	−.02				
16. Size of household	−.04	−.03	.01	−.04	−.02	**.15***	−.06	−.03	**.12***	−.09	.09	−.01	.02	**−.14***	−.06			
17. At least one friend from different sect	.09	.06	**.14***	.09	**−.11***	.07	**−.13***	−.04	−.09	.09	.01	−.07	−.04	**.12***	−.10	.01		
18. Small city of Bor	−.03	.01	**−.14***	−.02	.02	**.16***	.02	−.02	**.15***	−.01	.10	**.10***	−.01	.06	**.11***	.03	**−.11****	
19. Town of Ulukisla	−.01	**−.10***	**.17***	−.03	−.08	−.11	−.09	.04	**−.15***	−.10	−.02	.04	.08	.00	−.06	.02	.10	**−.22***

*Significant at the .05 level (two tailed).
[a]Reference categories were not involved in any deviant acts, not involved in violence, not used alcohol, low fate, reading 'non-religious' (more secular) newspapers, having leftist political identity, other TV channels which were not particularly Islamic, being men, never married, not having any friends from different sects, residing in the city of Nigde (its population was 105,702), Bor (its population was 37,566), Ulukisla (its population was 5,486) in 2009.

Table A4. Classic and logistic regression analyses of impacts of religion on current deviance, life-time deviance, violence and alcohol use in Nigde, Bor and Ulukisla (student sample).

Independent variables[a]	Current deviance (n = 341) Beta	Life-time deviance (n = 344) Beta	Violence (n = 380) Exp(B)	Alcohol use (n = 392) Exp(B)
Religion[a]				
Family's religiosity (high)	−0.06	0.04	1.293	0.855
Youth's religiosity	−0.17***	−0.21***	0.987	0.793***
Youth's belief in fate	−0.03	−0.02	1.000	1.002
Control variables				
Age	0.04	0.07	1.006	3.180***
Average total family monthly income (log.)	0.21***	0.19***	1.446	0.957
Gender (male)[b]	0.12**	0.18***	1.324	10.990***
Having deviant peer[b]	0.14**	0.11**	1.421	1.365
Grade (good)[b]	0.01	−0.09	0.920	0.942
Grade (very good)	0.04	0.01	2.039	1.531
Risk seeking	0.33**	0.29***	1.202***	1.346***
Family financial dissatisfaction	0.04	0.08	0.998	1.009
Duration of school (two-year college)[b]	−0.17***	−0.07	0.823	3.299***
Constant	14.179	2.054	−0.3.401	−5.176**
R^2/Nagelkerke R^2	0.31***	31***	0.100**	0.444***

*$p \leq .10$.
**$p \leq .05$.
***$p \leq .01$.
[a]While there was a question about being Alevi and Sunni, it was not included in the analysis due to the small number of the Alevi students in the sample (4.1%). Furthermore, although there were question about the importance of religion for the students, it was not included in the analysis owing to the highly skewed nature of its distribution.
[b]Reference categories were low religious family, being female, having non-deviant peer, low grade and four-year college.

Table A5. Logistic regression analyses of impacts of religion on deviance, violence, alcohol use in Nigde, Bor and Ulukisla (samples of academic and non-academic staff & shop owners).

Independent variables	University staff			Shop owners	
	Life-time deviance (n = 106) Exp(B)	Violence (n = 112) Exp(B)	Life-time deviance (n = 122) Exp(B)	Violence (n = 119) Exp(B)	Alcohol (n = 114) Exp(B)
Religion					
Importance of religion[a]	**0.130****	0.794	—	—	0.757
Fate (medium)[b]	2.004	0.332	2.789	2.203	0.595
Fate (high)	1.060	**0.186****	0.813	0.792	**0.290***
Ideology of newspaper read daily (AKP-Gulen-related newspapers)	2.254	0.891	0.623	0.924	0.428
Ideology of newspaper read daily (did not read)[c]	—	—	0.761	2.400	
Possessing religious symbols in one's office[d]	1.367	1.904	—	—	
Political identity (nationalist)[e]	—	—	0.960	0.255	0.584
Political identity (religious)	—	—	1.496	0.437	0.524
Political identity (apolitical)	—	—	4.421	3.682	0.471
Watching TV (Islamic channels)[f]	—	—	0.966	1.269	0.486
Control variables					
Age	1.010	1.010	**0.942****	**0.936****	0.967
Gender (female)	**0.225****	**0.096*****	**0.094*****	**0.080*****	**0.115****
Average total family monthly income (log.)[g]	—	—	0.942	1.195	0.715
Marital status (married)	0.432	1.226	0.702	0.723	1.318
Household size	1.084	0.697	0.976	1.210	1.175
Having friends from different sects (none)	1.981	0.862	**0.252****	**0.175*****	**0.342***
Occupational position[h] (administrative staff)	0.513	**0.244****	—	—	
Occupational position (academic staff)	**0.295***	**0.149****	—	—	

Location of residence (Bor)[i]	–	–	2.852	1.675	2.459	**0.253****
Location of residence (Ulukışla)	–	–	0.229*	1.822	1.625	0.797
Constant	2.477			3.660	2.326	3.766
Nagelkerke R^2	0.304**			0.372***	0.406***	0.385***

* $p \leq .10$.
** $p \leq .05$.
*** $p \leq .01$.

[a] Although a question about the importance of religion was asked in relation to the shop owners, the extremely skewed distribution of its responses did not allow to include it here. Also, one outlier was identified in relation to 'Deviance' as a dependent variable for the sample of the shop owners; it was deleted from the analysis.

[b] Reference categories were low fate, non-religious newspaper, having *at least* one friend from different sects, not possessing religious symbols in one's office, having leftist political identity, watching non-Islamic TV channels, being men, never married, working in the positions of lecturers or research assistants, living in the city centre of Niğde which had the population of 105,702, followed by the population of 37,566 in the centre of Bor and the population of 5486 in the centre of Ulukışla in 2009.

[c] 'Did not read' category had few cases for the sample of university staff ($n = 29$, % 8.2); it was not included in the analysis.

[d] The relevant question was not asked for the sample of the shop owners.

[e] While a question about the political ideology of the academic and non-academic staff was posed, its inclusion in the analyses reduced the sample size very much due to the missing cases; it, therefore, was not included in this table. Likewise, owing to the great number of missing cases, alcohol use of the university staff was dropped from the analysis.

[f] The TV question was not asked regarding the university staff.

[g] Because occupational position was viewed as an indicator of social class, as a result, income was not used for the sample of the university staff.

[h] This question was not relevant for the shop owners.

[i] Although this question was asked for the university staff, it was not as meaningful issue/question for them as it was for the shop owners. Also, an attempt was being made in the statistical analyses to have an equal number of control variables in relation to both the university staff and the shop owners.

Is there a natural rate of crime in India?

Jagadish Prasad Sahu and Chandan Kumar Mohanty

This paper examines the natural rate of crime hypothesis in the Indian context. We use annual time series data on aggregate as well as specific crime categories for the period 1953–2012. Various types of unit root tests – conventional as well as unit root test with endogenously determined structural breaks – are used to identify whether the respective crime rates are stationary. The empirical findings suggest that majority of the crime series are stationary with structural breaks implying the existence of a natural rate of crime in India in the long run. Specifically, total crimes along with individual crime types such as burglary, counterfeiting, criminal breach of trust, dacoity and theft are stationary with two structural breaks, whereas kidnapping & abduction and cheating are stationary with one break. Our findings are consistent with the literature which argues that crimes with pecuniary motives are more likely to have natural rates.

1. Introduction

The concept of natural rate of crime (henceforth NRC) is often used in the economics of crime literature to refer to the long-run equilibrium rate of crime (Buck, Gross, Hakim, & Weinblatt, 1983; Buck, Hakim, & Spiegel, 1985; Friedman, Hakim, & Spiegel, 1989). Drawing analogy with the natural rate of unemployment, the NRC is introduced in the analysis of crime to represent the long-run equilibrium crime rate which is the result of the structural characteristics of a given society. More precisely, the NRC refers to the presence of a certain level of crime in the long run despite several deterrent measures such as fine, imprisonment and police expenditure.

It is widely recognised that the structural factors like poverty, unemployment, inequality, lack of social security and the level of education are important determinants of crime in the long run. Therefore, the law enforcement expenditure alone cannot reduce crime beyond a certain level, known as the natural rate. Owing to the differences in structural characteristics, the natural rate varies across societies. Studies like Buck et al. (1983, 1985) and Friedman et al. (1989) argue that the existence of a natural rate is one possible reason why deterrent measures fail to reduce crime in the long run. The empirical evidence on the ineffectiveness of deterrent measures in the long run provides sufficient reason to examine whether a natural rate exists in the crime rate. The presence of a natural rate of crime entails that the deterrent measures have only temporary effects, and that crime rate reverts to its previous level in the long run. In other words, the law enforcement expenditures may not be effective to reduce crime in the long run unless the structural problems of the society are addressed.

The notion of NRC is derived from the natural rate hypothesis (hereafter denoted as NRH) formulated by Phelps (1967) and Friedman (1968). The NRH postulates that unemployment rate tends to revert to its equilibrium level (natural rate) in the long run, and characterises unemployment rate as a mean reversion process (i.e. integrated of order zero or stationary process). Simply put, the NRH asserts that shocks to the unemployment series are of temporary nature, and the unemployment rate finally returns to its equilibrium level in the long run. On the contrary, the hysteresis hypothesis proposed by Blanchard and Summers (1986, 1987) presumes that shocks have permanent effects on the level of unemployment rate due to labour market rigidities, and describes unemployment rate as a non-stationary or unit root process. These two competing hypotheses (hysteresis versus natural rate) have been examined extensively in the economics literature by employing unit root tests on the unemployment rate series.[1] Also, in the criminology literature, similar tests have been applied to investigate the nature of shocks in the crime series (Cook & Cook, 2011; Narayan, Nielsen, & Smyth, 2010). A non-stationary series of crime rate indicates that shocks to the series have permanent effect which provides evidence that the crime rate does not return to a natural rate (i.e. the equilibrium level) over time. However, a stationary time series of crime rate indicates that shocks to the series are of transitory nature, and subsequently, the series reverts to its equilibrium level in the long run.

In view of the fact that criminal activities impose a huge social cost, it is of paramount importance to understand the dynamics of crime rate for an efficient policy formulation. This paper investigates whether there is a natural rate of crime in India, utilising both total and specific types of crime data at the national level spanning 1953–2012. Being the second most populous country in the world with widespread poverty, inequality and unemployment, examining the behaviour of crime in India is of pedagogical interest. The literature on the NRC being sparse in the developing country context provides further motivation to carry out the present study. This paper is closely related to Narayan et al. (2010) and Cook and Cook (2011). Narayan et al. (2010) examine the natural rate of crime hypothesis in the context of developed countries including the US, while Cook and Cook (2011) investigate the time series behaviour of US crime rates without referring to the natural rate of crime concept. We provide a brief description of these papers in Section 2.

To the best of our knowledge, this paper is the first attempt to examine the NRC hypothesis in the Indian context. We use a number of unit root tests both conventional and unit root tests that account for endogenously determined structural breaks to identify the order of integration of the respective crime series. Particularly, in addition to the standard Augmented Dickey–Fuller (ADF) test and the generalised least squares (GLS) version of the Dickey–Fuller test, we employ the minimum Lagrange Multiplier (LM) unit root test of Lee and Strazicich (2003, 2004) to ascertain the order of integration of the specific crime categories over the sample period. The results of the Lee–Strazicich (LS) test show that most of the series are breakpoint stationary implying the existence of a natural rate of crime in India in the long run. To be precise, we find that total crime rate as well as specific criminal activities such as burglary, counterfeiting, criminal breach of trust (CBT), dacoity and theft are stationary with two structural breaks, whereas kidnapping & abduction (KA) and cheating are stationary with one break. The results suggest that the natural rate of crime hypothesis holds for majority of the criminal activities in India.

The remainder of the paper is structured as follows. In Section 2, we review the extant literature on the natural rate of crime including studies that examine the dynamic behaviour of criminal activities. Section 3 describes the data and empirical framework. The results are discussed in Section 4, and Section 5 concludes the paper.

2. Review of literature

The rational utility approach to crime argues that the potential offenders compare the costs and benefits of committing a crime before doing so (Becker, 1968). Following Becker (1968) and Ehrlich (1973), there is a large body of literature analysing the effects of deterrent measures such as police expenditure, capital punishment, fine and disposal of criminal cases on crime rate. However, several studies show that the deterrent measures have failed to reduce crime (Buck et al., 1983; Cameron, 1988; Cornwell & Trumbull, 1994; Myers, 1983). Buck et al. (1983, 1985) introduce the concept of NRC to explain the failure of deterrent measures to reduce crime in the long run. The socio-economic factors such as poverty, inequality, unemployment, level of education, percentage of adult population and sex ratio are important determinants of crime across space and time (Entorf & Spengler, 2000; Han, Bandyopadhyay, & Bhattacharya, 2013; Lin, 2008; Lochner, 1999; Raphael & Winter-Ebmer, 2001). The structural factors of the economy influence the likelihood of existence of a certain level of criminal activities in the long run. We briefly discus the few select papers related to the natural rate of crime in the following paragraphs. Though the concept of NRC dates back to 1980s, scholarly literature on this is extremely meagre. Investigating the differences in deterrent effects of policing on crime among various communities (rural, sub-urban and urban), Buck et al. (1983) find the presence of a natural rate of crime in the given community. Drawing analogy with the natural rate of unemployment, they argue that a certain level of property crime exists in the long run due to the high expected net return associated with it. Simply put, the central argument of the paper is that the expected net return of some property crime is too high that any reasonable increase in police expenditure would not substantially diminish the number of crimes in the long run. Subsequently, Buck et al. (1985) propose a theoretical model of natural rate of crime and provide empirical support for the same. The model predicts that the deterrent measures are effective only in the short run. Nonetheless, the potential offenders become more vigilant and find their targets by revising their actions in the long run. Given that the potential criminals are rational, learning by doing results in the presence of a certain level of criminal activities in the long run despite increasing police expenditure. Friedman et al. (1989) demonstrate that while police expenditure exhibits a deterring effect on crime in the short run, it fails to do so in the long run. In order to explain this phenomenon, they contend that the potential criminals learn from previous experiences and revise their strategies to tackle the new level of police effort that helps them to go back to the previous level of criminal activities.

Narayan et al. (2010) empirically examine the NRC hypothesis in the context of developed countries. Specifically, the paper investigates the existence of a natural rate of crime for the United Kingdom and the United States and for a panel of G7 countries (Canada, France, Germany, Italy, Japan, US and UK) and find evidence of the presence of a natural rate in several crime categories in these countries. Their results show that the null hypothesis of a unit root is rejected for most of the series for the UK when the Lee and Strazicich (2003) unit root test with two structural breaks is employed. In case of the UK, they find that violent crime, robbery, burglary, theft, criminal damage as well as total crimes are stationary with two structural breaks, and for the US, violent crime, assault and motor vehicle theft are stationary with one structural break. Finally, the panel unit root test results suggest that the aggregate crime rate is stationary with one structural break for the group of G7 countries. In a recent study, using the Lee and Strazicich (2003) unit root test with two breaks, Cook and Cook (2011) examine whether the US crime rates for the period 1960–2007 are characterised as unit root processes. They find that all classifications of criminal activity are non-stationary when traditional unit root tests without structural breaks are applied. However, their findings completely reverse, that is the null hypothesis of non-stationarity for all the series is rejected when the LS test with two structural breaks are utilised.

3. Data and methodology

3.1. *Data and variables*

We use the annual time series data on various types of crime in India for the period 1953–2012. Data on different types of crime incidences are taken from the annual reports of National Crime Record Bureau, Government of India. The present study considers both aggregate (total cognisable crimes) and specific crime categories under the Indian Penal Code (IPC). Precisely, our study includes the crime classifications, namely murder, culpable homicide not amounting to murder (CHNM), rape, KA, dacoity (violent robbery by a group of people), robbery, burglary, theft, riots,CBT, cheating, counterfeiting and other crimes.[2] The statistics on rape and CHNM are available only for the period 1971–2012. The incidences of CBT, cheating and counterfeiting are available for the period 1954–2012. For all other categories of crime, data are available for the full sample period, that is, 1953–2012. The population data are obtained from the Handbook of Statistics on Indian Economy, Reserve Bank of India. Our empirical analysis is based on crime rate which is defined as the number of crimes per 100,000 population. Table 1 reports the descriptive statistics of different crime categories. The average rate of total crime is 174 in the sample period. Other crimes top among the crime categories with an average of 68 incidences per one lakh population. Property crimes such as theft and burglary are high compared to other individual crime categories. Theft is the second highest crime with an average rate of 46, and counterfeiting is the lowest with an average rate of 0.2 over the sample period.

3.2. *Empirical strategy*

Our empirical strategy involves use of a variety of unit root tests – both conventional and unit root test which account for endogenously determined structural breaks – to ascertain the order of integration of each of the crime series. We begin the analysis with the use of ADF test and the GLS version of the Dickey–Fuller test of Elliott, Rothenberg, and Stock (1996, hereafter DF-GLS) to examine the stationarity of each of the series. The DF-GLS test is a two-step procedure. First, the

Table 1. Descriptive statistics.

Crime category	Obs.	Mean	Std. Dev.	Min.	Max.
Murder	60	3.13	0.58	2.32	4.60
CHNM	42	0.42	0.07	0.30	0.55
Rape	42	1.23	0.48	0.45	2.05
KA	60	2.00	0.51	1.39	3.91
Dacoity	60	1.19	0.55	0.35	2.31
Robbery	60	2.40	0.68	1.44	3.76
Burglary	60	20.85	9.62	7.60	38.89
Theft	60	46.40	15.56	22.88	73.68
Riots	60	9.30	3.37	5.05	15.95
CBT	59	2.76	1.14	1.22	4.73
Cheating	59	3.34	1.35	1.91	7.74
Counterfeiting	59	0.19	0.10	0.06	0.59
Other crimes	60	68.38	20.31	31.85	104.02
Total crimes	60	174.26	18.38	136.19	207.56

given time series is transformed via a GLS regression, and then (an augmented) Dickey–Fuller test is used to test for a unit root in the second step. Elliott et al. (1996) show that the DF-GLS test exhibits significantly greater power than the ADF test. For the reason that both the tests are extensively used in the literature, we do not describe them here. However, these unit root tests do not account for structural breaks in the given series. As a result, they have low power in the presence of structural breaks. Perron (1989) suggests that ignoring the presence of a structural break reduces the power to reject the null hypothesis of a unit root when the stationary alternative is true. In other words, the power of a unit root test declines substantially when the test does not account for the potential structural break in the series.[3] In order to overcome this drawback, a number of unit root tests have been devised to allow for structural break in the given series. The importance of allowing for structural breaks in the unit root test has been widely discussed in the literature (Lee & Strazicich, 2003; Lumsdaine & Papell, 1997; Perron, 1989; Zivot & Andrews, 1992).

Socio-economic time series data often exhibit structural breaks (abrupt changes) due to several reasons such as changes in the social structure, government policies and economic conditions. The breaks might occur in the level (intercept) or trend or both level and trend of the data series. Without taking into account the potential breaks in the series, the unit root tests would result in spurious inferences. Our data on various crime rates indicate the possibility of structural breaks in the respective series. With a view to taking into account the possible structural breaks, we employ the minimum LM unit root test proposed by Lee and Strazicich (2003, 2004) to determine the order of integration of each crime category. The LS unit root test determines the location of the breaks endogenously (i.e. the break dates are selected from the data as opposed to arbitrarily chosen breakpoints). The LS test allows for breaks under both the null and alternative hypotheses in a consistent manner. Consequently, rejection of the null hypothesis unambiguously implies that the series is trend stationary. Since the LS test is relatively new in the literature, we give a brief description of the same in the following paragraphs.

The LS unit root test is based on the principle of LM unit root test of Schmidt and Phillips (1992). The LS test equation takes the following form:

$$\Delta y_t = \delta' \Delta Z_t + \phi \tilde{S}_{t-1} + \sum_{i=1}^{k} \beta_i \Delta \tilde{S}_{t-i} + \varepsilon_t, \qquad (1)$$

where $\tilde{S}_t$ is a detrended version of the original series, $\tilde{S}_t = y_t - \tilde{\psi}_x - Z_t \tilde{\delta}$, $(t = 2, \ldots T)$; $\tilde{\delta}$ are coefficients in the regression of Δy_t on ΔZ_t; $\tilde{\psi}_x$ is given by $y_1 - Z_1 \tilde{\delta}$; y_1 and Z_1 denote the first observations of y_t and Z_t, respectively (see Lee & Strazicich, 2003). Z_t is a vector of exogenous variables and ε_t denotes an independently and identically distributed error term with zero mean and constant variance.

In general, alternative assumptions can be made to incorporate breaks in the test equation – shifts in the intercept or trend or both. In our estimation, we assume breaks to occur both in the intercept and time trend. In case of one shift in level and trend, Z_t takes the form $Z_t = [1, t, D_{1t}, DT_{1t}]$, whereas for two breaks, Z_t is described as $Z_t = [1, t, D_{1t}, D_{2t}, DT_{1t}, DT_{2t}]$, where 1 and t denote intercept and time trend, respectively, D_{1t} and D_{2t} represent break dummies in intercept, DT_{1t} and DT_{2t} are break dummies in time trend. D_{it} takes value 1 for $t \geq TB_i + 1 (i = 1, 2)$, and 0 otherwise. $DT_{it} = t - TB_i$ for $t \geq TB_i + 1 (i = 1, 2)$, and 0 otherwise, where TB_i denotes the time at which break occurs. The test allows both the intercept and trend to change at two points TB1 and TB2, which are determined from the data series instead of assigning the breakpoints exogenously. We include the lagged terms $\Delta \tilde{S}_{t-i}$ in the regression to correct for serial correlation. The optimal number of lagged first-differenced terms (k) is determined by following the general to specific procedure suggested by Ng and Perron (1995). Starting from a maximum of $k=8$, we examine the significance of the last augmented term (we use the 10% asymptotic value of 1.645 to determine the significance of the last term). If the last augmented term is found to be insignificant, we drop it and re-estimate the model with $k=7$. The procedure is repeated until we determine the optimal k.

The null hypothesis of a unit root is denoted as $\phi = 0$ in equation (1). The LM test statistic (τ) is the t-ratio testing the null hypothesis $\phi = 0$. For one break, the location of the breakpoint (TB) is determined by searching all possible breakpoints for the minimum (i.e. the most negative) LM test statistic. Similarly, for two breaks, all possible pairings of breakpoints are considered. The minimum LM unit root test determines the breakpoints endogenously by utilising a grid search as follows:

$$\mathrm{LM}_\tau = \inf_\lambda \tau(\lambda), \qquad (2)$$

where $\tau(\lambda)$ is the collection of test statistics for all possible breakpoints, $\lambda_i = \mathrm{TB}_i/T$ and T is the sample size. The grid search is carried out over the interval [0.10 T, 0.90 T]. In other words, all possible breakpoints are considered excluding observations in the first and last 10% of the sample. Finally, the null hypothesis is tested by comparing the computed values of the LM test statistic with the critical values derived by Lee and Strazicich (2003, 2004).

It is worth mentioning that a unit root test allowing for two endogenously determined structural breaks (when both breaks are statistically significant) has higher power than the one which allows for a single break (Lumsdaine & Papell, 1997). However, there are several instances where one break is appropriate instead of two breaks. Therefore, in the present study, we employ both one- and two- break minimum LM unit root test of Lee and Strazicich (2003, 2004) to identify the actual number of significant breaks, as including unnecessary breakpoints can lead to loss of power.

4. Empirical results and discussion

4.1. Unit root test results

First, we present the results of the conventional unit root tests and then discuss the LS test results. The ADF and DF-GLS test results are shown in Table 2. Both the tests suggest that all the series except counterfeiting are non-stationary at level. However, these tests do not account for structural breaks in the given series, and therefore, the results are not reliable.

We now turn to discuss the results of the LS unit root test which allows for changes in the level as well as trend. Table 3 reports the results of the LS test with one break. The results show that all the series but KA, and Cheating are non-stationary at level. The null hypothesis of unit root with one structural break is rejected for KA, and Cheating at the 1% and 5% levels of significance, respectively. The trend break is statistically significant at the 1% level for both the series. While the ADF and DF-GLS tests have failed to reject the unit root null for these series, the LS test suggests that both are stationary with one statistically significant structural break. This indicates the importance of allowing for potential structural break in the unit root test. However, considering a single break in the unit root test could lead to loss of information particularly when there is more than one break. For that reason, we perform the two-break LS unit root test to consider the possibility of two significant breaks in the given series.

Table 4 shows the results of the LS unit root test with two breaks.[4] The two-break LS test results overturn most of the previously presented results. We find that total crimes as well as

Table 2. Unit root test results.

	ADF test statistic		DF-GLS test statistic	
	Trend and intercept	Intercept	Trend and intercept	Intercept
Murder	−0.428 (0)	−1.427 (1)	−1.176 (1)	−1.176 (1)
CHNM	−1.756 (0)	−0.708 (0)	−1.613 (0)	−0.779 (0)
Rape	−2.479 (0)	−0.152 (0)	−2.538 (0)	1.567 (0)
KA	−0.567 (0)	0.942 (0)	−1.265 (0)	1.459 (0)
Dacoity	−1.504 (3)	−0.877 (3)	−1.497 (3)	−0.819 (3)
Robbery	−1.468 (0)	−1.488 (0)	−1.487 (0)	−1.483 (0)
Burglary	−2.109 (3)	−0.561 (3)	−2.216 (3)	0.590 (3)
Theft	−1.705 (0)	−1.042 (0)	−1.744 (0)	−0.189 (0)
Riots	−1.155 (0)	−1.305 (1)	−1.110 (1)	−0.874 (0)
CBT	−2.168 (4)	−0.831 (4)	−1.933 (4)	−0.238 (4)
Cheating	1.824 (0)	4.944 (0)	−0.236 (4)	4.610 (0)
Counterfeiting	−3.423 (1)*	−3.116 (1)**	−3.334 (1)**	−3.126 (1)***
Other crimes	−0.985 (0)	−1.376 (0)	−1.028 (0)	−0.474 (0)
Total crimes	−1.951 (0)	−1.553 (0)	−1.989 (0)	−1.281 (0)

Note: Lag length is in parenthesis.
***1% level of significance; **5% level of significance; *10% level of significance.

the individual crime series such as burglary, CBT, counterfeiting, dacoity, theft and other crimes are stationary with two breakpoints. Precisely, burglary and counterfeiting are found to be stationary at 1% level of significance, whereas CBT, dacoity, theft and total crimes are stationary at 5% level of significance. For each crime category, either the level break or the trend break or both are statistically significant.

To sum up, the ADF and DF-GLS tests provide little evidence against the null hypothesis of unit root for different crime categories. But, once we allow for structural breaks, we are able to reject the unit root null for most of the series at the 5% level or better. Our results show that crimes with financial motives are found to be stationary, while violent crimes like murder, rape and riots are non-stationary. The empirical findings suggest that the natural rate of crime hypothesis holds in case of crimes with economic motives in the Indian context, which is consistent with the NRC literature (Buck et al., 1983; Narayan et al., 2010).

4.2. Analysis of breaks in the Indian crime rates

The temporal pattern of different crime categories in India suggests that there is an overall increasing trend in the crime rates during 1960s through 1980s and subsequent decline in the post liberalisation (post-1991) era. Our findings of significant breakpoints in the respective crime series are discussed in view of the major socio-economic changes that have taken place in India. Analysing the changes in the time path of different crime rates, we find that crimes with pecuniary motive such as burglary, CBT, dacoity, robbery and theft have two significant breaks – first break in the late 1960s or early 1970s and the second break in the late 1980s or early 1990s. The break years for total crimes are 1971 and 1991, while the breakpoints for riots are 1974 and 1991. Although the exact break dates vary a little across crime categories, the dates are closely clustered for each of the two-break dates. However, the break timings are different for counterfeiting (fist break in 1989 and second break in 1999). In case of murder, breaks have occurred in 1987 and 2000. For most of the crime classifications, first break is an up break (i.e. average crime rate increases in the post-break period), whereas the second break is a down break (i.e. average crime rate decreases in

Table 3. Lee and Strazicich (2003) one-break unit root test.

	Murder	CHNM	Rape	KA	Dacoity	Robbery	Burglary
TB1	1987	1991	1996	1998	1991	1991	1981
S{1}	−0.288	−0.816	−1.138	−0.806***	−0.205	−0.291	−0.350
	(−3.001)	(−3.842)	(−3.349)	(−5.673)	(−2.995)	(−3.494)	(−4.147)
Constant	−0.047	0.010	−0.056	−0.013	0.048	0.046	0.115
	(−1.180)	(1.200)	(−1.616)	(−0.511)	(1.638)	(1.060)	(0.347)
D1	−0.094	0.121***	0.071	0.265	0.194	0.289	−1.193
	(−0.620)	(3.505)	(1.288)	(1.466)	(1.285)	(1.153)	(−0.851)
DT1	0.114	−0.056***	−0.033*	−0.312***	−0.133***	−0.224***	−1.114***
	(1.552)	(−3.552)	(−1.915)	(−3.494)	(−2.720)	(−2.835)	(−2.420)
k	6	8	8	5	6	7	

	Theft	Riots	CBT	Cheating	Counterfeiting	Other crimes	Total crimes
TB1	1991	1982	1979	1997	1988	1993	1991
S{1}	−0.362	−0.336	−0.320	−0.494**	−0.417	−0.398	−0.408
	(−3.862)	(−3.353)	(−3.145)	(−4.463)	(−3.966)	(−3.837)	(−3.651)
Constant	0.778	0.152	0.072	−0.202***	−0.023*	−0.470	0.553
	(1.152)	(0.794)	(1.467)	(−3.302)	(−1.804)	(−0.516)	(0.415)
D1	0.750	1.100	0.027	0.187	0.059	8.213*	3.838
	(0.213)	(1.283)	(0.189)	(1.017)	(1.029)	(1.841)	(0.513)
DT1	−3.488***	−0.978***	−0.247***	0.229***	0.033*	−5.882***	−6.727***
	(−2.731)	(−4.018)	(−2.806)	(4.319)	(1.748)	(−3.864)	(−2.735)
k	8	1	8	3	1	8	

Note: t-statistics are in parentheses.
***1% level of significance; **5% level of significance; *10% level of significance.

Table 4. Lee and Strazicich (2003) two-break unit root test.

	Murder	KA	Dacoity	Robbery	Burglary	Theft
TB1	1987	1998	1968	1969	1970	1971
TB2	2000	2003	1982	1992	1989	1991
$S\{1\}$	−0.708	−2.715***	−0.880**	−0.791	−1.311***	−1.108**
	(−5.069)	(−10.138)	(−5.822)	(−5.038)	(−6.762)	(−6.067)
Constant	−0.170***	−0.107***	−0.181***	−0.153**	−5.414***	−7.323***
	(−3.570)	(−5.253)	(−3.080)	(−1.974)	(−5.538)	(−4.433)
D1	−0.327**	−0.014	−0.482***	0.905***	−4.019***	−6.338*
	(−2.293)	(−0.132)	(−3.277)	(4.943)	(−2.662)	(−1.710)
DT1	0.445***	−0.026	0.628***	0.214**	6.040***	10.307***
	(4.290)	(−0.495)	(5.177)	(2.299)	(5.067)	(4.394)
D2	0.117	0.819***	0.172	0.013	1.877*	3.633
	(0.831)	(6.501)	(1.263)	(0.067)	(1.665)	(1.213)
DT2	−0.411***	−0.388***	−0.635***	−0.377***	−2.511***	−10.383***
	(−4.690)	(−4.356)	(−6.147)	(−4.299)	(−4.585)	(−5.188)
k	6	6	6	8	8	

	Riots	CBT	Cheating	Counterfeiting	Other crimes	Total crimes
TB1	1974	1973	1991	1989	1975	1971
TB2	1991	1995	2001	1999	1993	1991
$S\{1\}$	−0.567	−0.584**	−0.716	−1.665***	−0.756**	−0.941**
	(−4.700)	(−6.289)	(−5.129)	(−7.304)	(−6.336)	(−5.738)
Constant	−0.625**	0.104***	−0.226***	−0.157***	−1.303	−10.134***
	(−1.993)	(2.493)	(−3.843)	(−6.609)	(−1.346)	(−3.282)
D1	−3.946***	0.501***	0.074	−0.145***	−5.912*	−11.444
	(−4.785)	(4.018)	(0.441)	(−2.746)	(−1.694)	(−1.543)
DT1	1.588***	−0.247***	0.210***	0.265***	7.701***	16.907***
	(3.124)	(−4.845)	(3.158)	(6.149)	(4.733)	(4.051)
D2	1.039	0.073	−0.071	0.239***	15.094***	12.092*
	(1.422)	(0.655)	(−0.415)	(4.206)	(3.771)	(1.805)
DT2	−2.106***	0.062*	0.133*	−0.121***	−17.826***	−20.997***
	(−4.813)	(1.706)	(1.740)	(−4.268)	(−6.588)	(−5.223)
k	5	3	3	7	8	

Note: t-statistics are in parentheses.
***1% level of significance; **5% level of significance; *10% level of significance.

the post-break period). Contrary to other economic crimes, cheating has a different pattern. It has registered two up breaks (one in 1991 and the other in 2002), though the second break is weakly significant. In the one-break context, rape has witnessed a break in the year 1996, whereas CHNM has experienced a shift in the trend in 1991. KA has witnessed a down break in 1998.

We now turn to discuss the possible reasons for structural breaks in the Indian crime rates. Given the central arguments for the presence of a natural rate of crime, we focus on the underlying factors that determine the basic structure of a society. We argue that the effects of law enforcement mechanisms are conditional on the prevailing social structure of a country. In this context, we explain the evolution of crimes, particularly crimes of economic nature in view of the socio-economic transition in India over the past few decades. India experienced a prolonged period of low economic growth (famously known as the Hindu Rate of Growth)[5] for over three decades following its Independence (India's GDP growth rate averaged just 3.5% during 1951–1979). However, its economic growth increased considerably in the 1980s, rising to an annual average of 5.6% and increased further in the subsequent decades (5.8% in 1990s and 7.2% in 2000s).[6] The high growth rate in the past two decades is reflected in the declining trend of the share of population below poverty line. The incidence of poverty in India was quite high in the 1970s. The percentage of population below poverty line was 54.88% in 1973–1974 and 51.32 in 1977–1978. Nevertheless, the poverty ratio has declined consistently since 1980s.[7] Also, there is a steady rise in the urban population in India which increased from 19.99% in 1971 to 25.78% in 1991 and 31.28% in 2011.[8] Owing to inadequate job opportunities and lack of skills among the labour force, a large section of urban workers are increasingly being pushed into the informal sector, resulting in urban inequality (urban inequality measured as Gini coefficient of consumption distribution has increased from 0.30 in 1973–1974 to 0.38 in 2009–2010).[9] The growing sociocultural disparities in the 1970s and 1980s might have contributed to the increasing criminal activities during that period. Coming to the labour market characteristics, it can be noticed that the unemployment situation in India deteriorated during the 1970s and 1980s. But, there is a marked decline in the unemployment rate in the early 1990s and marginal improvement in the later period. The unemployment rate among the rural male increased from 12 (per 1000 labour force) in 1972–1973 to 18 in 1987–1988 and declined to 14 in 1993–1994. Similarly, the urban male unemployment rate increased from 48 to 52 and declined to 41 in the corresponding periods.[10] We find that breaks in economic crimes are consistent with the temporal pattern of unemployment rate in India.

The low economic growth during the 1970s and early 1980s accompanied by high rate of poverty, rising inequality and wide spread unemployment appears to contribute to the rising trend in the crime rates during this period. Nevertheless, the growth acceleration during the past two decades has resulted in an increase in per capita income, fall in poverty rate and improvement in the level of education. Overall, with better economic opportunities, we can expect an increase in the opportunity cost of crime, and hence a fall in the crime rates. This has essentially happened in case of India where most of the crime rates show a declining trend after 1990s. Nevertheless, violent crimes like murder and rape are driven by some psychological elements which cannot be explained entirely by the socio-economic factors.

5. Conclusion

In this paper, we examine whether there is a natural rate of crime in the Indian context. Using various unit root tests to identify the order of integration of each crime category, we find that most of the crime classifications are breakpoint stationary. The results imply the existence of a natural rate of crime in India, particularly in case of crimes with financial motives. To be precise, burglary, counterfeiting, CBT, dacoity and theft are found to be stationary with two structural breaks, whereas KA and cheating are stationary with one break. This suggests that a natural rate exists in these categories of criminal activities. Also, the categories, namely other crimes and total crimes are found to be stationary with two breaks. Our findings are consistent with the literature which argues that crimes with pecuniary motives are more likely to have natural rates.

Given these results, the ability of the traditional deterrent measures to reduce crime in the long run is questionable. We argue that law and enforcement expenditure alone cannot lessen crime in the long run. Therefore, the government should focus on policies to change the socio-economic structure of the country in order to reduce the level of crime in the long run. In particular, policies targeted towards employment generation, poverty reduction and enhancement of education would help create a pacified society.

Acknowledgements
We sincerely thank Professor David Canter (editor of this journal) and the anonymous reviewer for their valuable comments. We also thank Sitakanta Panda for his useful suggestions. Errors, if any, are ours.

Disclosure statement
No potential conflict of interest was reported by the authors.

Notes
1. A number of papers like Papell, Murray, and Ghiblawi (2000), Leon-Ledesma (2002), Gustavsson and Österholm (2006), Camarero, Carrión-i-Silvestre, and Tamarit (2006), Lee, Lee, and Chang (2009), Chang (2011), Mednik, Rodriguez, and Ruprah (2012), Cheng, Durmaz, Kim, and Stem (2012) and Chang and Su (2014) have examined these two competing hypotheses: hysteresis in unemployment versus a natural rate of unemployment.
2. The IPC defines dacoity as a type of robbery committed by a group (five or more) of people. The other crimes category constitutes criminal activities other than the major crime types under the IPC.
3. The unit root test proposed by Perron (1989) allows for an exogenously given structural break (i.e. the break date is known a priori). However, exogenously chosen breaks are subjective and ad hoc in nature. Therefore, subsequently proposed unit root tests consider identifying breaks endogenously (i.e. breaks are selected from the data series).
4. Since data for rape as well as culpable homicide not amounting to murder are available for the period 1971–2012, we do not consider these two series for the LS test with two structural breaks.
5. See Rodrik and Subramanian (2005) for details.
6. The real GDP data are obtained from the National Accounts Statistics, Central Statistical Organisation.
7. The Planning Commission, Government of India gives the estimates of poverty ratio based on the National Sample Survey (NSS) data. The proportion of population below poverty line was 44.48% in 1983, 38.86% in 1987–1988, 35.97% in 1993–1994 and 29.8% in 2009–2010.
8. The population data are obtained from various reports of the Census of India.
9. The statistics for unemployment rate are obtained from various rounds of NSS.
10. The Gini coefficient estimates are obtained from the Planning Commission, Government of India.

References

Becker, G. (1968). Crime and punishment: An economic approach. *Journal of Political Economy, 76*, 169–217.
Blanchard, O. J., & Summers, L. H. (1986). Hysteresis and the European unemployment problem. In S. Fischer (Ed.), *NBER macroeconomics annual* (Vol. 1, pp. 15–90). Cambridge: MIT Press.
Blanchard, O. J., & Summers, L. H. (1987). Hysteresis in unemployment. *European Economic Review, 31*, 288–295.
Buck, A. J., Gross, M., Hakim, S., & Weinblatt, J. (1983). The deterrence hypothesis revisited. *Regional Science and Urban Economics, 13*, 471–486.
Buck, A. J., Hakim, S., & Spiegel, U. (1985). The natural rate of crime by type of community. *Review of Social Economy, 43*, 245–259.
Camarero, M., Carrión-i-Silvestre, J. L., & Tamarit, C. (2006). Testing for hysteresis in unemployment in OECD countries: New evidence using stationarity panel tests with breaks. *Oxford Bulletin of Economics and Statistics, 68*, 167–182.
Cameron, S. (1988). The economics of crime deterrence: A survey of theory and evidence. *Kyklos, 41*, 301–323.
Chang, M.-J., & Su, C.-Y. (2014). Hysteresis versus natural rate in Taiwan's unemployment: Evidence from the educational attainment categories. *Economic Modelling, 43*, 293–304.
Chang, T. (2011). Hysteresis in unemployment for 17 OECD countries: Stationary test with a Fourier function. *Economic Modelling, 28*, 2208–2214.
Cheng, K. M., Durmaz, N., Kim, H., & Stern, M. L. (2012). Hysteresis vs. natural rate of US unemployment. *Economic Modelling, 29*, 428–434.
Cook, J., & Cook, S. (2011). Are US crime rates really unit root processes? *Journal of Quantitative Criminology, 27*, 299–314.
Cornwell, C., & Trumbull, W. N. (1994). Estimating the economic model of crime with panel data. *The Review of Economics and Statistics, 76*, 360–366.
Ehrlich, I. (1973). Participation in illegitimate activities: A theoretical and empirical investigation. *Journal of Political Economy, 81*, 521–565.
Elliott, G., Rothenberg, T. J., Stock, J. H. (1996). Efficient tests for an autoregressive unit root. *Econometrica, 64*, 813–836.
Entorf, H., & Spengler, H. (2000). Socioeconomic and demographic factors of crime in Germany: Evidence from panel data of the German states. *International Review of Law and Economics, 20*, 75–106.
Friedman, J., Hakim, S., & Spiegel, U. (1989). The difference between short and long run effects of police outlays on crime: Policing deters criminals initially, but later they may 'learn by doing'. *American Journal of Economics and Sociology, 48*, 177–191.
Friedman, M. (1968). The role of monetary policy. *American Economic Review, 58*, 1–17.
Gustavsson, M., & Österholm, P. (2006). Hysteresis and non-linearities in unemployment rates. *Applied Economics Letters, 13*, 545–548.
Han, L., Bandyopadhyay, S., & Bhattacharya, S. (2013). Determinants of violent and property crimes in England and Wales: A panel data analysis. *Applied Economics, 45*, 4820–4830.
Lee, J., & Strazicich, M. C. (2003). Minimum Lagrange multiplier unit root test with two structural breaks. *Review of Economics and Statistics, 85*, 1082–1089.
Lee, J., & Strazicich, M. C. (2004). *Minimum LM unit root test with one structural break* (Working Paper No. 04-17). Boone: Department of Economics, Appalachain State University.
Lee, J. D., Lee, C. C., & Chang, C. P. (2009). Hysteresis in unemployment revisited: Evidence from panel LM unit root tests with heterogeneous structural breaks. *Bulletin of Economic Research, 61*, 325–334.
Leon-Ledesma, M. A. (2002). Unemployment hysteresis in the US states and EU: A panel approach. *Bulletin of Economic Research, 54*, 95–103.
Lin, M.-J. (2008). Does unemployment increase crime? Evidence from US data 1974–2000. *Journal of Human Resources, 43*, 413–436.
Lochner, L. (1999). *Education, work, and crime: Theory and evidence* (Working Paper No. 465). New York, NY: Rochester Center for Economic Research, University of Rochester.

Lumsdaine, R., & Papell, D. (1997). Multiple trend breaks and the unit-root hypothesis. *Review of Economics and Statistics, 79*, 212–218.

Mednik, M., Rodriguez, C. M., & Ruprah, I. J. (2012). Hysteresis in unemployment: Evidence from Latin America. *Journal of International Development, 24*, 448–466.

Myers, S. (1983). Estimating the economic model of crime: Employment versus punishment effects. *The Quarterly Journal of Economics, 98*, 157–166.

Narayan, P. K., Nielsen, I., & Smyth, R. (2010). Is there a natural rate of crime? *American Journal of Economics and Sociology, 69*, 759–782.

Ng, S., & Perron, P. (1995). Unit root tests in ARMA models with data-dependent methods for the selection of the truncation lag. *Journal of the American Statistical Association, 90*, 268–281.

Papell, D., Murray, C., & Ghiblawi, H. (2000). The structure of unemployment. *Review of Economics and Statistics, 82*, 309–315.

Perron, P. (1989). The great crash, the oil price shock and the unit root hypothesis. *Econometrica, 57*, 1361–1401.

Phelps, E. S. (1967). Phillips curves, expectations of inflation and optimal unemployment over time. *Economica, 34*, 254–281.

Raphael, S., & Winter-Ebmer, R. (2001). Identifying the effect of unemployment on crime. *The Journal of Law and Economics, 44*, 259–283.

Rodrik, D., & Subramanian, A. (2005). From 'Hindu growth' to productivity surge: The mystery of the Indian growth transition. *IMF Staff Papers, 52*, 193–228.

Schmidt, P., & Phillips, P. C. (1992). LM tests for a unit root in the presence of deterministic trends. *Oxford Bulletin of Economics and Statistics, 54*, 257–287.

Zivot, E., & Andrews, D. (1992). Further evidence on the great crash, the oil price shock and the unit root hypothesis. *Journal of Business & Economic and Statistics, 10*, 251–270.

Use of drugs and criminal behaviour among female adolescent prostitutes in Lagos metropolis, Nigeria

Sogo Angel Olofinbiyi, Babatunde Ajayi Olofinbiyi and John Lekan Oyefara

> This paper demonstrates that a sizeable number of adolescent girls are often involved in the use of drugs in their various sex industries. There is much controversy as to whether criminal activities among the sex workers are influenced by drugs use. Cross-sectional survey and in-depth interviews were adopted to generate data from respondents. Findings show that sex workers are frequently engaged in drug use and criminality but their engagement in criminal activities is not significantly influenced by the use of drugs. The study recommends an urgent need to design and implement effective research studies, policies, prevention and intervention programmes to deal with the intricacies associated with drug use and criminality among adolescent girls in Nigeria.

1. Introduction

Several studies have established a link between prostitution and criminality over time and space. However, few or no studies have been able to state clearly that criminal activities ever observed among the commercial sex workers are influenced by the use of drugs. According to Child Labour Prevails in Ghana (2001), many prostitutes have been recorded to rob their clients during or after the sexual acts while the client is not expecting it. After all, the clients cannot call the police and tell them they are robbed by a prostitute as prostitution is illegal in this part of the world. According to Child Labour Prevails in Ghana (2001), prostitution is slowly taking over streets and many cities. After a few prostitutes set up and stalk a corner, before long, that whole street is nothing more than a prostitution ring and is filled with crimes including violence, rape, robbery, killings, drug abuse, thefts and many more egregious crimes (Child Labour Prevails in Ghana, 2001). Since these girls are offenders, they are nothing but the prime suspects of the police as they harbour criminals and also help in keeping weapons for the robbers and other criminals who bedevil the human society (see Sack, 1996).

The paper examines prostitution, use of drugs and criminality among the brothel-based adolescent sex workers in Lagos metropolis, Nigeria. The aim of the paper critically examines the relationship between use of drugs and tendency for criminal behaviour among female adolescent sex workers. The paper premised on Kompas' findings (1998) that prostitutes are divided into two categories: (a) those who are 'depraved', whose leanings towards prostitution were formed in the family; and (b) those who are 'casual', whose leanings towards prostitution were due to factors beyond their control. The research also provides insights into the various ways in which adolescents become involved in drugs use and criminality nowadays. These methods include: (i) through a newspaper advertisement, (ii) through the Internet, (iii) through modelling agencies, (iv) through friends and (v) taking part in filming pornographic movies (Kompas, 1998).

According to Wagner and Yatim (1997),

> adolescent prostitutes live in the same cities and towns as ordinary teenagers across the world at large. Their world is very different. They are here in our communities, and yet they are hidden from most people. They are kids, and yet the life they live separates them from most other kids and from normal teenage activities and concerns. They are criminals, but they are the victims of repeated crimes. They are family members, but most have not known a family's love and support. They have independence, but they do not have freedom. They are earning money, but they live in poverty. They are sexually active, but without intimacy.

They have escaped one set of rules but are forced to obey other harsher ones. Butcher (2003) argued along the same line asserting that adolescent prostitution is a kind of turn-around way of trying to get the financial support and love that the children need, but which their families have not been able to provide. Yet their families may cling to a respectable image that is not connected to the harsh realities their children must cope with on the street. Lacking parental support and love, these teens would have a very difficult time trying to cross back into the world where they grew up (Butcher, 2003).

The study investigates differences in drug use and criminal activities among adolescent prostitutes in Nigeria. According to The Nation (2009), there is evidence that the possible solution to the menace of drug use among female adolescents lies not only with the government but also with the parents who supervise their wards at schools more effectively since the authorities trusted with the job have failed. Moreover, religious groups such as Federation of Muslim Women's Associations of Nigeria (FOMWAN) and its Christian counterpart as well as other concerned groups should come up with effective campaigns against prostitution, drug use and criminality in our higher institutions and our societies at large ('Prostitution', 2000). The campaigns should aim at educating the students and all members of society on the negative effects of these acts on adolescents' career life, health and morals. Efforts like this might perhaps arrest the situation or at least save those who are yet to go beyond redemption.

2. Adolescent prostitution, drug use and criminality

The review of research on adolescent prostitution worldwide offers several explanations for their involvement in criminality and drug use, which spans from society to society. Reports from various researches have persistently shown that adolescent prostitution is a relatively new field of interest, and consequently there is a very little research work published on the issue of adolescent prostitution. We, however, need to know very much more about this category of people, the reality of their lives and the reasons for their active engagement in the use of drugs and criminality in the sex industry. Adolescents (people aged 10–19 years) constitute an important segment of a contemporary African population (Oyefara, 2011). In 1985, for instance, there were 122.4 million adolescents in the region. By 1990, this number had risen to 170.4 million and was projected to reach 223.7 million by the year 2010 (Njau et al., 1992). The current estimates of the United Nations show that at the beginning of the twenty-first century, about one out of every four people in Sub-Saharan Africa is between ages 10 and 19 years (UN, 1999, quoted in Oyefara,

2011). These essential data show the high proportion of adolescents in the total population of Sub-Saharan Africa.

Nigeria, the most populous country in Africa, shares with other countries in the region a youthful population structure, in which more than 40% of the total population is under the age of 20 (Oyefara, 2011). The National Population Commission report of 1998 revealed that adolescents make up around 30% of the total population of Nigeria (NPC, 1998).The existing data at the national level in the year 2000 showed that 27,805,138 (about 30 million) Nigerians were between ages 10 and 19 years (Population, Health and Nutrition Information Project [PHNIP], 2002). On the basis of 2.89% annual growth rate, their numbers are expected to double within the next 25 years to nearly 73 million. In terms of size alone, this is a significant group. These are the leaders of the country in particular and the continent in general, treasures and hope of tomorrow (Omololu & Dare, 1997).

All findings and theoretical evidences about adolescents point to the fact that the adolescent period is characterised by various transitory problems and the individual at this stage has to develop the appropriate coping strategies, otherwise everybody stands the risk of getting involved in one form of criminal behaviour or the other (Moru, 1989, pp. 27–28, quoted in Adams, 2002). Moreover, Hecker Geleerd (1945) looked at the adolescents as altruistic, solitary, idealistic, cynical, callous, sensitive, ascetic, pessimistic, optimistic, enthusiastic, indifferent, libertine and blindly submissive to a leader (see Olaogun & Ogundare, 2008). All of the above implies that adolescent period is said to be demanding, and to stress this more, Friendberg (1959) cited in Okpukpan (2006) noted that adolescence is a period of search for emotional and economic independence. It is a time for individuals to utilise a more mature and complex level, the ability to give and take, communicate with others and trust them, and to learn what is harmful and what is good for themselves and others.

With respect to risk behaviours among prostitutes, several scholars have submitted that most prostitutes use drugs frequently in order to be active towards subduing their depression and stigmatisation in the sex industry. Drug use involves the intake of chemical substances to change reality, alter behaviour and produce stimulation, relief or relaxation, unnecessary confidence or reactions; all that is contrary to the normal human behaviour (see FMHHS, 1992). The use of drugs such as alcohol or marijuana among adolescent prostitutes is associated with greater likelihood of involvement in all types of delinquent offences as well as myriads of risky sexual behaviours (Gilbert, 1996). Results as shown in Table 1 of this study revealed that 124 (42.8%) of the respondents who participated in the research work used alcohol/cigarette, 46 (15.9%) of them used alcohol/cigarette/Indian hemp, 37 (12.8%) used only cigarette, but 36 (12.4%) gave no response to the question, 31 (10.7%) of the respondents used alcohol, while 16 (5.5%) used

Table 1. Percentage distribution of respondents by the type of drug used and for what purpose.

Type of drug used and purpose for which it is used	Frequency	Percentage
Alcohol	31	10.7
Cigarette	37	12.8
Marijuana	16	5.5
Alcohol/cigarette	124	42.8
Alcohol/cigarette/Indian hemp	46	15.9
No response	36	12.4
Total	290	100.0

marijuana. Outcome of the research work showed that the majority of the respondents who participated in the research work used different types of drugs, and some in combination. The findings, thus, go on to buttress Gilbert's findings (1996) that an appreciable number of adolescent prostitutes in Nigeria engage in the use of drugs. The study identified sexual offences, murder of clients, deliberate spread of HIV/AIDS, reckless abortion, street fighting, public drinking, violence, theft, harbouring of criminals, keeping of weapons for criminals, as well as serving as agents for ritual perpetrations as the most prevalent criminal acts among adolescent prostitutes in Lagos metropolis, Nigeria.

Clearly, with this study we have been made to know that adolescents who use drugs are more likely to engage in a wide variety of criminal behaviours in the sex industry. For now, it is important to know that drug use and criminal acts are closely knit and tend to occur together.

The adolescent sex industry in Nigeria points to a fundamental injustice in the current materialist world order. It is an indication of a global willingness to sacrifice society's most vulnerable members for the sake of socio-economic and sexual gratifications. The truth is that with the involvement of the adolescents in prostitution, their future is being mortgaged (Marjorie, 1992). Unless there is a change in the economic situation of Nigeria, prostitution and other related offenses will continue to thrive across posterities.

3. Theoretical underpinning

The theoretical thrust of the study is anchored on two significant theories: economic theory and anomie theory.

3.1 *Economic theory*

Several studies have shown that certain economic conditions influence the level of crime in society. These studies argue that fluctuations resulting from economic conditions or business cycles affect the crime rate in one way or the other. Many of these studies have concentrated on the relationship between specific aspects of economy and crime. These aspects of economic condition include poverty, inequality, material deprivation and unemployment within the social structure. For example, earlier studies of crime and delinquency have found a causal relationship between poverty and crime (Bailey, 1984; William, 1984). They argued further that as the level of unemployment increases, so does poverty status, and there comes an increase in the level of frustration thereby generating crimes in society. They concluded stating that more crimes are committed in time of economic recession than in time of economic growth. The central idea of this theory is anchored on the fact that criminal behaviour results from the lack of or deprivation of basic economic needs. Regardless of these findings, it is generally assumed that poor people are potential criminals because of their desperate economic conditions. According to Townsend (1970), the poor consist of that section of the population whose resources are so depressed from the means as to be deprived of enjoying the benefits and participating in the activities which are customary in that society. Townsend sees poverty as a general form of relative deprivation which is the outcome of mal-administration of resources in society. Such people are said to live from hand to mouth to underscore the point that they live by scratching for food on a daily basis. This economic condition is said to have serious implications for various forms of criminal behaviour such as thefts of foodstuffs and related materials, robbery, prostitution, etc. (see Townsend, 1970). Relative deprivation, on the other hand, refers to the subjective feelings and comparisons by individuals of their presumed economic disadvantage or low socio-economic status *vis-à-vis* that of other comparable colleagues. This is sometimes referred to as 'inequality in the distribution of economic resources'. The individual here may not be seriously deprived as in absolute deprivation and indeed may be seen as better-off based on some visible characteristics. The feeling of relative deprivation is also said to be a source of crime (Radzinowiez, 1977 quoted in Igbo, 2007, p. 53). Concerning unemployment, it is generally believed, and it has been confirmed by some researchers, that unemployment leads to crime (Glaser & Rice, 1958 quoted in Igbo, 2007). The adage which says that 'an idle mind is a devil's workshop' aptly summarises this viewpoint, particularly for prostitutes in Nigeria. However, like the issue of poverty, not all unemployed persons commit crime. People who are gainfully employed also commit crimes and some of them take place in their places of employment (Sutherland, 1939 quoted in Igbo, 2007). It must, however, be pointed out that the consequences of unemployment may vary across societies and cultures depending on the socio-economic conditions. Unemployment may not provide a strong reason for crime in the advanced industrial societies where most people are employed. But in developing countries like Nigeria, where poverty and unemployment still represent extremes of deprivation, their influence upon people's behaviour could well be strong and thus push them into crimes (see Jones, 1981, p. 93).

Economic theory would assert that the main reason why prostitution still exists is due to the fact that women or young girls have not had enough access to economic opportunity and have had to rely on economic support from men (women have had to exchange sexual availability [a resource they control] for this support [a resource controlled by men]). More importantly, in this study, economic influences have been found significant in pushing adolescent girls to become prostitutes and tend to continue in the profession in the study area. Winick and Kinsie posited that a person's decision to become a prostitute is largely based on few work opportunities or jobs with little opportunity for advancement, as well as recognition of the income potential that cannot guarantee a living (see Haralambos & Holborn, 2008). However, irrespective of the type of prostitute or prostitution, this study established that the adolescents' primary motive of becoming a prostitute is the money it provides for the female individuals in order to solve a wide range of their economic problems.

According to Igbo (1992), studies that argue that poverty leads to crime have serious setbacks. One notable setback is the fact that not all poor persons commit crime. What is more, relatively rich persons also engage in crime just as the poor do. These facts have helped to question the poverty–unemployment thesis. Nevertheless, like the issue of poverty, not all unemployed persons commit crime. People who are gainfully employed also commit crimes and some of them take place at their places of employment (Sutherland, 1939 in Igbo, 2007). Likewise, women and young girls still have other legitimate means of income and some, particularly among the young girls, still come from averagely rich homes, yet they are involved in prostitution.

Despite the excellent merit of economic theory focusing all attention on economic issues such as poverty and unemployment, poor socio-economic background and financial instability, it fails to address other factors such as societal strain, structural inequality embedded within the social structure, peer group influence, etc. The theory also fails to address 'retreatist subculture', which socially and culturally detaches individuals from the lifestyle and everyday pre-occupation of the conventional world (see Merton, 1957, quoted in Haralambos & Holborn, 2008). By the same token, based on Merton's brilliant idea, the use of drugs for fun and pleasure is encouraged and expected within the prostitute subculture. On this note, the adoption of anomie theory thus becomes relevant to ask more comprehensive questions on the factors (other than the economic factors) that push adolescent girls into prostitution in Lagos metropolis, Nigeria.

3.2 *Anomie theory*

The theory has its origin in the works of the French sociologist Emile Durkheim, but was well elaborated upon and made popular by the American Sociologist Robert K. Merton in his book

Social theory and social structure (1968, first published, 1938; see Haralambos & Holborn, 2008). Merton looked at the problem of deviance from a sociological perspective; and he argued that deviance resulted from the culture and structure of society itself. Merton began from the standard functionalist position of value consensus, that is, all members of societies share the same values. However, members of the societies are placed in different positions in the social structure (e.g. people in society differ in terms of class position), and they do not have the same opportunities of realising the shared values as a result of 'structural inequality' embedded within the social structure. This situation, according to Merton, can generate deviance in society. In Merton's words, the social and cultural structure generates pressure for socially deviant behaviours upon people variously located in that structure (Haralambos & Holborn, 2008, p. 323). The central argument of this theory is that in a situation whereby there are no equal opportunities of achieving the success goals, people tend to deviate from the norms of the society in order to achieve the success goals, thereby leaving the society in a state of normlessness called anomie. Using American society as an example, Merton argued that the society sets up culturally defined goals that all members of it must strive to achieve; and this success goal is largely measured in terms of 'wealth' and 'material possessions'. Because the dream of America states that all members of society must have an equal opportunity of achieving the success goals, they device institutionalised means through which the success goals must be accomplished or reached. However, in America, such as we have in Nigeria, the accepted ways of achieving success are through educational qualification, talent, honesty, hard work, drive, determination and ambition. In a balanced society, an equal emphasis is placed upon both cultural goals and institutionalised means, and members of society are satisfied with both. But in an unbalanced society such as America, as well as Nigeria today, great importance is attached to the success goals while relatively little importance is attached to the accepted ways of achieving the goals (Haralambos & Holborn, 2008). The situation now becomes like a game of cards in which winning becomes so important that the rules are abandoned by some of the players. By the same token, when rules cease to operate, a situation of normlessness or anomie results. In this situation of 'anything goes', norms no longer direct behaviour and deviance is encouraged. However, individuals according to Merton will respond to a situation of anomie in five different ways and their response pattern will be shaped by their position in the social structure. These are Conformity, Innovation, Ritualism, Retreatism and Rebellion.

The study also presents important criticisms of anomie theory which served as the foundation for new theoretical developments in the sociological study of deviance and social control. These include: the theory fails to explain what conformity really is, it does not consider illegitimate opportunities shared by members of society, it overlooks social interaction and group processes, it assumes a common culture in the U.S., it ignores social control and overlooks crimes in the suites as emphasised by economic theory: crimes by the wealthy and powerful.

Despite all criticisms levelled against Merton's theory of anomie, the theory still deserves credit because it has given this study a very careful attempt to explain how socio-cultural structure exerts pressure on individual prostitutes in the study location; thereby causing them to exhibit various forms of socially deviant behaviour such as prostitution itself as well as involvement in the use of drugs and all sorts of criminal act. Drawing from Merton's words, the prostitutes in the study area claimed to have little access to the conventional and legitimate means of becoming successful due to their low educational qualifications, low social status as well as the kind of jobs they formerly had, which guaranteed them little opportunity for advancement. Since their way is blocked in this sense as Merton submitted, they 'innovate' turning to prostitution which promises greater rewards than the legitimate means.

The theory also provides explanations on how adolescent girls are denied equal opportunities of achieving the success goals of their societies irrespective of their little opportunity and low socio-economic status in the social structure. A situation that made them deviate on a daily basis from the norms of the society so as to achieve the stated goals. To the prostitutes, the situation has now become like 'survival of the fittest' in which making a headway now becomes so important that the rules of the society have to be abandoned by the adolescent girls. However, when these rules cease to operate, a situation of anomie erupts and prostitution begins to evolve and spread across Lagos metropolis.

4. Research methods

A good research design was developed to examine the topic of the study and specify the most appropriate methods employed to gather the richest possible data for the study. The study utilised data collected from a cross-sectional survey and ethnographic method of in-depth interview. The reason for this was to generate both quantitative and qualitative information for the study, which was eventually used to cross-check and compare the findings produced by both methods at the end of the research. This helped the richness of this study not only by probing further beyond the capacity of what questionnaires can cover but also by maximising the validity and reliability of the whole research. The study population covered those female adolescent sex workers who were within the age limit of 10–19 in Oyingbo and Yaba community of Lagos State. A total number of 300 copies of questionnaire were administered only to female adolescent sex workers within the age bracket 10–19 in the survey. A total of 300 female adolescent sex workers from 10 different brothels were interviewed in the general survey through a method of personal interview (230 female adolescent sex workers from 6 brothels in Oyingbo community and 70 female adolescent sex workers from 4 brothels in Yaba community). The survey questionnaire was structured in such a way that adequate information was elicited on research questions, objectives and hypotheses of the study; and the questionnaire was arranged in sections to capture the objectives of the study.

However, in the qualitative research method, focus was also placed on female adolescent sex workers within the same age bracket (10–19); and a total of eight in-depth interviews were conducted in the study using unstructured interview with 'guide' questions. The respondents interviewed in this section were as follows: six female adolescent sex workers, one brothel manager and one madam. The reason for including this set of people in the study was to know their own personal opinions towards this category of people they work with. It is also imperative to note that respondents for the in-depth interviews and survey were drawn from two sampled local government areas. This made the data generated from the technique represent a true picture of adolescent prostitution in Lagos metropolis, Nigeria.

A purposive sampling technique was utilised to select respondents in the survey, while in the in-depth interview, respondents were selected using both purposive and accidental sampling techniques (this selection method was based on convenience, chance, availability and relevance of the respondents to the theme of the study). Both descriptive and content analyses were utilised to analyse the generated data. For quantitative analytical method, chi-square using Statistical Packages for Social Sciences (SPSS/PC+) was adopted to analyse the collected data. The qualitative data generated in the study were analysed using 'content analysis'. This technique facilitated compressing inferences, by systematically and objectively identifying specified characteristics of messages (Holsti, 1969, p. 14; quoted in Oyefara, 2011). In doing this, the in-depth interviews recorded into the tapes were transcribed from a local language (i.e. Yoruba, Igbo or Pidgin) to English language. Responses to each question were summarised and important quotations were reported verbatim to complement our findings in the survey. It should be noted that the content analysis was done manually in order to enhance the explanatory clarity of findings.

5. Limitations of the study

(i) The major limitation encountered during the course of the study was the difficulty in getting the female adolescent sex workers to co-operate in answering the research questions. The research experience with this category of people threw more light on the notion that prostitutes, whether young or old, are very difficult to approach. This was largely due to fear of the police arrest, social insecurity, invasion of privacy, lack of confidence in the researchers, void of all interest, voluminous quantity of the questionnaires, time constraint, inferiority complex resulting from societal attitudes towards them, stigmatisation and the fact that the previous related studies by other researchers did not earn them any benefit. The researcher eventually submerged this problem through establishing a good rapport (friendly relationship based on personal contact and monetary reward), with the adolescent sex workers, their madams as well as the hotel managers.

(ii) However, a minor problem that featured during the course of the in-depth interview as almost all the respondents frowned at having their voices recorded on the tape for no reasons. It was after several persistent visits and persuasions by the researcher that pieces of information needed for the qualitative inquiries were released.

(iii) Another major limitation was the age limit of the female sex workers within which the study was conducted. This caused the researcher to explore 10 different brothels before there could be any successful administration of questionnaires. As it was a difficult task to get 300 adolescent prostitutes from 1 particular brothel, the study had to explore the entire community of Oyingbo and Yaba before the administration of questionnaires could be completed.

(iv) It was also discovered that some of the respondents could neither read nor write perfectly as they did not have a formal education. For this reason, the questionnaires were required to be interpreted to them in local languages and filled in for them by asking them questions in the languages they understood.

6. Results and discussion

6.1. *Demographic and socio-economic characteristics of the female adolescent sex workers*

The female adolescent sex workers were in the age group of 10–19 but the majority of them were between the ages of 15 and 19 years. However, Table 2 shows that the mean age of adolescent prostitutes in the study location was 16.9 years. This indicates that the average age of adolescents who are actively involved in the business of prostitution in Lagos Metropolis is 16.9 years old. Data show that 284 (97.9%) of the respondents who participated in the research study were of Christian faith, while 5 (1.7%) of the respondents were Muslims. When questioned about their ethnic background, 157 (54.1%) of the respondents were from various ethnic groups put together in Nigeria, 128 (44.1%) were from the Igbo ethnic group, followed

Table 2. Percentage distribution of respondents by age.

Age group	Frequency	Percentage
10–14 years	5	1.7
15–19 years	285	98.3
Total	290	100.0

by 4 (1.4%) of the Yoruba-speaking ethnic group. Only one (0.3%) of the respondents was of Hausa/Fulani ethnic group. The outcome shows that the practice of prostitution cuts across all ethnic groups in Nigeria. However, the study recorded that the practice was most common among the Igbo ethnic group, while the lowest percentage was recorded among the Yoruba and Hausa/Fulani ethnic groups. The study suggested that the reason for the low percentage of Yoruba ethnic group in the study does not really mean that the Yoruba girls are not involved in the practice, but might be connected with the fact that the study location is within the Yoruba socio-cultural setting, where the adolescents believe they might be quickly seen and openly recognised by their kith and kin. It was discovered that 263 (90.7%) of the respondents who participated in the research work had secondary education, 19 (6.6%) had primary education, 5 (1.7%) had Tertiary education, while 3 (1.0%) had no educational attainment. Outcome of the research shows that majority of the respondents were literate to a certain degree but not formally educated.

When questions were asked on their marital status, 283 (97.6%) of the respondents were single, 4 (1.4%) were married and 3 (1.0%) were divorced. Discussions with the very few married and divorced respondents indicated that they were deserted by their husbands and needed to support their children and their entire family. The data information on state of origin is distributed evenly across majority of the states in Nigeria with 70 (24.1%) from Edo, 37 (12.8%) from Enugu, 34 (11.7%) from Imo, 29 (10.0%) from Cross River, 25 (8.6%) from Anambra, 22 (7.65) from Benue, 17 (5.95) from Abia, 15 (5.2%) from Rivers, 14 (4.8%) from Akwa Ibom, 10 (3.4%) from Delta, 6 (2.1%) from Bayelsa, 3 (1.0%) from Ogun, 2 (0.7%) from Kaduna and Oyo, respectively, while 1 (0.3%) from Osun State. On nationality, as shown in the study, 279 (96.2%) of adolescent prostitutes were from Nigeria, while 11 (3.8%) were from other countries. The 3.8% of adolescent prostitutes, as revealed by this study, supports the findings of Ayodele (2000b) that adolescent girls are being secretly trafficked into African countries under the care of retired Nigerian prostitutes who pose as their madam. The outcome shows that the business of prostitution cuts across countries in varying magnitude.

Discussions with the respondents on how they were introduced to the profession confirmed that 133 (45.9%) were introduced through peer group influence at school, 106 (36.6%) through personal effort, 36 (12.4%) through peer group influence on the street, while 7 (2.4%) through mass media and 6 (2.1%) through a family member.

Findings from this study show that peer group influence plays a dominant role in paving ways for how female adolescents get into the business of prostitution in Nigeria. Studies have also shown that the peer group relations encourage adolescents to get involved in prostitution (Akinyele & Onifade, 2009). In this regard, the kind of friendship that an adolescent keeps at a

Table 3. Percentage distribution of respondents by weekly estimate of income in the business.

Weekly estimate of income in the business	Frequency	Percentage
₦10,000–15,000	4	1.4
₦20,000–25,000	148	51.0
₦30,000–35,000	101	34.8
₦40,000–45,000	14	4.8
₦50,000–55,000	8	2.8
₦60,000 and above	14	4.8
No response	1	0.3
Total	290	100.0

Table 4. Percentage distribution of respondents by reasons for involvement in the business.

Reasons for involvement in the business	Frequency	Percentage
For financial reason	263	90.7
For financial reason/social connection	3	1.0
For financial reason/to earn a living	23	7.9
No response	1	0.3
Total	290	100.0

point in time goes a long way in determining the kind of moral rectitude he or she will exhibit in society.

Data on weekly income in Table 3 of this study show that the majority of the respondents (51.0%) received between ₦20,000 and ₦25,000 as their weekly income and majority of them still struggled for their daily bread. Though unhappy with their lifestyle and their profession, they found no meaningful alternative to sustain their lives and that of their families other than this means.

Findings as shown in Table 4 confirmed that 263 (90.7%) of the respondents who participated in the research inquiry claimed that the reason for their involvement in the business was for financial gain, 23 (7.9%) of them said it was both for financial gain and to earn a living, and 3 (1.0%) said the reason was for both financial gain and social connection. Results show that majority of the respondents were in the business solely for financial gains. The above finding corroborates Kompas' (1998) findings that adolescents, particularly girls, have to work at an early age to support the family economically. They generally come from rural villages; therefore, they have little opportunity for education and employment. It is understandable that the quick and easy way for their parents to look for money is by selling children to agents or pimps who seem offering legitimate jobs and training opportunities. Similar studies have argued in line with Kompas' findings that poverty is the most common reason why most families sell the services of their female children to augment their income in order to buy food or clothes and other necessities of life (see Janssen, 2001, p. 10; Oyefara, 2007). The case of child labour is a typical factor that exposes children to prostitution. The hired female children are sent out to hawk food items on the streets, motor parks and mechanic garages thereby exposing them to rapes as well as sexual harassments.

Findings from in-depth interview show that most adolescents in prostitution enterprise are driven by poor financial conditions and socio-economic instability of their neighbourhood. To them, the only means to survive this condition is to go into prostitution which promises a quick and more promising reward. This finding also supports the view that adolescents are taken to prostitution due to sheer destitution (Barnes, 1959, p. 95, as quoted in Janssen, 2001). Awake (8 February 2003, p. 5) also reported along the same line that some street children resort to prostitution because they see it as their only means of survival.

Table 5. Relationship between the use of drugs and involvement in criminal activities.

Involvement in criminal activities	Use of drugs Yes	Use of drugs No	Total
Yes	16 (94.1%)	1 (5.9%)	17 (100.0%)
No	215 (86.3%)	34 (13.7%)	249 (100.0%)
Total	231 (86.8%)	35 (13.2%)	266 (100.0%)

$\chi^2 = .841^a$, $df = 1$, Asymp. Sig. (two-sided) = .359, contingency coefficient = .056.

Findings from the qualitative study showed that majority of the female adolescent sex workers are poor and have low socio-economic background with little or no opportunity for life advancement. They are living under the fear of harassment by the police and many of them get arrested and released as many times as possible during the course of the business.

6.2. *Use of drugs and criminal behaviour among female adolescent prostitutes*

Several studies have established a link between prostitution and criminality over time and space. However, few or no studies have been able to state clearly that criminal activities ever observed among the commercial sex workers are influenced by the use of drugs. Findings from the study have shown that sex workers are frequently engaged in the use of drugs, but their engagement has not in any way significantly connected with their involvement in criminal activities. Outcome of the study as expressed in Table 5 shows that there is no relationship between the use of drug and tendency for criminal behaviour among the female adolescent sex workers in the study area. This means that the use of drugs among this category of people is not significantly related to their tendency for criminal behaviour at .05 level of significance (Tables 6–11).

Discussions with an in-depth interview participant indicated that:

> It is a poor financial condition, not the use of drug that really pushes sex workers into criminal acts. She probed further that when prostitutes see that the financial reward is excellent, they may become unconsciously involved in criminal activities. For instance, we have heard of sex workers caught in the act of keeping weapons for robbers, providing a resting place for them after operation, killing their clients and make away with their money, selling indian hemp and marijuana to clients, and serving as agents for ritual perpetration in society. She stressed that prostitutes' involvement in criminality has nothing to do with the use of drugs; it all depends on individual desire for evil-doing. To her, being a sex worker does not mean that you must become a criminal, it is all about using what you have to get what you want in order to make a living.

When questioned about the relationship between the use of drugs and tendency for criminal behaviour, a 15-year-old sex worker answered:

> The use of drug as long as I know is totally unconnected with prostitutes' involvement in criminal acts. It is only the desire to earn more money in the business that we have ever recorded in various brothels to have influenced prostitutes into criminal activities. She probed further that most of us use one or two drugs including me, yet we do not, as a result, get involved in the mess of criminal activities.

Another in-depth interview participant was of the opinion that there is no significant relationship between the use of drug and tendency for criminal behaviour among female sex workers. It is recorded that those prostitutes ever caught in criminal activities did so on poor economic condition, not as a result of the influence of drug intake. In effect, most of my colleagues that use drugs in the business have never been found indulging in criminal ventures.

Table 6. Percentage distribution of respondents by belief in the use of drugs.

Belief in the use of drugs like alcohol, cigarette, etc.	Frequency	Percentage
Yes	241	83.1
No	43	14.8
No response	6	2.1
Total	290	100.0

Table 7. Percentage distribution of respondents by if they have ever used any of the drugs.

Perception of drugs ever used in the business	Frequency	Percentage
Yes	237	81.7
No	37	12.8
No response	16	5.5
Total	290	100.0

Table 8. Percentage distribution of respondents by duration of the use of the drug.

Duration of the use of drug	Frequency	Percentage
Less than 1 year	6	2.1
1 year	74	25.5
2–3 years	164	56.6
4–5 years	13	4.5
No response	33	11.4
Total	290	100.0

Table 9. Percentage distribution of respondents by who introduced them to the use of hard drug.

Introduction to the use of hard drug	Frequency	Percentage
Friend in the business	243	83.8
Friend at a school	4	1.4
Clients	2	0.7
No response	41	14.1
Total	290	100.0

Table 10. Percentage distribution of respondents by type of criminal activities they have been involved.

Type of criminal activities having been involved	Frequency	Percentage
Keeping weapons for criminals	2	0.7
Keeping hard drugs	7	2.4
Giving resting place to criminals after operation	6	2.1
Harbouring criminal during a police search	2	0.7
No response	273	94.1
Total	290	100.0

Table 11. Percentage distribution of respondents by which group of sex workers who are mostly involved in crime.

Groups of sex workers mostly involved in crime	Frequency	Percentage
Drug addicted sex workers	11	3.8
Sex workers with low rate of client patronage	14	4.8
Sex workers with low-income turnover	60	20.7
Drug addicted sex workers/sex workers with low rate of client patronage	128	44.1
Sex workers with low rate of client patronage/sex workers with low-income turnover	50	17.2
No response	27	9.3
Total	290	100.0

Source: MSc thesis research conducted and supervised in the Department of Sociology, University of Lagos, Nigeria.

A prostitute 'madam' from one of the brothels studied expressed that:

> Commercial sex workers are indeed actively involved in criminal activities. But in my own brothel, I usually discourage my girls from taking part in criminal acts, making them realize the adverse effects of crime on whosoever is caught in the act ... except for sometime ago that one of my girls was caught with hard drugs. We have heard from other brothels where sex workers were caught as agents selling sperm cells of her clients for money-making rituals. Whichever way this might have happened, it has not been established anywhere that the use of drug has influenced sex workers into criminal activities.

In-depth interview with a 'manager' of a brothel revealed that:

> The use of drugs does not predispose sex workers into criminal acts, substantiating his point by adding that many drug-addicted sex workers in our brothel have not been one day accused of any sort of crime. I will not say that drug effect cannot push sex workers into criminal act, it does; but the frequency of this occurrence is not as common as that of financial needs.

The findings above show that there is no significant relationship between the use of drugs and tendency for criminal activities in the study location. Though various facts from quantitative and qualitative research studies have justified adolescent prostitutes' frequent involvement in the use of drugs, no outcome of the studies has wholly reported that their widespread involvement in the use of drugs is accountable for their criminal activities.

7. Conclusion

The study reveals that a sizeable number of female adolescent sex workers in Nigeria are widely involved in the use of drugs and all sorts of criminal activities. The trend, if not checked, would become an anathema to the progress of the Nigerian state. Outcome of the research inquiry posits that the widespread involvement of adolescent prostitutes in the use of drugs tends not to influence the wide variety of criminal behaviours exhibited by this category of people. But to a larger extent, there is a clear-cut conclusion that sex workers are frequently engaged in drug use and criminality but their engagement in criminal activities is not significantly influenced by the use of drugs. In addition, the research outcome pinpointed drug use, sexual offences, murder of clients, deliberate spread of HIV/AIDS, reckless abortion, street fighting, public drinking, violence, theft, harbouring of criminals, keeping of weapons for criminals as well as serving as agents for ritual perpetrations as the most common criminal acts among adolescent prostitutes in Nigeria. This is an enough evidence to submit that prostitution is a powerful factor that contributes to the collapse of moral rectitude and encouragement of organised crime in society.

The study shows that little effort has been made or is being made to alleviate the various problems associated with adolescent prostitution in Nigeria. However, the current efforts made by this study leave a wide room for contributions from societies, governments, non-governmental organisations, parents and the young people themselves, so that the effects of such efforts can be maximal. In all, it is established that socio-economic constraints are the primary factors that push adolescent girls into prostitution in Nigeria; and these same factors were also observed to predispose them into various kinds of criminal behaviour in the sex industry.

From the stand point of this research, parents and adolescent girls involved in the business will have to be re-educated about prostitution and the use of drugs. They should be made to realise the adverse consequences of this act not only on the Nigerian societies at large but also as a weapon that can truncate the future of any children involved in the practice of prostitution. The study suggests that governments should put more resources together to ameliorate the conditions of young girls in general so that the future will not turn bleak for them, whether in Nigeria or abroad. The study recommends an urgent need to design and implement further effective research studies, policies, prevention and intervention programmes to deal with the intricacies associated with drug use and criminality among adolescent girls in Nigeria.

Disclosure statement

No potential conflict of interest was reported by the authors.

References

Adams, G. (2002). The study of adolescence: The past, present and the future. *SRA Newsletter, 1–2*, 1–8.
Akinyele, I. O., & Onifade, I. O. (2009). *Trends in social behaviour among secondary school adolescents in Ibadan: Institute of African Studies*. Ibadan: University of Ibadan.
Ayodele, S. (2000b, June 26). Cleric wants brothels shut down. *Nigerian Tribune*, p. 9.
Bailey, N. C. (1984). Poverty, inequality and city homicide rates: Some not expected findings. *Criminology, 22*, 531–550.
Butcher, K. (2003). Confusion between prostitution and sex trafficking. *Lancet, 361*(9373), 1921–1998.
Child Labour Prevails in Ghana. (2001, October 31). *Afrol News*. Retrieved from http:www.afrol.com/news2001/gha007_child_labour.htm
Child prostitution in the street: Implication for poor future of female adolescent girls in Nigeria. (2003, February 8). *Awake*, p. 14. Adopted by the United Nations General Assembly on December 18, 1979, and entered into force in September.

Federal Ministry of Health and Human Services. (1992). *National AIDS control programme: Nigeria bulletin of epidemiology*. Awka: Nnamdi Azikiwe University.

Gilbert, L. (1996). *Drug abuse among children and adolescents*. Jakarta: PKBI DKI, YPSI, UNICEF.

Haralambos, M., & Holborn, M. (2008). *Sociology: Themes and perspectives* (7th ed.). London: Harper Collins.

Igbo, E. U. M. (1992). Development and crime in Nigeria. *African Journal of Sociology, 2*, 110–120.

Igbo, E. U. M. (2007). *Introduction to criminology*. Nsukka: University of Nigeria Press, Department of Sociology and Anthropology, University of Nigeria.

Janssen, K. (2001). *Causes of child prostitution in Owerri municipal council*. Owerri: Ibtissam Bagoz Publication.

Jones, H. (1981). *Crime, race and culture. A study in developing country*. Chichester: Wiley.

Kompas. (1998, July 22). *Adolescent prostitution in Indonesia: The effect on their reproductive health*. Jakarta: Central Bureau of Statistics (CBS).

Marjorie, M. A. (1992). Mother sells food, daughter sells her body: The cultural continuity of prostitution. *Journal of Social Science & Medicine, 35*, 891–901.

National Population Commission. (1998, April). *1991 population census of the Federal Republic of Nigeria: Analytical report at the national level*. Abuja.

Njau, W., Radney, S., & Muganda, R. (1992, March 24–27). A summary of the proceedings of first inter-African conference on adolescent health, Nairobi.

Okpukpan, E. A. (2006). The socio-economic background and school population: A survey of the background of children in three types of school in the western state of Nigeria. In *Psychological guidance of the school children* (pp. 16–32). London: Evans and Brothers.

Olaogun, J. A., & Ogundare, C. F. (2008). *Fundamentals of sociology*. Ikeja: Bolabay Publications, Department of Sociology, University of Ado-Ekiti.

Omololu, F. O., & Dare, O. O. (1997). Prospects and future for the Nigerian youth. In *Status of adolescents and young adults in Nigeria* (pp. 498–504). CHESTRAD- Ibadan in Collaboration with NPHCDA. Lagos: CSS Press.

Oyefara, J. L. (2007). *Food insecurity, HIV/AIDS pandemic and sexual behaviour of female commercial sex workers in Lagos Metropolis*. Lagos: Concept.

Oyefara, J. L. (2011). *Socio-cultural context of adolescent fertility in Yoruba society: Insight from Osun State, Nigeria*. Lagos: Concept.

Population, Health and Nutrition Information Project. (2002, March), *PHNIP. Country health statistical report: Nigeria*. Washington, DC.

Prostitution: Envoy chides Benin girls. Nigeria. (2000, February 29). *The Punch*, p. 35.

Sack, A. (1996). *Child prostitution: The Asian reality* (p. 1). Women in Action.

Townsend, P. (1970). Measures and explanations of poverty in high income and low income countries: The problems of operationalizing concepts of development, class and poverty. In P. Townsend (Ed.), *The concepts of poverty* (pp. 74–80). London: Heinemann.

Wagner, & Yatim. (1997, July 22). *Adolescent prostitution in Indonesia: The effect on their reproductive health*. Jakarta: Central Bureau of Statistics (CBS).

Why Nigerian students find a vocation in prostitution? Nigeria. (2009, March 23). *The Nation*, p. 9.

Williams, K. (1984,). Economic sources of homicide: Re-estimating the effect of poverty and inequality. *American Sociological Review, 49*, 283–289.

A reason for reasonable doubt in social justice: the weight of poverty, race and gender in lopsided homicide case clearances outcomes

Alonzo DeCarlo

Threats to and lack of social justice in response to homicide victims in the USA is one of the most provocative topics of inquiry. The current study empirically scrutinises a decade of data and statistical trends regarding case clearances for homicide victims. The relationship between a homicide victim's race, age, gender and poverty status of their residential area was examined. Analysis of the circumstances and type of weapon used were also examined in conjunction with the status of the offender. The investigation of patterns over 10 years reveal that homicide victims who live in cities with high poverty and who happen to be young, African-American and male are less likely to have their case solved or cleared.

The American public has been conditioned, albeit somewhat weakly, that they should presume equal treatment under the law irrespective of their social and economic status. This expectation falls within the sphere of social justice fundamentals, which involves guaranteeing the protection of equal access to rights, liberties and opportunities for disadvantaged members of society (Rawls, 1958, 1971). But in reality, the American public stands at an intensely disputed crossroads where race relations intersect with the rules that govern the apprehension and punishment of criminals. Hence, to many American citizens, particularly African-Americans, this social justice imperative is little more than a contestable ideal. This may be due to the lack of perceived legitimacy, technical competence and ability to perform efficiently prescribed duties by agents of the US criminal justice system, especially as it relates to communities with high-poverty rates and ethnic minority individuals. For example, research has indicated that African-Americans believe they are treated unfairly in criminal legal formalities and actual practice (Brunson, 2007). This reinforces the idea of anticipatory injustice (AI), that is, the extent to which individuals presume unfair or discriminatory procedures and outcomes in judicial and law enforcement circumstances (Shapiro & Kirkman, 2001). In fact, robust research findings by Wolard, Harvell, and Graham (2008) revealed that African-Americans have higher levels of AI than other ethnic minority groups and Caucasian Americans. A study by Pastore and Maguire (2007) showed that 41% of African-Americans had confidence in the US law enforcement system as compared to 71% of Caucasian Americans. Indeed, Tonry (1995) suggested that there exists a 'malign neglect' within the criminal justice system relative to racial and ethnic minorities. Research has shown that the principal injury suffered by ethnic minority victims in relation to criminal matters is simple underenforcement of the law. This paper examines the extralegal factors such as metropolises' poverty proportions and size, race, gender and age as contributing influences to the disparate percentage of unsolved murders or lack of homicide case clearances.

To clear an offense (including homicide cases) within the Federal Bureau of Investigation's (FBI) guidelines, certain criteria must be met; including at least one person (a) arrested, (b) charged with the commission of the offense and (c) turned over to the court for prosecution whether following arrest, court summons or police notice (FBI, 2011). A study by Corsianos (2003) indicated that law enforcement officials often consider crimes involving minority victims as low priority and consequently give less time, energy and resources to solve their cases. This perception is consistent with Black's (1976) seminal work on law and behaviour, which posits that homicide case clearance, to a large degree, is connected to the status of the parties. According to Black (1976), extralegal factors such as racial identity, gender and age of the victim affect the outcome of homicide case clearances. Thus, victims with higher socioeconomic status are likely to receive more attention and subsequently have higher homicide case clearance rates than those with lower socioeconomic status. These extralegal factors contribute categorically to the decline in what Khodyakov (2007) labelled 'institutional trust', which is based on perceived institutional legitimacy, technical competence and the ability to perform its duties efficiently.

In general, versions of three explanatory theoretical frameworks have emerged from the professional literature regarding homicide case clearance. Perennially cited is the devaluation perspective by Black (1976), which suggests that there is a differential in the dispensation of effort and resources for homicide cases often resulting in low case clearances for the economically vulnerable and ethnic minority groups. Next is the event characteristics perspective (Klinger, 1997) that posits that the variance in homicide case clearance is contingent upon the quantity of available evidence. The third and most recent conception can be described as the blaming the victim perspective (Rydberg & Pizarro, 2014); it highlights the lifestyle activities of the victim in a deviant context as major contributors in the difficulty of resolving homicide cases. The aforementioned theoretical positions have merit, but none adequately examine the gender and race variance in homicide case clearance rates in large metropolises with high-poverty proportions across the USA.

Research has highlighted that poor homicide case clearance rates affect deterrent value, reduce police morale and intensify trauma and fear in families of victims (Riedel & Boulahanis, 2007). They also influence perception of corruption within law enforcement agencies (Sparrow, Moore, & Kennedy, 1990; Walker & Katz, 2002) and heighten the suspicion that case clearance is in part based on the victim's race, ethnicity and status (Black, 1980; Borg & Parker, 2001; Lee, 2005; Peterson & Hagan, 1984; Roberts & Lyon, 2011). In their pioneering research on procedural justice, Thibaut and Walker (1975) proposed that individuals are as concerned about how their cases are managed as they are about the actual outcome. Similarly, Tyler's (2001) study demonstrated that people weigh procedural fairness in terms of two issues: (a) how legal authorities treat them and (b) whether or not those legal authorities make fair decisions about their cases.

Sarat (1977) argued, 'The perception of unequal treatment is the single most important source of popular dissatisfaction within the American legal system' (p. 434). Contemporary studies have confirmed that the fundamental factor that forms the public's perceptions about the law is appraisal of the fairness of the processes, regardless of whether the emphasis is on the courts or the police (Tyler, 2001; Tyler & Lind, 2001). In 2004, Bendixen found that 88% of African-Americans and 75% of American Indians believed that the criminal justice system favours wealthy individuals. Bias and tolerance of racial discrimination within the criminal justice system have reinforced the public's apprehension about its true objectivity and effectiveness. Many ethnic minorities' faith in the criminal justice system is tenuous due to extenuating extra-legal factors impacting poor homicide case clearance rates.

A quarter of a century has passed since Stark (1987) stated that urban underenforcement is one of those problems that everyone knows about, but for which there is no firm evidence. Since then, confirmation that the criminal justice system was less likely to clear cases of African-American victims between 1965 and 1995 has emerged (Litwin & Xu, 2007). However, the perceived biases in law enforcement against minorities have existed for decades (Bayley & Mendesohn, 1969; Roberts & Stalans, 1997; Weitzer & Tuch, 1999). There are also empirical data documenting that law enforcement officers engage in some form of biases against African-Americans (see Wiley, 2001, for a review of relevant studies). Such studies lend credence to the belief that enforcement of the law does not occur without prejudice. Thus, homicide case clearances are often used as a barometer of police performance, but this rational may be incongruous (Maguire, King, Johnson, & Katz, 2010).

Studies have also stressed that population density and percentage of non-Caucasian individuals are both inversely related to homicide case clearance rates (Keel, Jarvis, & Muirhead, 2009). However, there is paucity in the macro-level homicide research regarding this critical relationship between the national scope of community area characteristics and homicide clearance rates. Accordingly, there are little empirical data revealing the combined depth of difference in homicide case clearance rates as a function of economics status, race and gender. This study examines that relationship and expounds upon social justice attitudes in this context.

Methodology

Data sources and research questions

The 2000–2009 editions of the Uniform Crime Reporting (UCR) containing data (143,443 records) from the FBI were obtained to conduct an exploratory analysis of homicide characteristics in crimes committed by young African-American males (ages 13–24). Young Caucasian male offenders were identified to serve as a direct comparison group. The remaining cases were to serve as an additional comparison sample to be classified by gender, race and age group. This step in data management revealed a large amount of missing offender data, ranging from 35% of the cases in 2009 to 39% of the cases in 2003. Because of this magnitude of missing data, the emphasis for this study was changed to questions regarding differences between victims with known offenders and victims for whom offenders were not known. Was age of victim related to identification of the offender? Was the gender of the victim related to identification of the offender? Was race of the victim related to identification of the offender? Was the circumstance of the homicide associated with knowledge of offenders? Was weapon type associated with knowledge of offenders? Was law enforcement agency location associated with knowledge of the offenders? Were results consistent across the 10-year span? Frequencies, chi-square and logistic regression were used to answer the research questions, Table 1.

Analysis and results

The answer was a significant 'yes' to each of the above questions: younger homicide victims were more likely to have unknown offenders; male homicide victims were more likely to have unknown offenders; African-American homicide victims were more likely to have unknown offenders. Use of guns in the homicide was also significantly related to lack of knowledge of the offender. Additionally, homicides from the top 40 poverty cities had the highest percentage

Table 1. Variable coding.

Variable	Definition/coding
Dependent variable	
Offender status	Offender status was coded as 0 for known and 1 for unknown. Only victims in whose situation category, as reported in the UCR, was single victim with a single known offender or single victim with single unknown offender were included when their gender, age and race were known Independent variables
Independent variables	
Victim gender	Females = 0 and males = 1
Victim race	Caucasians = 1; African-Americans = 2 and Other = 3
Victim age	Years 0–12 = 0; Years 13–24 = 2; Years 25–50 and greater = 3
Circumstances	Felony = 1; non-felony = 2; justified = 3; manslaughter = 4 and unknown = 5
Weapon	Gun = 1; knife = 2 blunt object = 3 bodily force = 4 and all others = 5
Year	Data were for a 10-year span, from 2000 to 2009
Agency location	The location variable was based on a combination of the FBI size of population groups included in the UCR and a coding of cities as to poverty status based on data provided by Andrew A. Beveridge, a demographer at Queens College and reported in the New York Times on page A23 of the February 18, 2012, edition as the cities with populations over 250,000 and the highest percentages of poverty. Poverty cities with a population greater than 250,000 were coded as 1; other cities with population greater than 250,000 were coded as 2. The remaining cities continued the sequence with cities 100,000–249,999 coded as 3, cities 50,000–99,999 coded as 4; cities 25,000–49,999 coded as 5 and cities with population less than 25,000 coded as 6

of victims with unknown offenders. As was expected and affirming the validity of the data, in almost every case, justified homicides were associated with known offenders

Victim gender: For each of the 10 years, the percentages of known and unknown offenders were computed within victim gender. Each year, the chi-square was significant beyond the .001 level, indicating a strong relationship between gender and knowledge of the offender. Males consistently demonstrated the higher percentage of unknown offenders. Merging all 10 years into 1 analysis, the percentage of unknown offenders for 87,342 males was 42.2%; for 25,288 females, 21.7%. The overall chi-square was 3504.263

Victim race: For each of the 10 years, the percentages of known and unknown offenders were computed within each of the race categories. Each year, the chi-square was significant beyond the .001 level, indicating a strong relationship between race and case closure, with African-Americans presenting the highest percentage of unknown offenders. When all 10 years are pooled, the percentage with an unknown offender for the 54,059 African-Americans was 44.8%; for the 54,678 Caucasians, 30.3% and for the remaining 2,844 others, 32.3%. The overall chi-square was 2471.685, $p < .001$.

Victim age: Victim age categories were 0–12 ($N = 5,113$), 13–24 ($N = 33,665$), 25–50 ($N = 57,891$) and greater than 50 years of age ($N = 14,300$). For each of the 10 years, the percentages of known and unknown offenders were calculated within each victim age group. Each year, the chi-square was significant beyond the .001 level, indicating a strong relationship between age and case closure, with the age group 13–24 constantly presenting the highest percentage of unknown offenders, and the youngest age group exhibiting the lowest percentage. Combining all 10 years, the unknown offender percentages for the 4 age groups were 26.6% for ages 0–12, 43.8% for ages 13–24, 38.0% for ages 25–50 and 29.3% for ages greater than 50. The overall chi-square was 1211.911, $p < .001$

Circumstance: As with the victim demographics, known and unknown status of the homicide varied with circumstance (chi-square = 25,150.412, $p < .001$). The most frequent circumstantial category was non-felony (47.8% of the cases). The second most frequent category was 'unknown,' accounting for 34.0% of the cases. When the offender was known, 62.4% of the cases were non-felony, compared with 23.6% when the offender was unknown. For the unknown circumstances, the percentages were reversed: 60.5% of the unknown offender cases were in the unknown circumstance category; while 18.0% of the known offender cases were in that category. Using the types of circumstance as the base, the results for the comparisons between known and unknown offenders were, for 14,417 felonies, 44.2% had an unknown offender and 55.8% had a known offender; for 53,928

Table 2. Logistic regression, predicting offender status as unknown ($N = 109{,}630$).

	B	SE	Sig.	Exp (B)	95% CI for exp (B) Lower	Upper
Location[a]			.000			
Poverty cities > 250,000	1.324	.027	.000	3.758	3.563	3.963
Other cities > 250,000	1.168	.034	.000	3.215	3.006	3.438
Cities 100,000 to 249,999	0.848	.028	.000	2.336	2.209	2.469
Cities 50,000 to 99,999	0.827	.035	.000	2.286	2.135	2.448
Cities 25,000 to 49,999	0.205	.034	.000	1.228	1.149	1.311
Weapon[b]			.000			
Any kind of gun	−0.200	.028	.000	0.819	0.775	0.864
Knife	−1.030	.034	.000	0.357	0.334	0.382
Blunt object	−0.424	.043	.000	0.655	0.602	0.712
Bodily force	−0.808	.041	.000	0.446	0.411	0.483
Circumstance[c]			.000			
Felony	−1.024	.022	.000	0.359	0.344	0.375
Non-felony	−2.144	.017	.000	0.117	0.113	0.121
Justified	−3.693	.061	.000	0.025	0.022	0.028
Manslaughter	−3.707	.129	.000	0.025	0.019	0.032
Victim gender	0.768	.020	**.000**	2.154	2.070	2.242
Victim race[d]			.002			
Caucasian	0.046	.016	.003	1.048	1.016	1.081
African-American	0.121	.048	.013	1.128	1.026	1.241
Victim age[e]			.000			
13–24	0.649	.045	.000	1.914	1.753	2.089
25–50	0.480	.044	.000	1.616	1.484	1.760
> 50	0.280	.047	.000	1.323	1.206	1.450
Year[f]			.000			
2001	−0.060	.034	.077	0.942	0.881	1.006
2002	−0.065	.034	.053	0.937	0.877	1.001
2003	−0.009	.034	.787	0.991	0.928	1.058
2004	−0.024	.034	.472	0.976	0.914	1.043
2005	−0.187	.034	.000	0.829	0.776	0.886
2006	−0.107	.033	.001	0.899	0.842	0.960
2007	−0.039	.033	.249	0.962	0.901	1.027
2008	−0.085	.034	.012	0.919	0.860	0.982
2009	−0.122	.034	.000	0.885	0.827	0.947
Constant	−0.899	.057	.000	0.407		

[a]Reference group: Cities < 25,000.
[b]Reference group: All other weapons.
[c]Reference group: Unknown circumstance.
[d]Reference group: Other races.
[e]Reference group: 0–12.
[f]Reference group: 2000.

Table 3. Proportions of homicide victims with an unknown offender as a function of year, location/poverty, race and handgun involvement.

Location size	Victim race	Handgun used	2000	2001	2002	2003	2004	2005	2006	2007	2008	2009
Poverty Cities, 250,000+	African-American	Yes	.48	.45	.49	.54	.52	.49	.45	.50	.50	.50
		No	.43	.42	.43	.41	.37	.46	.47	.42	.44	.42
	Caucasian	Yes	.37	.39	.37	.46	.44	.42	.39	.44	.42	.36
		No	.40	.38	.34	.36	.36	.37	.38	.34	.34	.35
Cities, 250,000+	African-American	Yes	.43	.44	.44	.41	.48	.41	.47	.39	.48	.49
		No	.39	.42	.38	.39	.49	.47	.43	.53	.45	.38
	Caucasian	Yes	.31	.30	.35	.39	.35	.36	.39	.33	.35	.25
		No	.34	.31	.34	.34	.27	.29	.30	.34	.27	.24
100,000–249,999	African-American	Yes	.39	.41	.43	.43	.43	.39	.43	.43	.39	.37
		No	.33	.37	.35	.34	.34	.31	.32	.33	.32	.32
	Caucasian	Yes	.32	.30	.33	.38	.36	.36	.35	.38	.33	.34
		No	.26	.31	.22	.25	.26	.24	.23	.23	.23	.25
50,000–99,999	African-American	Yes	.43	.42	.42	.32	.45	.50	.37	.46	.47	.41
		No	.32	.32	.34	.32	.32	.29	.31	.27	.38	.28
	Caucasian	Yes	.32	.35	.32	.34	.33	.31	.29	.34	.31	.26
		No	.20	.20	.21	.20	.16	.18	.18	.22	.22	.20
25,000–49,999	African-American	Yes	.26	.24	.22	.20	.19	.22	.22	.21	.29	.28
		No	.26	.25	.27	.26	.26	.27	.18	.29	.22	.25
	Caucasian	Yes	.18	.16	.21	.17	.18	.17	.16	.22	.16	.17
		No	.17	.19	.17	.16	.19	.13	.15	.15	.17	.16
<25,000	African-American	Yes	.18	.18	.18	.20	.18	.15	.16	.22	.21	.20
		No	.19	.22	.20	.23	.21	.22	.25	.20	.23	.24
	Caucasian	Yes	.12	.14	.15	.13	.13	.15	.12	.12	.16	.13
		No	.13	.14	.15	.14	.13	.13	.14	.15	.14	.12

Notes: For Year, $F(9,129,125) = 2.017, p = .033$; For Location, $F(5,129,125) = 894.689, p < .001$; For Race, $F(1,129,125) = 824.551, p < .001$ and For Handgun, $F(1,129,125) = 209.879, p < .001$. One large interaction: Handgun and Location $F(1,129,125) = 48.403, p < .001$.

non-felonies, the corresponding percentages were 18.6% unknown offenders and 81.4% known offenders; for 1,601 manslaughters, 4.5% unknown offenders and 95.5% known offenders; for the 38,380 unknown circumstances, 66.9% unknown offenders and 33.1% known offenders; and, for 4,531 justified homicides, 7.0% unknown offenders and 93.0% known offenders. These last two circumstance categories provide a degree of affirmation for the validity of the database, as identification of the circumstance would imply a more thorough knowledge of the case, perhaps leading to its closure.

Weapon: Cases with unknown offenders differed significantly from cases with known offenders (chi-square = 4324.769, $p < .001$). Guns as weapon was more prevalent within unknown offender homicides: 74.8% of the unknown offenders used guns while 59.1% of known offenders used guns. In contrast, known offenders were more closely associated with knives (17.2% vs. 7.5%) and bodily force (10.2% vs. 3.8%). In the homicides involving knives, 79.2% had known offenders. In the homicides involving bodily force, 81.6% had known offenders. 'Up close and personal' weapons were more prevalent in homicides with known offenders, which could more easily lead to identification of the offender.

Agency location: Large cities with highest poverty levels had the highest percentages of unknown offenders; the smaller locations consistently showed the lower percentages of unknown offenders compared to known offenders. Percentages with an unknown offender decreased with location size, the largest percentage for the large poverty cities (45.9%) decreasing to 6.6% for the smallest location (population less than 25,000). The overall chi-square was 6172.594, $p < .001$.

Multivariate results – logistic regression: As there were clear differences between known and unknown offenders at the bivariate level, logistic regression was then used to assess these differences while controlling for the remaining variables. The results of the significant logistic regression (−2 log likelihood = 110,153.706, chi-square = 35,341.418, df 28, $p < .001$) are presented in Table 2. Even when controlling for the effects of other variables, the bivariate results

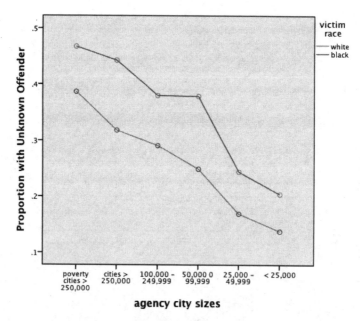

Figure 1. Unknown offender as function of victim race and location size over a 10-year period.

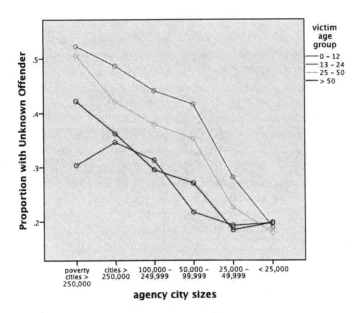

Figure 2. Unknown offender as function of victim age and location size over a 10-year period.

remain intact. As is evident from the increase in the odds [Exp(B)], African-American males in the age range of 13–24 years, living in a large, high-poverty city are more likely to be killed in a felonious situation by a firearm and not to have a known offender, regardless of year of the homicide. The estimated R-squared (Nagelkerke) was .375, and the prediction accuracy was 82.6% for victims with known offenders and 63.0% for victims with unknown offenders. The overall predictive percentage correct was 75.2%.

By way of summary, the proportions of unknown offenders, which served as the dependent variable for an analysis of variance using as independent variables year, location, race and a handgun weapon, are presented in Table 3. These proportions help anchor the logistic regression results. Furthermore, Figure 1 presents the proportion of victims with unknown offenders as a function of the agency location size and victim race. Figure 2 shows the proportion of victims with unknown offenders as a function of the agency location size and age. As results are consistent across the 10 years, all years have been aggregated in Figures 1 and 2. Regardless of race, unknown offender status decreases with size of the location. Regardless of location, unknown offenders are more prevalent for African-American victims.

Discussion and conclusion

The notion that 'equal justice under law' is one of the most firmly embedded and widely violated legal principles in the USA (Rhode, 2001) may be supported by data from this study, which provide statistical substantiation of underenforcement of the law in homicide case clearances. The present study examined the relationship between poverty, race, age, gender and identification of the offender in homicide cases. The questions raised in this study are a response to a perceived absence of uniform social justice, especially where solving homicide crimes are concerned. Consistent with some research findings, in homicides where the victim was elderly, the cases are unlikely to be solved or the offender is unknown (Addington, 2006; Alderden & Lavery, 2007; Lee, 2005). Other studies have found significant gender effects and have concluded that female victims are more likely to have their homicide cases solved (Roberts & Lyons, 2011). Those findings were supported in this study. Moreover, if the homicide victim is young, African-American, male and poor, it is highly unlikely that the killer in that case will be found and prosecuted as illustrated in Figures 1 and 2.

These circumstances are similar to Puckett and Lundman's (2003) research which showed that homicides are less likely to be cleared by arrest in predominantly African-American census tracts. This finding is consistent in large American cities that have high percentages of poverty. The data from this research show an extremely high probability that homicide offenders were unknown in top poverty cities when a firearm was used as the murder weapon. Cities with large poverty percentages are likely to have a disproportionate number of homicide victim cases that are not justified. These types of data may help explain why African-Americans are willing to acknowledge or accept the view of malign neglect and discriminatory procedures in the American law enforcement system.

That homicide clearance rates have dropped nearly 30% since the 1960s is a national concern. The idea that this trend may be disproportionally distributed among the poor is disquieting. The argument that attaining social justice is a function of the economic status of the individual and/or their residential municipalities has been made more convincing in view of the findings of this study. Data from this investigation may explain in part why underprivileged African-Americans have an implicit negative expectation about how they may be treated under the law. African-Americans' normative orientation about law enforcement thus has become rife with cynicism. Under these conditions, it will be extremely difficult to convince African-Americans that the arbiters for US systems of modern jurisprudence have an interest in correcting the institutional culture of law enforcement without prejudice. The issue of exposed empirical regularities of disparities in homicide case clearances calls for further research and attention. The results of this study provide tentative confirmation that the race of homicide victims and the economic status of their communities reveal a pattern of features regarding the relationship between homicide case clearances and race, gender and poverty.

Although these features are critical to understanding and possible intervention, there are a number of methodological obstacles. One major limitation is that homicide case clearance data sources may be incomplete. The FBI's Uniform Crime Report data set is a nationwide collection of crime statistics data gathered from over 18,000 law enforcement agencies. However, these law enforcement agencies submit their statistics on a voluntary basis, which accounts for missing data. The FBI's uniform crime report data set is the most comprehensive one available for researchers. Another possible limitation is that the data sets do not provide information on the complexity and difficulty of each case. Notwithstanding these limitations, there is ample evidence to draw important inferences about the nature of social justice disparities in homicide case clearances for victims. Paramount among possible inferences is the need to use the uncompromised exemplar of equal treatment under the law as a lodestar to social justice regardless of race, class and gender.

References

Addington, L. A. (2006). Using national incident-based reporting system murder data to evaluate clearance predictors a research note. *Homicide Studies, 10*(2), 140–152. doi:10.1177/1088767905285439

Alderden, M. A., & Lavery, T. A. (2007). Predicting homicide clearances in Chicago investigating disparities in predictors across different types of homicide. *Homicide Studies, 11*(2), 115–132. doi:10.1177/1088767907300505

Bayley, D. H., & Mendelsohn, H. A. (1969). *Minorities and the police: Confrontation in America* (p. 91). New York: Free Press.

Black, D. J. (1976). *The behavior of law*. New York: Academic Press.

Black, D. J., & African-American, D. (1980). *The manners and customs of the police*. New York: Academic Press.

Borg, M. J., & Parker, K. F. (2001). Mobilizing law in urban areas: The social structure of homicide clearance rates. *Law and Society Review, 35*(2), 435–466.

Brunson, R. K. (2007). "Police don't like African American people": African-American young men's accumulated police experiences. *Criminology & Public Policy, 6*(1), 71–101. doi:10.1111/j.1745-9133.2007.00423.x

Corsianos, M. (2003). Discretion in detectives' decision-making and high profile cases. *Police Practice and Research, 4*(3), 301–314. doi:10.1080/1561426032000113893

FBI. (2011). *Crime in the United States*. Washington, DC: U.S. Department of Justice, Federal Bureau of Investigation.

Keel, T. G., Jarvis, J. P., & Muirhead, Y. E. (2009). An exploratory analysis of factors affecting homicide investigations examining the dynamics of murder clearance rates. *Homicide Studies, 13*(1), 50–68. doi:10.1177/1088767908326903

Khodyakov, D. (2007). Trust as a process a three-dimensional approach. *Sociology, 41*(1), 115–132. doi:10.1177/0038038507072285

Klinger, D. A. (1997). Negotiating order in patrol work: An ecological theory of police response to deviance. *Criminology, 35*, 277–306.

Lee, C. (2005). The value of life in death: Multiple regression and event history analyses of homicide clearance in Los Angeles County. *Journal of Criminal Justice, 33*(6), 527–534. doi:10.1016/j.jcrimjus.2005.08.002

Litwin, K. J., & Xu, Y. (2007). The dynamic nature of homicide clearances a multilevel model comparison of three time periods. *Homicide Studies, 11*(2), 94–114. doi:10.1177/1088767907300759

Maguire, E. R., King, W. R., Johnson, D., & Katz, C. M. (2010). Why homicide clearance rates decrease: Evidence from the Caribbean. *Policing & Society, 20*(4), 373–400. doi:10.1080/10439463.2010.507869

Pastore, A. L., & Maguire, K. (2007). *Sourcebook of criminal justice statistics*. Washington, DC: U.S. Department of Justice, Bureau of Statistics.

Peterson, R. D., & Hagan, J. (1984). Changing conceptions of race: Towards an account of anomalous findings of sentencing research. *American Sociological Review, 49*(1), 56–70. doi:10.2307/2095557

Puckett, J. L., & Lundman, R. J. (2003). Factors affecting homicide clearances: Multivariate analysis of a more complete conceptual framework. *Journal of Research in Crime and Delinquency, 40*(2), 171–193. doi:10.1177/0022427803251125

Rawls, J. (1958). Justice as fairness. *The Philosophical Review, 67*(2), 164–194. doi:10.2307/2182612

Rawls, J. (1971). *A theory of justice*. Cambridge, MA: Harvard University.

Rhode, D. L. (2001). Access to justice. Fordham law. *Review, 69*(5), 1785–1819.

Riedel, M., & Boulahanis, J. G. (2007). Homicides exceptionally cleared and cleared by arrest an exploratory study of police/prosecutor outcomes. *Homicide Studies, 11*(2), 151–164. doi:10.1177/1088767907300747

Roberts, A., & Lyons, C. J. (2011). Hispanic victims and homicide clearance by arrest. *Homicide Studies, 15*(1), 48–73. doi:10.1177/1088767910397278

Roberts, J. V., & Stalans, L. J. (1997). *Public opinion, crime, and criminal justice*. Boulder, CO: Westview Press.

Rydberg, J., & Pizarro, J. M. (2014). Victim lifestyle as a correlate of homicide clearance. *Homicide Studies*, doi:1088767914521813

Sarat, A. (1977). Studying American legal culture: An assessment of survey evidence. *Law & Society Review, 11*, 427–488.

Shapiro, D. L., & Kirkman, B. L. (2001). Anticipatory injustice: The consequences of expecting injustice in the workplace. *Advances in organizational justice, 32*(5), 152–178.

Sparrow, M. K., Moore, M. H., & Kennedy, D. (1990). *Beyond 911: A new era for policing*. New York: Basic Books.
Stark, R. (1987). Deviant places: A theory of the ecology of crime. *Criminology, 25*(4), 893–910. doi:10.1111/j.1745-9125.1987.tb00824.x
Thibaut, J., & Walker, L. (1975). *Procedural justice*. Hillsdale, NJ: Lawrence Erlbaum.
Tonry, M. (1995). *Malign neglect: Race, crime, and punishment in America*. New York: Oxford University Press.
Tyler, T. R. (2001). Public trust and confidence in legal authorities: What do majority and minority group members want from the law and legal institutions? *Behavioral Sciences & the Law, 19*(2), 215–235. doi:10.1002/bsl.438
Tyler, T. R. & Lind, E. A. (2001). Procedural justice. In J. Sanders & V. L. Hamilton (Eds.), *Handbook of justice research in law* (pp. 65–92). Boston, MA: Kluwer Academic/Plenum Publishers.
Walker, S., & Katz, C. M. (2002). *Policing in America: An introduction* (4th ed.). New York: McGraw Hill.
Weitzer, R., & Tuch, S. A. (1999). Race, class, and perceptions of discrimination by the police. *Crime & Delinquency, 45*(4), 494–507. doi:10.1177/0011128799045004006
Wiley, D. C. (2001). African American and white differences in the perception of justice. *Behavioral Sciences & the Law, 19*(5–6), 649–655. doi:10.1002/bsl.463
Wolard, J. L., Harvell, S., & Graham, S. (2008). Anticipatory injustice among adolescents: Age and racial/ethnic differences in perceived unfairness of the justice system. *Behavioral Sciences & the Law, 26*(2), 207–226. doi:10.1002/bsl.805

A consideration of the social impact of cybercrime: examples from hacking, piracy, and child abuse material online

Mary Aiken, Ciaran Mc Mahon, Ciaran Haughton, Laura O'Neill and Edward O'Carroll

> Contemporary news headlines seem to play regular host to treatments of one form of *cybercrime* or another, whether it be fraud, hacking, malware, piracy or child abuse material online. In this paper, the meaning of that term is unpacked, social impact is considered and possible future developments are discussed. Given the pervasive and profound influence of the Internet, it is important to acknowledge that in terms of criminology, what happens online can impact on the real world and vice versa. Consequently, real-world and cyber social impacts in relation to cybercrime will be examined.

Introduction

Technology is now ubiquitous, the Internet specifically is an increasingly pervasive phenomenon with approximately 3.2 billion people (almost 40%) of the world's population now online (International Telecommunications Union, 2015). While the Internet offers abundant opportunities for education, networking and communication as an information superhighway, it can also manifest risk particularly regarding criminal activity, which in turn has implications in both real and virtual worlds. As such, the purpose of this article is to discuss the social impact of forensic phenomena in this new sphere: *cybercrime*.

Social impact and social context of cybercrime

'Social impact' per se is a fickle concept, which can be treated on both a macro scale – for example, the 'economic and social impact of the arts' (Reeves, 2002), the political effects of rumors (Huang, 2015) – and a micro scale – ' ... changes in physiological states and subjective feelings, motives and emotions, cognitions and beliefs, values and behavior, that occur in an individual, human or animal, as a result of the real, implied, or imagined presence or actions of other individuals' (Latane, 1981, p. 343). Consequently, there lies within our exploratory toolkit a whole range of factors to hand – from economic, cultural, psychological and interpersonal – which is useful, because, as will be discussed cybercrime explodes the notion of social impact. It is an implicit argument within this paper that such an explosion of the understanding of 'social impact' is necessary in the study of cybercrime, because, quite frankly, of the nature of the environment in which it occurs.

Human interaction in cyberspace, while usually carried out in physical isolation, is almost immediately public and permanent: users are both alone and hyper-connected, all at once. As such, given the social context of cybercrime, its social impact has quite unusual properties. Slane (2007, p. 97) has noted:

> Claims for the independence of cyberspace sound quaint and idealistic, largely because they are based on a false dichotomy between virtual and physical phenomena. Physical and virtual are not opposed; rather the virtual complicates the physical, and vice versa.

This complication of virtual and physical – a sort of 'augmented reality' (Jurgenson, 2011) – represents a new problem for the study of environmental behaviours such as crime. The difficult task is therefore to study problems as they are naturally occurring in everyday life (Proshansky, 1987), a point which is particularly relevant in the study of cybercrime. Proshansky states that it is important, however, for the environmental researcher to utilise all aspects of research and analysis of the findings and to take into account both the general and individualised aspects of the problems. However, Proshansky (1987) only considered environment in terms of a 'real-world' construct, understandably his research at the time did not extend into cyberspace. Subsequently, Suler (2004) presents an evolving conceptual framework for understanding how people react to and behave in cyberspace, arguing that the experience created by computers and computer networks should in many ways be understood as a psychological 'space' – ergo, 'cyberspace'. How the learnings of environmental psychology, like Proshansky (1987), be applied to Suler's (2004) remains to be seen, though this paper, like some other tentative steps (Aiken & Mc Mahon, 2014), should be seen in that light.

Such theoretical developments naturally produce corollary methodological issues. For example, Aiken and Mc Mahon (2014, p. 3) assert that 'traditional research methodology ... is beginning to look quaint' in the light of rapid developments in information communication technology and how that effects the social science research process. There are important questions which researchers must reflect upon, such as the level of digital literacy of the researcher, the source of their ethical guidance, the evangelism which envelopes public messaging on the use of technology and how close the researcher can or should come to the lived experience of the research subjects (Aiken & Mc Mahon, 2014). Such reflections are particularly useful in the context of the social impact of cybercrime, but equally so in a broader conversation on the academic treatment of its social context. Vishik (as cited in '4th World Cyber Security Technology Research Summit Report,' 2014) noted that 'the multi-disciplinary nature of cyber security attacks is important, attacks happen for different reasons, only some of which are technical, other reasons include, for example, socioeconomic issues' (p. 8). What is also important, in addition to inter-disciplinarity, is the construct of trans-disciplinarity in cyberspace (Suler, 2013). There is a long-standing tradition of this in the context of cybercrime, in the guise of applied studies such as forensic and investigative psychology, and as such, cyberpsychology is yet another exemplification of how this can be achieved, drawing from social science and computer science, but also similarly recent enterprises such as network science and digital humanities.

With regard to the current treatment, the most salient cyberpsychological theoretical perspective to note is the concept of online disinhibition (Suler, 2004). In exploring how people tend to do and say things while on the Internet, which they would not be likely to do in a real-world face-to-face context. Suler (2004) details several factors at play in this phenomenon, including dissociative anonymity, and minimisation of status and authority online. Suler notes that the text-heavy nature of online environments occludes many of the effects of authority as presented in the physical environment – dress, physical stature, trappings of officialdom and so on. Moreover, there is a long-standing Internet social philosophy which holds that 'everyone is an equal, that the purpose of the net is to share ideas and resources among peers' (Suler, 2004, p. 324). Consequently, with society's normal hierarchies and powers flattened somewhat, it could be argued that the online environment is one which naturally lends itself to criminal or at least unusual behaviour. Minimisation of authority should be viewed in addition to what Suler terms 'dissociative imagination' – the idea that 'one's online persona along with the online others live in a make-believe dimension, separate and apart from the demands and responsibilities of the real world' (2004, p. 323). As such, even without tackling the problematic issue of anonymity, scenarios may manifest online which are quite unlike those where real-world physical crimes occur.

When the notion of authority is developed more specifically with regard to cybercrime, there are a number of corollaries. On the one hand, with no observable authority figures, or in an apparently hierarchy-free context, a lower barrier to crime participation may be envisaged. Moreover, where there is the possibility that all participants in this environment may not fully appreciate it as a real environment, the words of the infamous hacker, Kevin Mitnick may be appreciated: '... the human factor is truly security's weakest link' (Mitnick & Simon, 2002, p. 16). Fundamentally, even following installation of sophisticated information security technology, practices and training, a company will still be vulnerable. This is because people tend to underestimate the severity of potential cyber threats and this complacency may lead to successful cyber-attacks (Paganini, 2012).

As such, from the perspective of the victims of cybercrime, concepts such as *herd immunity* may need to be considered (Rosenzweig, 2013) – where not every member of a population needs to be inoculated to prevent the spread of infection – with regard to human behaviour in cyberspace. Some work has been done with regard to modelling the spread of viruses in computer networks (Asllani & Ali, 2012), but this concept should be considered in relation to a wider variety of phenomena: perhaps people fall victim to cybercrime because they assume that the rest of the herd will take care of security for them? This also has parallels with what is known as the Peltzman effect (1975) – whereby paradoxically increased safety regulation seems to reduce safety behaviours. Fundamentally, while not wishing to engage in digital dualism (Jurgenson, 2011), people should be open to the possibility that denizens of cyberspace, either not fully believing it to be 'real', or assuming that its security will be taken care of elsewhere, may leave themselves open to some forms of criminal attack. At the outset, a preliminary social impact of the phenomenon of cybercrime should be noted: a culture of unreality and novelty still pervades in cyberspace, which continues to be readily exploited by adversaries.

Such an illusory context however, has concomitant risk. Wilde (1998) proposed the hypothesis of risk homeostasis, suggesting that people maximise their benefit by comparing the expected costs and benefits of safer and riskier behaviour. Thus, any situation which is perceived as safe will allow people to take more risks, resulting in equilibrium: as the dangers of the Internet can be intangible, a false sense of security can develop. This allows cybercriminals to take bigger risks online, while at the same time, in a social context, enables their victims to be less protective of themselves and their information online. In an industry context, a lot of cybercrimes go unreported to authorities and thus, the majority of information is held in the private sector by businesses or their IT partners (Bradley, 2014). Businesses seek to minimise public panic when they are attacked, and are concerned about liabilities from disclosing internal information (Groenfeldt, 2013). In early 2015, the British telecommunications company, Talktalk, had a security breach and lost valuable customer data. The hack was not publically disclosed and therefore hackers were then able to contact customers, quote personal information, gain remote access to their computers, thus allowing the hackers to steal in excess of £3000 per customer (Brignall, 2015). Some feel that they cannot risk reporting to the authorities, and instead opt for 'frontier justice' – counter attacks (which shut down the server an attack is originating from) known in cyber security industry as 'active defence' or 'striking back' (Deloitte, 2014). To combat rogue security and encourage sharing with law enforcement, Deloitte, amongst others, has suggested a clearinghouse model (2014). Private companies worried about seizure of servers, public trust and competitors taking advantage could submit data to the clearinghouse, which would analyse it to share with action-taking authorities and also to warn other companies in similar industries of potential risks (Deloitte, 2014). Information sources such as SurfWatch are on this path, collecting data to better inform industries and allow them to compare information about cybercrime and related issues (SecurityWeek, 2015). But there is very much a sense of primitiveness in how this is being dealt with: as if all are still in the early days of understanding how to collectively organise a response to these threats.

Cybercrime defined

At the outset, it is worth noting that the relatively recent phenomenon of cybercrime is steadfastly resisting an accepted definition. Popular media treatments mentioning cybercrime usually involve imagery of masked hackers typing green screen text in dark rooms, but scholarly treatment of the concept is far more mundane. On the one hand, there is the general understanding that cybercrime refers to ' … any activity occurring online which has intended negative consequences for others … ' (Kirwan & Power, 2012, p. 2). To specify in some more detail, a three-stage classification is provided by the US Department of Justice:

(1) Crimes in which the computer or computer network is the target of the criminal activity. For example, hacking, malware and Distributed Denial of Service (DDoS) attacks.
(2) Existing offences where the computer is a tool used to commit the crime. For example, child pornography, stalking, criminal copyright infringement and fraud.
(3) Crimes in which the use of the computer is an incidental aspect of the commission of the crime but may afford evidence of the crime (Clough, 2010, p. 10).

Alternatively, Kirwan and Power (2013, p. 3) state that ' … cybercrime can be divided into "property crimes" (such as identity theft, fraud and copyright infringement) and "crimes against the person" (such as cybercrimes involving the sexual abuse of children)'. Kirwan and Power (2013, p. 3) outline a basic typology of cybercrime, classified as 'Internet-enabled crimes', 'Internet-specific crimes' and 'Crime in virtual worlds'. For the purposes of this article, via a cyberpsychological lens, a wide variety of phenomena will be examined along an ad hoc structure: while these definitions and typologies are useful, none have considered cybercrime from a perspective of social impact.

Hacking, malware, dark net, black markets and more

One of the more highly publicised categories of cybercrime involves hacking, which can be defined as ' … activities involved in attempting or gaining unauthorised access to IT systems' (Furnell, 2009, p. 173). Hacking is used as a broad term in the media and could be considered as too simplistic as there are a number of different sub-groups. For example, a white hat or ethical hacker infiltrates a system without causing any damage in the process and such an individual can be hired by companies to find weaknesses in security systems. Alternatively, some hackers unrequested, infiltrate systems in order to highlight frailties and report it to the organisation in order for them to improve their security. While there is obviously a benign motivation for such activity, it is still an illegal act (as a form of trespassing) and hackers can be prosecuted even without having done any damage. Conversely, black hat hackers penetrate computer systems with the specific purpose of causing damage or accessing unauthorised information. Grey hat hackers may seek opportunities to exploit systems in the hope of obtaining a monetary reward and may cause malicious damage to an individual or organisation they deem to be unethical. Kirwan and Power (2012, p. 57) discuss the 'dark figure' of hacking – that is, the difficulty of knowing just how much hacking occurs due to issues in completing methodical surveys, attackers not wanting to incriminate themselves, victims' disinclined to report hacking, and victims who may even be unaware and therefore unable to report.

Given such secrecy and intrigue around the topic, it might be difficult to ascertain any broader social aspects to these phenomena. On the one hand, there exists early research which notes that hacking was associated with 'intellectual curiosity and fascination with the technology' (Bissett & Shipton, 1999, p. 904), and even further back Hayes (1989) suggests that teenage hackers are rarely politically motivated. Yet more recently this has transitioned into an 'obsession to make all information free and accessible to everyone … no secrets' (Kirwan & Power, 2012, p. 55). Moreover, at the same time, this occurs alongside an 'anti-authority impulse [which] begins to manifest itself in response to commercial or legal obstacles – illegal aspects … begin to appear' (Kirwan & Power, 2012, p. 55).

Labelling theory (Becker, 1997), from the sociological theory of crime, may be applicable in that defining a person in a certain light may allow the definition to become a means of defence to them (Rock, 2007). For example, Appleby (2010) states that that the way in which muslims are sometimes banded together under the same umbrella as militant Islamists may cause them to feel alienated and eventually cause them to sympathise with said group. Similarly, Kirwan and Power (2012) suggest that it is possible that media coverage of all hackers as black hat hackers might impact white/grey hat hackers and alter their behaviours. Warren and Leitch (2009) draw a comparison between hackers who 'tag' themselves in site they have gained access to, and offline 'taggers' in graffiti culture – an interesting interrelationship between online and offline vandalism.

In terms of social developments, what has emerged in recent years is an unusually strong political culture in hacking. There now exists the figure of the *hacktivist* – an individual who draws 'on the creative use of computer technology for the purposes of facilitating online protests, performing civil disobedience in cyberspace … ' (Gunkel, 2005, p. 595). An example in that light is the Aaron Swartz hacktivism case involving mass downloading JSTOR ('Journal Storage') of scientific research documents, which he believed should be made freely available for everyone, not just those who could afford them (Naughton, 2015). This was deemed a felony by US prosecutors (*United States of America v. Aaron Swartz*, 2012). Facing up to 35 years in prison and a fine of up to $1 million (US Attorney's Office District of Massachusetts, 2011), Swartz took his own life while awaiting trial, his memory has become a *cause celebré* for hacktivists worldwide. There is now an increase politically motivated Denial of Service (DoS) or DDoS attacks (Nazario, 2009), a DoS attack is where a system or website is flooded with requests, slowing or stopping normal operations, whereas a DDoS attack is where a botnet (remote-controlled group of computers, possibly surreptitiously compromised by a hacker) attacks such a service or website (Cid, 2014). As such, whereas hacking began as an 'intellectual curiosity' arguably with hints of vandalistic overtones, it now has distinct overtones of political and social protest.

However, at the same time, such exploits require reasonably high levels of technical expertise – but such is not necessarily required in order to gain access to a system. *Social engineering*, where people are a system's weakest point, has been utilised by hackers such as the aforementioned Kevin Mitnick (Mitnick & Simon, 2011). Examples of exploiting social convention to hack include: finding out someone's birthday and sending them an email with a masked and malicious link and so on. This kind of *socio-technical approach* runs through the whole phenomenon of *malware* (malicious software), and other cybercrime tools such as worms, Trojans, spyware, keyloggers, ransomware and rootkits to name a few. Bocij (2006) discusses the switch from curiosity to financial motives in malware writers, as well as a move to the more profitable spyware. A white paper published in 2012 by Trend Micro gives insight into cybercrime originating in Russia, showing the prices of popular hacking services and software:

Trojan for bank account stealing – US$1300
Credit card checker – US$70
Fakes of different programs – US$15–25. (Goncharov, 2012)

Cyber criminals offer consulting and programming services, installation options and spamming/phishing schemes and viruses/malware such as Trojans or rootkits. What is curious to note, in terms of a narrow understanding of social impact (Latane, 1981), is the development of CaaS – 'Cybercrime as a Service' (Europol, 2014a; Manky, 2013). In other words, the technical expertise barrier to individual participation in cybercrime has been removed, replaced with a low financial cost and a service-based model.

Such a phenomenon is new, but does not appear to be under threat of law enforcement, perhaps due to the globalised nature of cybercrime. With an apparent lax attitude to IP and copyright, and a disinterest in prosecuting for international cybercrimes (Plesser, 2014), Russia's cybercrime market reached a conservative estimate of US$1.9 billion in 2012 (Volkov et al., 2013). At one global estimate, where victims lose around €290 billion each year worldwide as a result, cybercrime is more profitable than the global trade in marijuana, cocaine and heroin combined (Europol, 2014b). Other estimates put the economic impact of cybercrime at $445 billion worldwide, and between 15% and 20% of the value created by the Internet ('McAfee and CSIS: Stopping Cybercrime Can Positively Impact World Economies,' 2014) In general, however, it is incredibly difficult to find hard, empirical data on how much profit cybercriminals are making, additionally an often cited estimate of $1 trillion global cost of cybercrime has been queried (Maass & Rajagopalan, 2012).

In a financial and corporate context, the threat of cybercrime has been a substantial fear for quite some time, with references to the Internet being a 'wild west' type of environment stretching back at least 20 years (Amiran, Unsworth, & Chaski, 1992; Gozzi, 1994; Meyer, 1995). That idea, with its associations with general lawlessness, still recurs in information security literature (Moraski, 2011). The 2014 hack of the multi-billion dollar company Sony offers a prime example of the cost of cybercrime, the attack ended up costing the company over $35 million (Hornyak, 2015; Seal, 2015). Consequently, it is no overstatement to say that cybercrime presents a very clear and present danger to all companies.

Interestingly, according to the Director of the Federal Bureau of Investigation, 'there are only two types of companies: those that have been hacked, and those that will be' (Mueller, 2012, para. 63). What is curious to note is not necessarily how blunt or pessimistic that assessment is – but how odd it would seem if it were made in the context of real-world physical security.

For most private individuals, on finding out their house or car was broken into, or wallet containing money and personal information was stolen, the first call would be to the police. Yet, articles offering information to victims of hacking advise them to contact the group with whom they hold the compromised account, with no mention of contacting law enforcement (e.g. Gibbs, 2014). Similarly, in a business context, advice to private enterprises with regard to information security is quite low on reference to state security. With no real geo-political borders, asking nations to police their own 'area' of cyberspace can be confusing, and next-to-impossible in a lot of cases. If you, as a UK citizen, are in Germany on holidays, and have your Gmail account (with servers in Ireland) hacked by Russians, who are working off servers hosted somewhere in the Caribbean, which country is responsible for protecting you online? Who do you report digital theft to?

Companies have however acted on their own initiative and have made efforts themselves in terms of corporate social responsibility. Microsoft, for example, have taken their own action, founding their Digital Crimes Unit (DCU), focusing on technology-facilitated child sexual exploitation crimes, malicious software crimes and piracy and intellectual property (IP) crimes (Campbell, 2015). Barclays Bank have a link with Europol where they are sharing all information they have of being hacked to help better understand how hackers work. This information is vital for future cyber safety (Nicholls, 2015).

However, for many businesses, IT security companies are the first call when they discover cybercrimes (Selby, 2012). These 'digital bodyguards' are tasked with hunting down intruders and protecting systems from attack when there is no statutory alternative – for example, Mandiant was recently profiled under the Ghostbusters-esque title of 'Who you gonna call?' (Stone & Riley, 2013). While some companies may wish to press legal charges, exposing a security breach may deter them from reporting, and the inherent global nature of the Internet makes it difficult to track down offenders, and even more difficult to prosecute them under local laws (Dye, Ax, & Finkle, 2013). According to Richard Boscovich, senior attorney with Microsoft's DCU, 'the number one issue is that there is simply no homogenous legislation worldwide' (as quoted in Moraski, 2011). It would appear that the risks involved in cybercrime are minimal, especially when compared to other criminal acts. The former Chief Security Advisor for Microsoft UK, Ed Gibson, maintains:

> If you commit a cybercrime there's almost no chance you'll get caught; if caught there's almost no chance you'll get prosecuted; get prosecuted and there's slim chance you'll get time; get time and there's no chance you'll serve anything like the whole ride. Under those conditions, what possible reason would there be not to commit cybercrime? (as cited in Kassner, 2014, para. 11)

As such, with smaller acts of cybercrime (e.g. music piracy, below) a person's attitude to risk is not as important a factor, as the acts are not even perceived as 'real' crimes, and therefore carry little or no risk (Nandedkar & Midha, 2012). For more advanced cybercriminals, the risk is evaluated on a cost basis, 'the greater the overall gain from any particular behaviour, the more likely it is to be carried out' (Feldman & Feldman, 1993, p. 224). The social consequences of this are seen as the cost-benefit of any cybercrime is extremely appealing; it is more likely to be carried out. There is often a disconnect between the potential danger online and the awareness of such danger felt by Internet users, who are often connecting to the Internet from a familiar, safe environment such as home or office. Arguably this may lead to a user base that is notably lax about cyber security, and therefore ripe for exploitation and victimisation. As private companies and authorities try to make the Internet a safer place, it seems that users may defer responsibility for their own security, and take more risks in keeping with the belief that is it safe to do so (McAfee Enterprise, 2013).

On the other hand, cybercriminals have become adept in hiding their illegal activity online. It is important to remember that what is commonly called 'the Web' is really just the surface Internet, beneath that surface content lies a vast, mostly uncharted area known as the 'Deep Web'. It is estimated that the surface web accounts for only about 1% of all content online; the remaining 99% is housed in the deep web (Pagliery, 2014). Tor ('The Onion Router', so-called because of its many layers of security) is one of the gateways to purposefully hidden information in the Deep Web (Kotenko, 2014). Designed to anonymise users, it also has a function for whistleblowers, activists and confidential sources (Kotenko, 2014). Deep web and Tor protocols were arguably originally intended for sensitive communications including political dissent; however, in the last decade they have become hubs for criminal black markets that distribute drugs, counterfeit pharmaceuticals, stolen credit cards, child pornography online, pirated media and more ('Going Dark: The Internet Behind The Internet,' 2014). Open-source software based currency such as *bitcoins* can be used to facilitate transactions on the deep web, drugs can be purchased, money can be laundered and assassins can be hired (Pagliery, 2014), and consequently there is some speculation it has been compromised by the FBI (Poulsen, 2013).

Up until its closure in 2008 (Davies, 2010), DarkMarket was one of the largest English-speaking online black markets. The Silk Road, residing on the Deep Web and accessible via Tor, was shut down in 2013 (*United States Of America v. Ross Ulbricht*, 2014). Without a doubt, other markets have sprung up to capture their market share (Goodman, 2013). With black markets similar to eBay and Amazon available, cyber criminals can buy and sell credit cards, identities, financial information, as well as new hacking software tools with relative ease (Goodman, 2013). The very odd social feature of these black markets is not only how accurately they copy the 'look and feel' of their surface web, public and legal counterparts, but that apparently, they have great customer service (Bartlett, 2014). Bartlett (2014) notes that, despite them being dens of inordinate criminality, social interactions on deep web illicit markets display a large amount of self-policing and monitoring by it is community of users. Such an observation lends itself to a corollary on the social impact of this cybercrime: the potential normalisation of online drug sales. An example of this phenomenon is highlighted by the fact that many teenagers have been found posting pictures on social media and bragging about the drugs they have purchased on the deep web (O'Neill, 2013).

Piracy

While the preceding section dealt with cybercriminals of a relatively small population of individuals, the most prevailing offences by ordinarily law-abiding citizens concerns illegal file-sharing or piracy (Kirwan & Power, 2012). Piracy therefore probably presents one of the best opportunities to discuss the social impact of cybercrime. Online piracy is understood to involve the unauthorised copying, distribution and selling of works that are in copyright (Yar, 2005). Copyright piracy has existed for decades but relied on hard-copy distribution, for example, physical CDs/DVDs being duplicated and sold on the black market. Modern piracy has been facilitated by the explosion of faster Internet speeds and the availability of popular illegal file-sharing websites such as 'Napster' (now a legitimate site) and 'The Pirate Bay', which were established in 1999 and 2003, respectively. Through sites such as these, the Internet has expanded people's resources to the point where anyone with a basic knowledge of computers has the ability to download any copyrighted material such as music, films and games for free.

In terms of a social context, a 2013 British Phonographic Institute report (BPI) found that 14.5% of Britons were using piracy networks and 4 million people were regularly file-sharing in the UK (2013). The BPI believes that £980 million in physical music sales is lost annually to illegal downloading (Robinson, 2010). The Federation Against Copyright Theft (FACT), as cited in Yar (2005), estimates an annual loss of £400 million for the British Film Industry (BFI). However, it must be noted that the preponderance of facts made publicly available are published by organisations with a vested interest in highlighting the seriousness of the problem and there is some research that suggests that some artists can benefit from illegal downloading (Bounie, Bourreau, & Waelbroeck, 2006; McKenzie, 2009; Shang, Chen, & Chen, 2007). Nevertheless, the majority of the studies in the field tend to find a negative association between illegal downloading and genuine sales (Smith & Telang, 2012). However with illegal downloading affecting the revenues of major corporations it was only a matter of time before online piracy drew significant attention from the law.

Despite highly publicised court cases brought forward by the music industry in order to deter file-sharing, millions of people around the world continue to illegally download and share music.

In 1999, Napster, the first major online file-sharing service, made its debut and at the peak of its popularity could boast 60 million registered users (Goldman, 2010). The Recording Industry Association of America (RIAA) took 'Napster' to court and was successful in forcing the company into liquidation. Individual file sharers have also been pursued. The most recent case involved Paul Mahoney of Northern Ireland being sentenced to four years in prison for facilitating the streaming of movies online, costing the film industry an estimated £120 million (Deeney, 2015).

So why do millions of people continue to break the law? Altschuller and Benbunan-Fich (2009) state that from a social outlook, it might be expected that the laws in place sufficiently reflect the moral perceptions of society and in turn will be observed by the bulk of its citizens. Events however suggest that the law does not reflect what the general public considers to be legal or even moral in the case of digital music downloading. Research suggests that deterrence attempts, such as the legal proceedings mentioned above, are likely to fail in this context because, once again, the chances of being caught are slim and participants perceive the prevalence of the criminal act makes it extremely difficult to take action against every individual file sharer (Wingrove, Korpas, & Weisz, 2011). As long as a punishment seems unlikely, offending behaviour is probably going to continue (Kirwan & Power, 2013). The number of 'neutralisation' techniques as put forward by Sykes and Matza (1957) are also used by offenders to justify offending behaviour. Respondents in some studies state a belief that illegal downloading is a victimless act, that it causes no harm to artists and the record companies could afford the financial loss (Altschuller & Benbunan-Fich, 2009; Selwyn, 2007).

Social learning theory suggests individuals tend to pick up deviant behaviour from their peers (Bandura, 1977). Peer norms have a strong impact on the intentions to illegal download music (Levin, Dato-on, & Manolis, 2007). Individuals may place higher values on their social group norms rather than on legal norms, which is blurring the line between a moral and immoral act. Svensson and Larsson's (2012) study in Sweden found that there are no social norms to back up the judicial system in this field. The question must be posed: how can compliance to the law be maintained when it is not supported by social norms? Such is a continuing observation in the study of the social impact of cybercrime. This would explain why overwhelming evidence suggests that most Internet users view such downloading behaviours as morally acceptable despite the law (Selwyn, 2007; Shang et al., 2007; Sirkeci & Magnúsdóttir, 2011). Individuals may not be able to evaluate or recognise infringing on IP rights as an ethical dilemma when it comes to non-tangible goods such as digital files. Evidence of this is well highlighted in studies such as Lysonski and Durvasula (2008), who examined opposing ethical beliefs systems regarding hard-copy (CD) shop lifting and digital 'soft lifting'. Here researchers found that their participant's ethical beliefs would prohibit them from stealing a CD from a record store; however, the same partakers were ambivalent towards downloading pirated material. Moores and Chang (2006) suggest that there is a disconnection between real-world ethical orientations and online downloading behaviour. Suler's (2004) online disinhibition effect can help us to explain how computer-mediated environments can create ethical ambiguity through dissociative anonymity and lead to a minimisation of authority. The potential disconnect between the law and personal ethics can often be due to fast-pace changes in technology and their impacts on society (Altschuller & Benbunan-Fich, 2009).

The war between the entertainment industries and online file sharers has had a considerable effect on society and the generation who grew up file-sharing. A new technology emerged which on the one hand was heralded by the vast population and on the other, derided as deviant by corporate record companies and the law. Harvard Universities Lawrence Lessig in Winter's (2013) film 'Downloaded' states it created:

> ... a war which has basically criminalized a whole generation, it is *culture's Vietnam* ... the only people who have gotten paid are the lawyers who have been presiding over expanding legal actions against people who are only using culture the way technology encourages them to use it.

It seemed at one stage that along with the general population, major media organisations were changing their stance on the morality of piracy. This can be highlighted by the HBO show 'Game of Thrones', which broke a piracy world record in 2013 when an episode was shared 1.5 million times within the first 12 hours of its airing (Tassi, 2013). The CEO of Time Warner Jeff Bewkes, as cited in Tassi (2013, para. 5), addressed this piracy and highlighted how it could be portrayed as a positive; ' ... if you go around the world, I think you're right; Game of Thrones is the most pirated show in the world. Well, you know, that's better than an Emmy'. Fast forward to 2015, this time four out of ten episodes in the Game of Thrones series could be downloaded from torrent sites two days before being aired on HBO. Contrary to their previous stance, HBO promptly sent out legal letters to users who were suspected of downloading the episodes (Kain, 2015). This example highlights the paradoxical nature of attitudes to piracy. If the producers of content cannot make up their minds about whether piracy is good or bad, is it any wonder that the people who download it generally do not feel like they are doing anything wrong.

There has been a decline in illegally copied files and this has been ascribed to the rise of legal alternatives, such as streaming service Spotify for music and Netflix for film, which offer consumers a more reliable experience than peer-to-peer file-sharing sites (Sherwin, 2013). Figures released by the BPI (2013) showed that legally acquired music surpassed file-sharing by 13.2%, and for the first time in history digital music had outsold all other types of physical formats. These statistics seemed to demonstrate that tougher anti-piracy laws, demanded by music and film companies, were no longer required, since the market was driving file-sharing to the margins (Sherwin, 2013). With this in mind, it would appear that the British government has decided to effectively decriminalise the downloading of copyright material. From 2015 onwards, individuals found downloading copyrighted content will be sent four warning letters that are aimed at educating the offender; however no legal action will be pursued even if that individual was to continue downloading illegally (Green, 2014). Society's norms have in a sense dictated the law, in that what was once deemed deviant will now have no legal ramifications in the UK. Perhaps the pirates have won.

Child pornography online, self-produced indecent images of minors and sexting

During the past 10 years over 132 million child pornography images have been seized by police and sent to the National Centre for Missing and Exploited Children (NCMEC, 2015). Of the 5375 victims that have been identified and classified by NCMEC investigators, 70% of these images were classified as child pornography, 16% as online enticement (grooming) and 14% as 'self-production'.

The U.S. Department of Justice (2010) outlined that 'child pornography' refers to the possession, trade, advertising and production of images that depict the sexual abuse of children. The term child pornography is a legal term for images of child sexual abuse; however, a report by the U.S. Department of Justice (2010, p. 8) maintains that,

> ... many experts in the field believe that use of that term contributes to a fundamental misunderstanding of the crime – one that focuses on the possession or trading of a picture and leaves the impression that what is depicted in the photograph is pornography. Child pornography is unrelated to adult pornography; it clearly involves the criminal depiction and memorializing of the sexual assault of children and the criminal sharing, collecting, and marketing of the images.

In terms of describing the offence, there is a growing movement to utilise the words 'Child Abuse Material' (CAM) (Aiken, Moran, & Berry, 2011). The term child pornography is however consistently used in the majority of laws and policy documents internationally (Akdeniz, 2008), and attempts to change terminology are thought by some to be inadequate in terms of capturing the complex nature and of the material (Lanning, 2008). Terminology differs by jurisdiction, in the UK the wording 'Indecent Images of Children' is used in The Protection of Children Act (PCA, 1978) and the legislative term 'Prohibited Images of children' is employed in Section 62 of the Coroners and Justice Act (2009). Akdeniz (2008) notes the role of the Internet in the production, collection and distribution of 'Internet Child Pornography', pointing out that in recent years there is a general consensus that the Internet has increased the range, volume and accessibility of child-related pornographic imagery. The delicate social implications of appropriate and acceptable terminology illustrate the complexity of this cybercrime. Given these sensitivities for the purposes of this paper, the term CAM will be utilised.

The use of the Internet regarding this abusive material of minors has been a growing concern, there is a paucity of up-to-date data regarding the volume and criminal value of this material. In 2009 the criminal commercial 'market' for CAM was estimated to be worth in excess of $20 billion annually (Bourke & Hernandez, 2009). Cooper, Delmonico, and Burg (2000) first discussed the accessibility, affordability and anonymity (Triple A Engine) of the Internet and its impact on availability of CAM. Notably, research indicates that complex social networks can form, not dissimilar to peer-to-peer networks, concerning collecting and sharing of CAM online (Moran, 2010). Aiken et al. (2011) describe the social networking phenomenon of 'sharers' and 'leechers' in CAM trading communities online, which are comparable to 'seeders' and 'leechers' on networks such as 'The Pirate Bay'. Regarding these CAM communities, Aiken et al. (2011) point out an apparent *cyber social order* – in that expert groups develop a distinct hierarchy; jobs include administrators, technology advisors, security personnel and intelligence experts: a daunting prospect for law enforcement.

Minors are at risk as a result of the self-production of indecent images/videos, which may be distributed online. While there are cases of children being extorted into producing such media (Hainsworth & Sterling, 2014), others may engage in this behaviour as a result of online disinhibition (Suler, 2004), or simply in the course of normative adolescent social and developmental behaviour (Wolak & Finkelhor, 2011). Leary (2010) stresses the importance of the subject, pointing out that social problems that exist at the intersection of adolescence sex, technology and criminology require immediate investigation. This uploading of self-produced inappropriate material by Internet users, including many children and adolescents, is a growing phenomenon (Lenhart, 2009; Temple et al., 2012), resulting in youth engaging in increasingly risky behaviour (Leary, 2010; Wolak, Finkelhor, & Mitchell, 2011). This can even lead minors to produce and distribute images of themselves that are similar to child pornography (Quayle & Jones, 2011). The self-production of indecent images is also known as *sexting*. Specifically sexting is a form of mobile text messaging in which people send pictures of a sexual nature or sexually explicit text. Youth sexting has been described as the creating, sharing and forwarding of sexually suggestive nude or nearly nude images by minors (Lenhart, 2009). However, in many jurisdictions, senders are in danger of being charged with possession and distribution of child pornography (Leary, 2010), notwithstanding the fact that they are minors, and that the pictures are often of themselves (Zhang, 2010). A recent case in North Carolina highlighted issues in this area when a 17-year-old was prosecuted for having naked photos of himself on his phone (Brennan, 2015). Cormega Copening was sixteen at the time the photos were taken and was accused of committing a sexual offense against himself, he took a plea deal in order to avoid going to prison and having to register as a sex offender (Brennan, 2015).

From a criminal social justice perspective, Ostrager (2010) has suggested that the legal system needs to distinguish between sexting as a serious offence posing a danger to others, and when it is simply normative adolescent romantic activity (Wolak & Finkelhor, 2011). Typically, youths are taking photographs of themselves and posting them on social network sites, in chat room forums, or transmitting them on mobile phones via Multimedia Messaging Services (Ringrose, Gill, Livingstone, & Harvey, 2012).

One of the social challenges of this problem is to attempt to understand why youth engage in this form of cyber behaviour. The Barnes (2006) model of the cyberpsychology 'privacy paradox' suggests that young people may not always be aware of the public nature of the Internet. The privacy paradox is the disconnect between how users feel about privacy online, how they act, and how they react to the consequences of an unintended breach of privacy (Barnes, 2006; Viégas, 2006). Generally teens are aware that the Internet is not private; however, some act as though it is, and freely give up often personal information (Barnes, 2006; Gross, Acquisti, & Heinz, 2005). Additionally people share much of their lives online, revealing intimate thoughts and information, but are often unclear of the boundaries between public and private space (Barnes, 2006). Once an item is placed on the Internet, it can be distributed worldwide especially if it goes viral, while the individual concerned is under the impression that his/her boyfriend/girlfriend is the only recipient of their exchanges of images/ photographs. However the question must be asked if youth can be really be so disconnected from the issue? Phippen (2009) reports that most youth are fully aware of the concept of sexting, and a significant subset are actively engaged in the practice. The author notes that 'what is particularly worrying is the somewhat blasé attitude to the subject' (Phippen, 2009, p. 2). Ringrose et al. (2012) report that quantitative research on sexting has found rates varying from 15% to 40% among young people, depending on age, methodology and the definition of sexting employed. Temple et al. (2012) report that 28% of youth are engaging in the behaviour; however, Mitchell, Finkelhor, Jones, and Wolak (2012) argue that that only 1% of content in their study was actually sexually explicit. Discrepancies in terms of defining, investigating and academic reporting of sexting require clarification. The legal overlap between sexting and child pornography requires further investigation. From a sociological perspective the issue is a complex one, ranging from the production and distribution of child pornography (which is a criminal act) to the self-production and dissemination of indecent images by minors, which is arguably a social as opposed to policing issue; that said, given the nature of the material, it remains de facto a crime. Once again similarly to piracy, it is a question of weight of numbers, there exists a cybercrime which is illegal, that is, the production and distribution of explicit content by minors, but would appear to be socially acceptable amongst those who engage in the practice.

Policy and policing

In terms of addressing cybercrime, Kirwan and Power (2012, p. xvii) point out that 'governments attempt to respond with law, corporations with policies and procedures, suppliers with terms and conditions, users with peer pressure, technologists with code' and this perhaps illustrates one of the core issues, and that is the multiplicity of approaches to the problem space. Physical presence and visibility have been a cornerstone of policing policy to date. The lack of visibility of police online may arguably be a factor in the facilitation of cybercrime (Suler, 2004). An interesting initiative may now address this lack of visibility. In September 2014 Europol launched a trial of the first fully international cybercrime task force, the *Joint Cybercrime Action Taskforce* (J-CAT), results of which are still under review at the time of writing. Based in the Netherlands, it will be led by the deputy head of the UK's National Crime Agency's National Cyber Crime Unit, Andy Archibald (Schwartz, 2014). Paul Gillen (head of operations of the European Cybercrime Centre) has stated that 'everyone has woken up to the fact that we can no longer stay within our own borders and enforce the law, we have to reach out to each other' (as cited in Schwartz, 2014, para. 4). Referring to the difficulties inherent in multinational cooperation against cybercrime, he states that 'in the European Union we have 28 different countries, 23 different languages, 28 different legal systems, and law enforcement ... is not the most integrated part of the European Union' (as cited in Schwartz, 2014, para. 7). This new initiative is a significant step in the right direction in terms of 'joined up thinking' and a globally co-ordinated policing approach in cyberspace.

In terms of deterrents, amendments to UK legislation have increased the seriousness of penalties for certain cybercrime offences, up to life imprisonment (Serious Crime Act, 2015). However, it is yet to be seen if traditional criminal deterrent measures such as incarceration will be effective as digital space evolves. Notably, Chris Burchett of Credant Technologies states, 'Legislative bureaucracies tend to move slowly, whereas the attackers have shown a spectacular capacity for adaptation and innovation' (as cited in Moraski, 2011, p. 21).

There is a vast amount of data and literature regarding real-world crime; however everything has changed concerning the emergence of cybercrime, ranging from hacking to malware, and from piracy to the self-production of CAM by minors. In terms of criminal investigation, arguably there has been a paradigm shift, key police investigative aides such as eye witness testimony, and physical forensic evidence (e.g. DNA and fingerprints) are no longer relevant in cyber contexts. In terms of future research, cyber methodological approach will be critical in order to empirically investigate this new environment, cyberspace. An interdisciplinary or transdisciplinary research and investigative approach may result in optimum results and insights. Additionally, learnings from the field of cyberpsychology to date and going forward will arguably be invaluable in terms of illuminating human behaviour impacted by emerging technologies.

Detailed consideration of the social impact of cybercrime is a complex issue. There exists a vast body of knowledge regarding real-world crime; however, as crime has evolved online some of that knowledge may now be redundant, and therefore more research is required to rebuild the knowledge base. Given the evolving and adaptive nature of the phenomenon, unexpected events such as the increasing decriminalisation of piracy and the spontaneous generation of CAM by minors, evidently there exist significant challenges in terms of investigating cybercrime and any associated social impact. Going forward it may be observed that if a crime even vaguely involves cyber technologies at some point, it could be labelled a 'cybercrime'. Moreover, taking this position to a not-too-distant future, it is quite easy to imagine a context where all crime may be some form of cybercrime (Mc Mahon, 2013). Given the proliferation of networked surveillance devices, the question must be asked, how easy will it be to commit a crime in the future or indeed the present, *without* there being some 'cyber' aspect – that is, without leaving some digital forensic trace? The corollary to such an observation is that when everyone is carrying a smartphone or similar device (loaded with valuable personal data), coupled with an ever increasing presence of privatised Unmanned Aerial Vehicles (UAVs) in the skies, people may hypothetically enter a state of ubiquitous high-risk victimology. Both might seem like straightforward observations from a criminological standpoint, but are considerably more troublesome from a social impact perspective.

References

Aiken, M., & Mc Mahon, C. (2014). A primer on research in mediated environments: Reflections on cyber-methodology. *Social Sceince Research Network*. Retrieved from http://papers.ssrn.com/abstract=2462700

Aiken, M., Moran, M., & Berry, M. J. (2011, September 5–7). *Child abuse material and the Internet: Cyberpsychology of online child related sex offending*. 29th Meeting of the INTERPOL Specialist Group on Crimes against Children (pp. 1–22), Lyon.

Akdeniz, Y. (2008). *Internet child pornography and the law: National and international responses* (4th ed.). Hampshire: Ashgate.

Altschuller, S., & Benbunan-Fich, R. (2009). Is music downloading the new prohibition? What students reveal through an ethical dilemma. *Ethics and Information Technology*, *11*(1), 49–56. doi:10.1007/s10676-008-9179-1

Amiran, E., Unsworth, J., & Chaski, C. (1992). Networked academic publishing and the rhetorics of its reception. *Centennial Review*, *36*(1), 43–58.

Appleby, N. (2010). Labelling the innocent: How government counter-terrorism advice creates labels that contribute to the problem. *Critical Studies on Terrorism*, *3*(3), 421–436. doi:10.1080/17539153.2010.521643

Asllani, A., & Ali, A. (2012). Using simulation to investigate virus propagation in computer networks. *Network and Communication Technologies*, *1*(2), 76–85. doi:10.5539/nct.v1n2p76

Bandura, A. (1977). *Social learning theory*. Oxford: Prentice-Hall.

Barnes, S. B. (2006). A privace paradox: Social networking in the United States. *A Privacy Paradox*, *11*(9). doi:10.5210/fm.v11i9.1394

Bartlett, J. (2014). *Dark net drug markets kept alive by great customer service*. Retrieved September 23, 2014, from http://www.wired.co.uk/news/archive/2014-08/21/buying-drugs-on-the-dark-net/viewgallery/284

Becker, H. S. (1997). *Outsiders: Studies in the sociology of deviance*. New York, NY: Simon & Schuster.

Bissett, A., & Shipton, G. (1999). Some human dimensions of computer virus creation and infection. *International Journal of Human-Computer Studies*, *52*, 899–913. doi:10.1006/ijhc.1999.0361

Bocij, P. (2006). *The dark side of the internet: Protecting yourself and your family from online criminals*. Greenwood Publishing Group. Retrieved from http://books.google.com/books?hl=en&lr=&id=o5h2qwyDzRsC&pgis=1

Bounie, D., Bourreau, M., & Waelbroeck, P. (2006). Piracy and demands for films: Analysis of piracy behavior in French universities. *Review of Economic Research on Copyright Issues*, *3*(2), 15–27. Retrieved from http://papers.ssrn.com/sol3/papers.cfm?abstract_id=936049

Bourke, M. L., & Hernandez, A. E. (2009). The "Butner Study" Redux: A report of the incidence of hands-on child victimization by child pornography offenders. *Journal of Family Violence*, *24*, 183–191.

BPI. (2013). *BPI digital music nation*. London. Retrieved from http://www.ukmusic.org/assets/general/Digital_Music_Nation_2013_LR.PDF

Bradley, K. (2014). *Speech to the finance services' cybercrime summit*. Finance Services' Cybercrime Summit. London. Retrieved from https://www.gov.uk/government/speeches/karen-bradleys-speech-to-the-finance-services-cybercrime-summit

Brennan, C. (2015). *An American teenager has barely escaped prosecution for sexually exploiting ... himself*. Retrieved September 24, 2015, from http://www.thejournal.ie/naked-selfie-prosecution-2344010-Sep2015/?utm_source=facebook_short

Brignall, M. (2015, March 14). TalkTalk won't listen as another fraud victim fights for compensation. *The Guardian*. London.

Campbell, A. (2015). *Inside Microsoft's digital crimes unit*. Retrieved September 25, 2015, from http://smallbiztrends.com/2015/04/microsoft-digital-crimes-unit.html

Cid, D. (2014). *More than 162,000 wordpress sites used for distributed denial of service attack*. Retrieved September 28, 2015, from https://blog.sucuri.net/2014/03/more-than-162000-wordpress-sites-used-for-distributed-denial-of-service-attack.html

Clough, J. (2010). *Principles of cybercrime*. New York, NY: Cambridge University Press.

Cooper, A., Delmonico, D. L., & Burg, R. (2000). Cybersex users, abusers, and compulsives: New findings and implications. *Sexual Addiction and Compulsivity*, *7*, 5–29.

Coroners and Justice Act 2009 (c 25), s. 62, *The Crown Prosecution Service*, UK.

Davies, C. (2010, January). Welcome to DarkMarket – global one-stop shop for cybercrime and banking fraud. *The Guardian*. Retrieved from http://www.theguardian.com/technology/2010/jan/14/darkmarket-online-fraud-trial-wembley

Deeney, D. (2015). *Shy fraudster who pocketed almost £300k from his "sophisticated" film-streaming website jailed for four years*. Retrieved September 23, 2015, from http://www.belfasttelegraph.co.uk/news/northern-ireland/shy-fraudster-who-pocketed-almost-300k-from-his-sophisticated-filmstreaming-website-jailed-for-four-years-31512777.html

Deloitte. (2014, February 26). Banding together to fight cyber crime. *The Wall Street Journal*. Retrieved from http://deloitte.wsj.com/cio/2013/02/26/band-together-to-fight-cyber-crime/

Dye, J., Ax, J., & Finkle, J. (2013). *Huge cyber bank theft spans 27 countries*. Retrieved September 4, 2014, from http://www.reuters.com/article/2013/05/09/net-us-usa-crime-cybercrime-idUSBRE9480PZ20130509

Europol. (2014a) *Europol iOCTA: Threat assessment (abridged): Internet facilitated organised crime*. The Hague. Retrieved September 10, 2015 https://www.europol.europa.eu/content/internet-organised-crime-threat-assesment-iocta

Europol. (2014b). *European cybercrime centre cybercrime: A growing global problem*. Retrieved from https://www.europol.europa.eu/ec3old

Feldman, P., & Feldman, M. P. (1993). *The psychology of crime: A social science textbook*. New York, NY: Cambridge University Press. Retrieved from http://books.google.ie/books/about/The_Psychology_of_Crime.html?id=aqjSf3lLMzoC&pgis=1

Furnell, S. (2009). Hackers, viruses and malicious software. In Y. Jewkes & M. Yar (Eds.), *Handbook of internet crime* (pp. 173–193). New York, NY: Willan.

Gibbs, S. (2014, February 14). What to do if your email gets hacked – and how to prevent it. *The Guardian*. Retrieved from http://www.theguardian.com/technology/2014/feb/03/what-to-do-email-hacked-how-to-prevent

Going Dark: The Internet Behind The Internet. (2014). Retrieved September 23, 2015, from http://www.npr.org/sections/alltechconsidered/2014/05/25/315821415/going-dark-the-internet-behind-the-internet

Goldman, D. (2010). *Music's lost decade: Sales cut in half*. Retrieved July 23, 2014, from http://money.cnn.com/2010/02/02/news/companies/napster_music_industry/

Goncharov, M. (2012). *Russian underground 101. Trend micro incorporated*. Cupertino. Retrieved from http://dl.packetstormsecurity.net/papers/general/wp-russian-underground-101.pdf

Goodman, K. (2013). *The dark net: The new face of black markets and organized crime*. Retrieved September 4, 2014, from http://www.huffingtonpost.com/kevin-goodman/internet-black-markets_b_4111000.html

Gozzi, R. J. (1994). *The cyberspace metaphor*. Retrieved August 26, 2014, from http://www.thefreelibrary.com/The+cyberspace+metaphor.-a015543199

Green, C. (2014, July 23). New internet piracy warning letters rules dismissed as "toothless." *The Independent*. Retrieved from http://www.independent.co.uk/life-style/gadgets-and-tech/news/new-internet-piracy-warning-letters-rules-dismissed-as-toothless-9623907.html

Groenfeldt, T. (2013). *Hackers collaborate, now white hats can share cybercrime info*. Retrieved September 4, 2014, from http://www.forbes.com/sites/tomgroenfeldt/2013/11/04/hackers-collaborate-now-white-hats-can-share-cyber-crime-info/

Gross, R., Acquisti, A., & Heinz, H. J. (2005). *Information revelation and privacy in online social networks*. Proceedings of the 2005 ACM workshop on Privacy in the electronic society – WPES '05 (p. 71). New York, NY: ACM Press. doi:10.1145/1102199.1102214

Gunkel, D. J. (2005). Editorial: Introduction to hacking and hacktivism. *New Media & Society*, 7, 595–597. doi:10.1177/1461444805056007

Hainsworth, J., & Sterling, T. (2014). *Dutch man's case linked to Amanda Todd*. Retrieved September 29, 2015, from https://www.bostonglobe.com/news/world/2014/04/18/dutch-man-case-linked-amanda-todd/39eIi53AFtgqc79yqH8JTJ/story.html

Hayes, D. (1989). *Behind the silicon curtain: The seductions of work in a lonely era*. London: Free Association Books.

Hornyak, T. (2015). *Hack to cost Sony $35 million in IT repairs*. Retrieved September 24, 2015, from http://www.networkworld.com/article/2879814/data-center/sony-hack-cost-15-million-but-earnings-unaffected.html

Huang, H. (2015). A war of (mis)information: The political effects of rumors and rumor rebuttals in an authoritarian country. *British Journal of Political Science*. Advance online publication doi:10.1017/S0007123415000253

International Telecommunications Union. (2015). *ICT facts and figures – The world in 2015*. Retrieved from http://www.itu.int/en/ITU-D/Statistics/Pages/facts/default.aspx

Jurgenson, N. (2011). Digital dualism versus augmented reality. *Cyborgology, 24*. doi:10.1089/cyber.2009.0226

Kain, E. (2015). *HBO is going after "game of thrones" pirates*. Retrieved September 23, 2015, from http://www.forbes.com/sites/erikkain/2015/04/19/hbo-is-going-after-game-of-thrones-pirates/

Kassner, M. (2014). *TEDx Birmingham: Call the police on cybercrime*. Retrieved September 4, 2014, from http://www.techrepublic.com/article/tedx-birmingham-call-the-police-on-cybercrime/

Kirwan, G., & Power, A. (2012). *The psychology of cybercrime: Concepts and principles*. Cambridge: Cambridge University Press.

Kirwan, G., & Power, A. (2013). *Cybercrime: The psychology of online offenders*. New York: Cambridge University Press.

Kotenko, J. (2014). *What is Tor? A beginner's guide to the underground internet*. Retrieved September 23, 2015, from http://www.digitaltrends.com/computing/a-beginners-guide-to-tor-how-to-navigate-through-the-underground-internet/

Lanning, K. V. (2008). *Child pornography*. Paper presented at the Child Pornography Roundtable, National Center for Missing and Exploited Children, Washington, DC.

Latane, B. (1981). The psychology of social impact. *American Psychologist, 36*(4), 343–356. doi:10.1037/0003-066X.36.4.343

Leary, M. (2010). Sexting or self-produced child pornography? The dialogue continues – structured prosecutorial discretion within a multidisciplinary response. *Virginia Journal of Social Policy and the Law, 17*, 486–566.

Lenhart, A. (2009). *Adults and social network websites*. Retrieved September 9, 2014, from http://www.pewinternet.org/2009/01/14/adults-and-social-network-websites/

Levin, A. M., Dato-on, M. C., & Manolis, C. (2007). Deterring illegal downloading: The effects of threat appeals, past behavior, subjective norms, and attributions of harm. *Journal of Consumer Behaviour, 6*(2–3), 111–122. doi:10.1002/cb.211

Lysonski, S., & Durvasula, S. (2008). Digital piracy of MP3s: Consumer and ethical predispositions. *Journal of Consumer Marketing, 25*(3), 167–178. doi:10.1108/07363760810870662

Maass, P., & Rajagopalan, M. (2012). *Does cybercrime really cost $1 trillion?* Retrieved September 23, 2015, from http://www.propublica.org/article/does-cybercrime-really-cost-1-trillion

Manky, D. (2013). Cybercrime as a service: A very modern business. *Computer Fraud & Security, 6*, 9–13. doi:10.1016/S1361-3723(13)70053-8

McAfee and CSIS: Stopping Cybercrime Can Positively Impact World Economies. (2014). Retrieved September 23, 2015, from http://www.mcafee.com/us/about/news/2014/q2/20140609-01.aspx

McAfee Enterprise. (2013). *SMBs false sense of security: How this is putting their businesses in Jeopardy*. Retrieved September 4, 2014, from https://blogs.mcafee.com/business/smbs-false-sense-of-security-how-is-this-putting-their-business-in-jeopardy/

McKenzie, J. (2009). Illegal music downloading and its impact on legitimate sales: Australian empirical evidence. *Australian Economic Papers, 48*(4), 296–307. http://doi.wiley.com/10.1111/j.1467-8454.2009.00377.x

Mc Mahon, C. (2013, December 13). *All crime is cybercrime*. An Garda Síochána Analyst Service Annual Conference. Dublin, Ireland.

Meyer, M. (1995, February). Stop! Cyberthief! *Newsweek*, 36–38. Retrieved from http://www.d.umn.edu/~pcannan/mikemeyer.pdf

Mitchell, K. J., Finkelhor, D., Jones, L. M., & Wolak, J. (2012). Prevalence and characteristics of youth sexting: A national study. *Pediatrics, 129*(1), 13–20. doi:10.1542/peds.2011-1730

Mitnick, K. D., & Simon, W. L. (2002). *The art of deception: Controlling the human element of security*. Wiley & Sons. Retrieved from http://books.google.ie/books/about/The_Art_of_Deception.html?id=VR_aVP0KKh8C&pgis=1

Mitnick, K. D., & Simon, W. (2011). *Ghost in the wires: My adventures as the world's most wanted hacker*. New York, NY: Little, Brown and Company.

Moores, T. T., & Chang, J. C.-J. (2006). Ethical decision making in software piracy: Initial development and test of a four-component model. *MIS Quarterly, 30*(1), 167–180. Retrieved from http://dl.acm.org/citation.cfm?id=2017284.2017294

Moran, M. (2010). *Online child abuse material offenders: Are we assigning law enforcement expertise appropriately?* Unpublished manuscript. Dublin, Ireland: University College Dublin.

Moraski, L. (2011). Cybercrime knows no borders. *Infosecurity*, 8(2), 20–23. doi:10.1016/S1754-4548(11)70021-3

Mueller, R. S. I. (2012). *Combating threats in the cyber world: Outsmarting terrorists, hackers, and spies.* Retrieved from http://www.fbi.gov/news/speeches/combating-threats-in-the-cyber-world-outsmarting-terrorists-hackers-and-spies

Nandedkar, A., & Midha, V. (2012). It won't happen to me: An assessment of optimism bias in music piracy. *Computers in Human Behavior*, 28(1), 41–48. doi:10.1016/j.chb.2011.08.009

Naughton, J. (2015, February 7). Aaron Swartz stood up for freedom and fairness – and was hounded to his death. *The Guardian*. Retrieved from http://www.theguardian.com/commentisfree/2015/feb/07/aaron-swartz-suicide-internets-own-boy

Nazario, J. (2009). Politically motivated denial of service attacks. In C. Czosseck & K. Geers (Eds.), *The virtual battlefield* (pp. 163–181). Amsterdam: IOS Press.

NCMEC. (2015). *National Center for Missing and Exploited Children.* Retrieved March 12, 2015 http://www.missingkids.com/home

Nicholls, J. (2015). *Europol backs Barclays as pair commit to cybercrime fight.* Retrieved September 28, 2015, from http://www.cbronline.com/news/cybersecurity/business/europol-backs-barclays-as-pair-commit-to-cybercrime-fight-4612750

O'Neill, P. H. (2013). *Teens on Tumblr can't stop bragging about silk road drug deals.* Retrieved September 23, 2015, from http://www.dailydot.com/crime/tumblr-teens-silk-road-drug-deals/

Ostrager, B. (2010). SMS. OMG! LOL! TTYL: Translating the law to accomodate today's teens and the evolution from texting to sexting. *Family Court Review*, 48(4), 712–726. http://doi.wiley.com/10.1111/j.1744-1617.2010.01345.x

Paganini, P. (2012). *Why humans could be the weakest link in cyber security chain?* Retrieved August 21, 2015, from http://securityaffairs.co/wordpress/9076/social-networks/why-humans-could-be-the-weakest-link-in-cyber-security-chain.html

Pagliery, J. (2014). *The deep web you don't know about.* Retrieved September 23, 2014, from http://money.cnn.com/2014/03/10/technology/deep-web/index.html

Peltzman, S. (1975). The effects of automobile safety regulation. *Journal of Political Economy*, 83(4), 677–726. Retrieved from http://www.jstor.org/discover/10.2307/1830396?uid=17134080&uid=3738232&uid=2&uid=3&uid=67&uid=18761664&uid=62&sid=21104621298313

Phippen, A. (2009). *Sharing personal images and videos among young people.* Exeter. Retrieved from http://www.blackpoollscb.org.uk/contents/documents/sexting-detail.pdf

Plesser, B. (2014). *Skilled, cheap Russian hackers power American cybercrime* – NBC News.com. Retrieved September 4, 2014, from http://www.nbcnews.com/news/world/skilled-cheap-russian-hackers-power-american-cybercrime-n22371

Poulsen, K. (2013). *FBI admits it controlled tor servers behind mass malware attack.* Retrieved September 9, 2014, from http://www.wired.com/2013/09/freedom-hosting-fbi/

Proshansky, H. M. (1987). The field of environmental psychology: Securing its future. *Handbook of Environmental Psychology*, 2, 1467–1488.

Protection of Children Act 1978 (c 37), s.1, The Crown Prosecution Service, UK.

Quayle, E., & Jones, T. (2011). Sexualized images of children on the Internet. *Sexual Abuse: A Journal of Research and Treatment*, 23(1), 7–21. doi:10.1177/1079063210392596

Reeves, M. (2002). *Measuring the economic and social impact of the arts: A review.* London: Arts Council of England. Retrieved from http://culturability.org/wp-content/blogs.dir/1/files_mf/1271761227measuringtheeconomicandsocialimpactofthearts.pdf

Ringrose, J., Gill, R., Livingstone, S., & Harvey, L. (2012). *A qualitative study of children, young people and "sexting."* London. Retrieved from http://eprints.lse.ac.uk/44216/1/__Libfile_repository_Content_Livingstone, S_A qualitative study of children, young people and "sexting" (LSE RO).pdf

Robinson, J. (2010, December 16). Britons "downloaded 1.2bn illegal tracks this year" | Media | theguardian.com. *The Guardian*. Retrieved from http://www.theguardian.com/media/2010/dec/16/illegal-music-downloading-online-piracy

Rock, P. (2007). Sociological theories of crime. In M. Maguire, R. Morgan, & R. Reiner (Eds.), *The Oxford handbook of criminology* (pp. 3–42). Oxford: Oxford University Press.

Rosenzweig, P. (2013). *Cyber warfare: How conflicts in cyberspace are challenging America and changing the world.* Retrieved from http://books.google.ie/books?hl=en&lr=&id=teZ8pAHJUa8C&oi=fnd&pg=PP2&dq=rosenzweig+books+cyber+warfare&ots=5-NPcIPT6C&sig=FjIUgIrkbwXEWPmTXcGXVAtxEA&redir_esc=y#v=onepage&q=rosenzweig books cyber warfare&f=false

Schwartz, M. (2014). *EU to roll out cybercrime taskforce*. Retrieved September 5, 2014, from http://www.bankinfosecurity.com/eu-to-roll-out-cybercrime-taskforce-a-7093/op-1

Seal, M. (2015, March). An exclusive look at Sony's hacking Saga. *Vanity Fair*. Retrieved from http://www.vanityfair.com/hollywood/2015/02/sony-hacking-seth-rogen-evan-goldberg

SecurityWeek. (2015). *SurfWatch labs enables intelligence sharing across extended enterprise*. Retrieved September 23, 2015, from http://www.securityweek.com/surfwatch-labs-enables-intelligence-sharing-across-extended-enterprise

Selby, N. (2012). *There's No 911 for cybercrime, but would anyone call if there were?* Retrieved September 28, 2015, from http://www.pcworld.com/article/254499/theres_no_911_for_cybercrime_but_would_anyone_call_if_there_were_.html

Selwyn, N. (2007). A safe haven for misbehaving?: An investigation of online misbehavior among university students. *Social Science Computer Review, 26*(4), 446–465. doi:10.1177/0894439307313515

Serious Crime Act 2015, s. 41–44, *Home Office*, UK.

Shang, R.-A., Chen, Y.-C., & Chen, P.-C. (2007). Ethical decisions about sharing music files in the P2P environment. *Journal of Business Ethics, 80*(2), 349–365. doi:10.1007/s10551-007-9424-2

Sherwin, A. (2013). *Music and film industries winning war on piracy, says report*. Retrieved July 23, 2014, from http://www.independent.co.uk/arts-entertainment/music/news/music-and-film-industries-winning-war-on-piracy-says-report-8714499.html

Sirkeci, I., & Magnúsdóttir, L. B. (2011). Understanding illegal music downloading in the UK: A multi-attribute model. *Journal of Research in Interactive Marketing, 5*(1), 90–110. Retrieved from http://www.academia.edu/491842/Understanding_illegal_music_downloading_in_the_UK_A_multi-attribute_model

Slane, A. (2007). Democracy, social space, and the internet. *University of Toronto Law Journal, 57*(1), 81–105. doi:10.1353/tlj.2007.0003

Smith, M. D., & Telang, R. (2012). Assessing the academic literature regarding the impact of media piracy on sales. *SSRN Electronic Journal*. Retrieved from http://papers.ssrn.com/abstract=2132153

Stone, B., & Riley, M. (2013, February). *Hacked? Who ya gonna call?* Retrieved September 4, 2014, from https://dl.mandiant.com/EE/library/businessweek_eprint.pdf

Suler, J. (2004). The online disinhibition effect. *Cyberpsychology & Behavior: The Impact of the Internet, Multimedia and Virtual Reality on Behavior and Society, 7*(3), 321–326. doi:10.1089/1094931041291295

Suler, J. (2013). *Cyberpsychology as interdisciplinary, applied, and experiential*. Retrieved September 4, 2014, from http://cypsy.com/News/Cyberpsychology_as_Interdisciplinary

Svensson, M., & Larsson, S. (2012). Intellectual property law compliance in Europe: Illegal file sharing and the role of social norms. *New Media & Society, 14*(7), 1147–1163. doi:10.1177/1461444812439553

Sykes, G. M., & Matza, D. (1957). Techniques of neutralization: A theory of delinquency. *American Sociological Review, 22*(6), 664–670. Retrieved from http://www.jstor.org/stable/2089195?seq=1#page_scan_tab_contents

Tassi, P. (2013, April). "Game of Thrones" sets piracy world record, but does HBO care? *Forbes*. Retrieved from http://www.forbes.com/sites/insertcoin/2014/04/15/game-of-thrones-sets-piracy-world-record-but-does-hbo-care/

Temple, J. R., Paul, J. A., van den Berg, P., Le, V. D., McElhany, A., & Temple, B. W. (2012). Teen sexting and its association with sexual behaviors. *Archives of Pediatrics & Adolescent Medicine, 166*(9), 828–833. doi:10.1001/archpediatrics.2012.835

The Centre for Secure Information Technologies (CSIT). (2014). *4th world cyber security technology research summit: Securing our digital tomorrow*. Belfast. Retrieved from http://www.csit.qub.ac.uk/News/Events/Belfast2014/Fileutoupload,450092,en.pdf

United States of America v. Ross Ulbricht, 1:13-mj-02328. (2014). *New York Southern District Court*. Retrieved from http://www.justice.gov/usao/nys/pressreleases/February14/RossUlbrichtIndictmentPR/US v. Ross Ulbricht Indictment.pdf

US Attorney's Office District of Massachusetts. (2011). *Alleged hacker charged with stealing over four million documents from MIT network*. U.S. Department of Justice. The U.S. Attorney's Office Massachusetts. Retrieved from http://www.justice.gov/archive/usao/ma/news/2011/July/SwartzAaronPR.html

U.S. Department of Justice. (2010). *The national strategy for child exploitation prevention and interdiction: A report to congress*. Retrieved from http://www.justice.gov/sites/default/files/psc/docs/natstrategyreport.pdf

Viégas, F. B. (2006). Bloggers' expectations of privacy and accountability: An initial survey. *Journal of Computer-Mediated Communication, 10*(3). doi:10.1111/j.1083-6101.2005.tb00260.x

Volkov, D., Grudinov, S., Skripkar, T., Kislitsin, N., Belov, V., & Kalinin, A. (2013). *Group-IB Threat Intelligence Report 2012-2013 H1*. Retrieved from http://report2013.group-ib.com/

Warren, M., & Leitch, S. (2009). Hacker taggers: A new type of hackers. *Information Systems Frontiers*. doi:10.1007/s10796-009-9203y

Wilde, G. J. S. (1998). Risk homeostasis theory: An overview. *Injury Prevention, 4*(2), 89–91. doi:10.1136/ip.4.2.89

Wingrove, T., Korpas, A. L., & Weisz, V. (2011). Why were millions of people not obeying the law? Motivational influences on non-compliance with the law in the case of music piracy. *Psychology, Crime & Law, 17*(3), 261–276. http://dx.doi.org/10.1080/10683160903179526

Winter, A. (2013). *Downloaded*. United States: Trouper Productions.

Wolak, J., & Finkelhor, D. (2011) *'Sexting: A typology'*. Research Bulletin (March), University of New Hampshire: Crimes Against Children Research Center.

Wolak, J., Finkelhor, D., & Mitchell, K. (2011). Child pornography possessors: Trends in offender and case characteristics. *Sexual Abuse: A Journal of Research and Treatment, 23*(1), 22–42. doi:10.1177/1079063210372143

Yar, M. (2005). The global "epidemic" of movie "piracy": Crime-wave or social construction? *Media, Culture & Society, 27*(5), 677–696. doi:10.1177/0163443705055723

Zhang, X. (2010). Charging children with child pornography – using the legal system to handle the problem of "sexting." *Computer Law & Security Review, 26*(3), 251–259. doi:10.1016/j.clsr.2010.03.005

The impacts of organised crime in the EU: some preliminary thoughts on measurement difficulties

Michael Levi

This article analyses the social construction of the problem of organised crime and associated problems of measurement. It reports on a study conducted for the European Parliament which had three principal aims:
1. To produce a critical assessment of the state-of-the-art in terms of what is and is not known about the prevalence and distribution of different forms of organised crime.
2. To set out a robust conceptual framework which would enable us to think more clearly and coherently about the costs of organised crime going forward.
3. To use this assessment and framework to interrogate empirical data on the costs of organised crime in the EU, where it is available and is judged to be reasonably valid and reliable, to produce informed estimates of what these social and economic costs might be.

It comments on the conceptual and empirical problems involved in this exercise and the policy issues that arise in the context of it.

Background and introduction

There is consistent and widespread concern across the EU institutions and EU Member State (MS) governments about the negative impacts that organised crime has upon the security of individual citizens, communities, businesses and MS. Set against this backdrop, the European Parliament commissioned a study to synthesise the research evidence base in an effort to produce a reasoned estimate of the costs of organised crime across the EU, against which to develop policy responses (though it is the view of this author that policy responses are seldom actually or even normatively deducible from harm data). Many estimates of organised crime and money laundering represent what Reuter (1984) termed 'mythical numbers' and van Duyne and Levi (2005) termed 'facts by repetition', that is, they have little plausibility but become facts by dint of being regularly picked up by electronic media trawls and repeated. They are also institutionally useful as 'problem amplifiers' to those making claims for more resources, powers and attention. Indeed, once some numbers – mythical or not – exist, then this creates pressure for other numbers to be created, in order that those other areas of criminal activity are not disadvantaged compared with those for which large numbers exist.

In a number of areas, suitable data to prepare informed estimates of cost are lacking wholly, or in part, due to figures being produced via methodologies that render them unreliable. However, this does not mean that social harms cannot be identified, without producing imaginary numbers. For example, there are the human costs of collapsed bridges, buildings and roads due to bad construction combined with corrupt construction contracts: commonplace in developed and developing countries where Mafias with political connections are able to monopolise large public contracts, including those from the EU (Transcrime, 2013). The economic and social costs of these far exceed the illegal profits made, to which we should add the social anxieties of citizens who have no one they can turn to, to deal with exploitation, and the destruction of entrepreneurial drive that such criminal monopoly or oligopoly creates.

Organised crime is an ambiguous and contested concept. If the crimes and their apparent (possibly concealed) organisation do not fit the imagery of cunning, trafficking and violence, then most citizens would think that there was not a problem of 'organised crime'. On the other hand, the UN Convention Against Transnational Organized Crime signed in Palermo in 2000 sets a far lower standard for the label, to the extent that 'organised crime' can be three burglars and a window cleaning service or even lower criteria used in the UK government's Organised Crime Strategy 2013, which notes (para 2.5) that 'For the purposes of this strategy, organised crime is serious crime planned, coordinated and conducted by people working together on a continuing basis. Their motivation is often, but not always, financial gain'. Although there may be nothing disorganised about their conduct, such a business is far from the popular or the police image of organised crime. Conversely, major frauds committed by less than three people would not count even if they took billions by fraud. This author has introduced the phrase 'The Organisation of Serious Crimes for Gain' (Levi, 2012), which tries to capture the complexities better, just as the UK and Europol have made 'serious' an alternative or supplement to 'organised' as a basis for intervention. Such attempts notwithstanding, however, 'organised crime' is not easily dispensed with as a term, because it is the antithesis of 'opportunistic-individual' crime and also precisely because of its evocative connotations of interpersonal and social threat; and membership of a criminal organisation (however tricky to define operationally – see the Home Office's Serious Crime Act 2015) triggers greater investigative powers and tougher sentences in many countries, particularly in the EU. This article seeks to tease out the nature and extent of harms associated with organised crime, and concludes with the implications of the study.

Aim

This study had three principal aims:

(1) To produce a critical assessment of the state-of-the-art in terms of what is and is not known about the prevalence and distribution of different forms of organised crime.
(2) To set out a robust conceptual framework which would enable us to think more clearly and coherently about the costs of organised crime going forward.
(3) To use this assessment and framework to interrogate empirical data on the costs of organised crime in the EU, where it is available and is judged to be reasonably valid and reliable, to produce informed estimates of what these social and economic costs might be.

Methodology

The research itself involved a multi-lingual evidence search and appraisal exercise, in which we reviewed studies that made claims about costs of organised crime generally or particular activities, in the EU and in individual MS. In engaging with the aims outlined above, we identified a number of cross-cutting problems with the current knowledge base that profoundly limit our ability to guide decision-making with soundly based knowledge of what the costs of organised crime are. These gravitate around a number of core issues using the well-known Political, Economic, Social, Technological, Legal and Environmental (PESTLE) framework, including

- Political – there are priorities that may be agreed across the EU, for example, via the Serious and Organised Crime Threat Assessment policy cycle. However, the very different political contexts that exist across EU MS shape what other issues and problems are defined as priorities in practice by enforcement and other agencies and institutions that can have a preventative function. There are also different traditions of national and local data collection. Consistent data are seldom available across different problem types for many MS, making meaningful comparisons difficult.
- Economic – the economic situations of different EU MS shape their exposure to different organised crime risks. For example, some states have difficulties because they are points of origin for trafficked human beings, where others are points of destination. This makes it a mistake to extrapolate even from relatively robust data produced in one MS to estimate the problem across the whole of the EU.
- Legal – different legal regimens and traditions (including data matching in the private and the public sectors, and proceeds of crime seizure and confiscation regimes) alter the costs and possibilities of responding to organised crimes of different kinds, as well as the organisational inputs that are involved in effecting any such responses.

The analytical approach

There are at least two ways of defining 'organised crime'. The first is to focus on Mafia-type associations – the image (and legal category in Italian law) that most graphically captures what many people think of when they use the term. The second is a looser set of networks with far less stability or hierarchy whose participants supply markets with illicit goods and services they desire: this represents the reality of 'organised crime' in most areas of most EU MS. The Mafia-type associations have activities in other MS, but we cannot easily identify a particular sets of costs attached to it, except in Italy and up to a point in Bulgaria. Therefore, we chose to look primarily at the costs arising from the looser networked 'organised crime'. One of the problems in this field is that different types of crime have different levels of visibility, and the plausibility of their attribution to 'organised crime' is also variable. VAT frauds involving missing traders, for example, are hard to imagine without being 'organised crime', and this may be generally true of extortion whether offline or online, via ransomware. Other areas may be more problematic and we stress that this exercise involves both estimating the volume of hard-to-measure crimes *and* working out how much of those crimes is the product of 'organised crime'.

Informed by published and other readily available data on different forms of organised criminal activity across the EU MS, Levi, Innes, Reuter, and Gundur (2013) outlined an innovative analytic framework that can present a systematic and structured picture of the various types of costs associated with organised crime. The analytic framework draws distinctions between:

- Predatory (crimes with specific victims) and market-based organised crimes (like drugs and people smuggling);
- direct and indirect costs;
- 'Upstream' and 'downstream' control/response costs.

In particular, it may be helpful to distinguish between:

- Private costs: which impact upon individuals directly connected to the victim.
- Parochial costs (Hunter, 1985): that are born through community ties, for example, extortion threats or Ponzi fraud against a particular business community or ethnic group.
- Public costs: are where the impacts are shared between citizens who are not directly connected to each other.

The principal advantage of introducing such an approach is that it steers attention in meaningful ways to those who are exposed to any such costs and could contribute data to fill in our understandings. For example, some forms of fraud tend to predominantly involve private costs – the victims are dispersed individual citizens of the EU. The main targets of other fraud types are small businesses, social enterprises and individuals who are inter-connected, and so involve parochial costs. In addition, some frauds, against EU institutions for instance, involve public costs (House of Lords, 2013; Levi, Burrows, Fleming, Hopkins, & Matthews, 2007; NFA, 2013; OLAF, 2013).

This emergent framework builds up a picture of the different kinds of costs induced by organised crime, taking account of data availability and quality, enabling a way of progressively widening the scope of what is included in the count of costs. Unfortunately, there are so many gaps in the data available that this short scoping study was unable to fulfil loftier ambitions and produce actual estimates for most offenses.

What are we seeking to measure?

Is the target of anti-organised crime measures a broad range of acts (such as the full range of crimes that 'organised criminals' may be involved in committing), a specific set of acts (like 'human slavery' or 'payment card fraud') or a particular set of actors who constitute a threat and their 'enablers', both intentional and reckless/careless. It is seldom easy to know how much of that damage is caused by any particular set of actors and there is a tendency for both public and private sector actors to engage in what security professionals term 'shroud-waving' in order to attract resources to their issues, to enhance resources and powers.

Perceptions of organised crime

Perceptions of threat are distinct from evidence about actual risks and costs, though insecurity is a cost in itself and has political impacts (as does its absence in lack of support for control measures). When Scots were asked which crimes they associate with 'organised crime', the three crimes highlighted by respondents were drugs (use and selling) (72%), money laundering (20%) and people trafficking (18%) (IPSOS MORI, 2013). Yet, of the 10% who stated that they had been affected by organised crime in Scotland in the past three years, theft and burglary ranked relatively high, while drugs and payment card fraud were the only crimes that featured in the perceptions list above. Whereas most Scots consider organised crime to be a serious issue 'in Scotland' – creating fear and drug abuse – only a third considered it to be a problem in their area. So, it appears that the government and police have not convinced many of the public that organised crime affects them personally, even if they agree that it is a more abstract threat to the nation. So, unless people think that there is a highly organised Mafia (like in *The Godfather* or *The Sopranos*), they do not accept that there is 'organised crime' where they live. The construction of this in Scotland is likely to be very different from that in Bulgaria or Italy (see Antonopoulos & Hall, 2015; Dugato, Favarin, & Giommoni, 2015; Savona, 2014), and this is both a fascination for sociologists and social psychologists and a problem for policy-makers and enforcement officials who may consider that the public underappreciates the threat posed by organised crime in the UK.

Costs of organised crime

Translation of harms into money can be a way of disciplining subjectivism (Greenfield & Paoli, 2013; Paoli & Greenfield, 2013), and in principle, 'willingness to pay to prevent harm x' – is a way of revealed preferences (though in the real world, differences in ability to pay may make more practical impact). The history of 'threat assessments' is one of largely political (with a small 'p') judgements dressed up as scientific ones, but there are ongoing efforts (refs) to make these more rigorous. Estimating the costs and harms of particular issues is different from estimating what criminals make from crime and how much of those proceeds they are laundering. The harms from crime may be far greater (or far less) than the benefits to offenders: toxic waste dumping and some forms of counterfeiting that do not involve physical harms are examples. Others are highly contested: the boundaries between sex work, people smuggling and trafficking for example. Much crime – even as part of 'organised crime activities' – might better be described as 'offend to spend' rather than 'offend to save and legitimise'. In short, estimates of the cost of organised crime and of laundering must be looked at with a sceptical eye and can even be counterproductive, given that the gap between the proceeds of crime confiscation (worldwide, maximum $2 billion annually) and the estimated proceeds of crime, which is guesstimated/thought to be in the trillions or – more conservatively – multi-billions of dollars. Realistically, such a gap cannot be bridged. The most pressing question, therefore, is what the practical implications of this gap are for strategies and tactics.

Research in this field is still at an early stage. Our study conducted for the European Parliament (Levi et al., 2013) identified minimum total costs of organised-crime activities in the European Union to be €126.3 billion; €1.2 billion for identified budget enforcement costs (excluding most national agencies); and €34 billion for costs related to drug treatment. More specifically, these costs were broken down into different areas of criminal activity on which there are variable data both about levels of harm and about the organisational contexts in which they occur. These latter issues are important because they are affected by the social organisation of crime prevention and data matching (or rejection thereof for privacy reasons). The integration of payment card data (by banks), credit applications (via the not-for-profit CIFAS and by for-profit credit reference agencies) and insurance claims (via the industry mutual body the Insurance Fraud Bureau) have transformed our assessment of the financial transactions as frauds rather than losses/claims, and social network analysis using data integration packages has shown that what formerly were regarded as individual acts of either non-criminal loss or fraud were in fact connected as fraud rings such as Crash-for-Cash rackets (IFB, 2013; Levi, 2008). In other European countries, the more hostile legislation and cultural attitudes to data sharing for crime prevention make such integration (and awareness of 'organised crime') impossible, so losses there may be greater, but awareness of them as 'organised crime' are far less. (Though that may not stop assertions about their vast scale – simply that there is a poorer evidence base for their magic numbers.)

Table 1 shows the estimated direct economic costs of some organised-crime activities within the EU. More detailed analysis of individual components may be found in Levi et al. (2013). The social and economic costs of organised crime in the UK alone were estimated by a recent Home Office study at £24 billion (Mills, Skodbo, & Blyth, 2013): 'drugs supply (£10.7 billion), organised fraud (£8.9 billion) and organised immigration crime types (£1.0 billion) have major impacts on the UK, and other less visible crimes also cause substantial harm'. The Home Office study, like its predecessors, attributes all of the consequences of drug misuse to organised crime, implicitly (and, given the UN definition, arguably) on the grounds that without organised crime there would

Table 1. Estimate of the minimum identifiable direct economic costs of selected activities of organised crime in the EU in 2012.

Organised-crime activities	Direct economic cost (€)
Human trafficking	30 billion
Fraud against EU (cigaret smuggling)	11.3 billion
Fraud against EU (VAT/MTIC fraud)	20 billion
Fraud against EU (agricultural and structural funds)	3 billion
Fraud against EU individuals	97 billion
Unrecovered motor vehicle theft	4.25 billion
Payment card fraud	1.16 billion
Insurance fraud	1 billion (in UK alone). Other EU countries' insurance sectors do not collect these data

be little or no illegal drugs available. Thus, for example, deaths from illegal drug use and their economic consequences – notwithstanding the low economic productivity of many drug users – are attributed to organised crime. Levi et al. (2013) argue, however, that the harms from illegal drug taking are significantly affected by how one treats the commodity and its suppliers and users. On this logic, it would be a mistake to lump the iatrogenic impacts of drug policy into the category of 'organised crime costs'. If successes in the reduction of supply lead to more inconsistent and toxic 'cutting' of products whose purity is not standardised and is not visible to users, there will be more fatalities and serious injuries. No economically rational drug dealer would kill off purchasers (though some do make misjudgements about the effects of their cost-cutting measures, as do some alcohol counterfeiters and otherwise legitimate businesspeople); and killing off criminal rivals attracts too much media and police 'heat' unless the group is strong enough to threaten or resist the state, as sometimes happens, at least episodically.

The economic and social harm of human trafficking might rationally be compared with its opportunity cost for those in poverty and war-damaged zones from which many victims originate. The main legal differences between trafficking and smuggling are that migrants usually pay to be smuggled, but traffickers generate money from the ongoing exploitation of their victims, even when originally paid to smuggle them voluntarily. Smugglers only generate money from the movement and illegal entry phases, and smuggling must involve illegally crossing a border, whereas trafficking can also occur within a country. The tragic loss of lives – especially at sea but also in trucks – has highlighted the huge market in smuggled people, for whom large investments in search of a better life or flight from an imperilled life constitute a rational choice. The costs and benefits of people smuggling accrue in different places: some may see harms to the UK labour market, for example, but businesspeople and illegal migrants may see this as enthusiastic and cheap labour. There would be a much smaller market for illegal emigration if those extended families who raised funds to pay the smugglers were not usually repaid by the migrants afterwards: otherwise (except where death and torture were the alternatives), it would be irrational for the families to invest such (proportionately vast) sums in their collective futures. Even many of those trafficked send some funds back to their families. It is unknown whether the better communication of risks to people living in developing countries would have much impact – an aspect that remains underexplored.

Human trafficking is a different matter, as it can entail rape and slavery (often after voluntary migration), and its socio-economic costs have been estimated to be high in all studies. However, the very real issues inherent in people trafficking notwithstanding, it is not clear in what sense the

2340 victims who were referred to the UK authorities in 2013 (National Crime Agency, 2015) – an increase from the 1746 in 2013, 1186 in 2012 and 946 in 2011 – constitute a real rise in numbers rather than better identification and recording; or represent a national security threat to the UK, as opposed to a human security threat to those individuals. Much of the human-trafficking/modern slavery debate is over highly contested estimates – especially over the numbers of people trafficked to various parts of the world – which have become a political football between IGOs, NGOs, religious groups and other interested parties.

Similar observations apply to the very different field of cybercrime, where business interested in selling software services to the public (Symantec, 2013) and to business and government (BAE Detica, 2011) has been alleged to have improperly amplified the scale of 'the problem' by mixing up highly speculative scale estimates of some types of e-crime (especially commercial espionage and Intellectual Property Theft) with some real data (Anderson et al., 2012; McAfee, 2014), in a way previously done by financial consulting firms with fraud generally (Levi et al., 2007). Tax gap estimates and the role played by intentional frauds in them remain a matter of controversy, at both national and EU levels (CASE, 2013; HMRC, 2012; Reckon, 2009), but their impact on national budgets is significant.

While most criminal activities are threatening, their impact varies widely by social group and by region. It would be a mistake to focus on individual incidents, though some 'signal crimes' (Innes, 2014) can have a symbolic effect in transforming political assessments of harm which, in turn, motivates action at the political level and in society more widely. Instead, decision-makers must determine at what frequency and level of seriousness organised-crime acts become a threat to some important national interest (be it social values or economic interests).

There are many sorts of harms arising from crime, whether organised in Mafia-type Associations or not. The additional harms of 'organisation' consist of political and enforcement corruption, and the sub-standard, overpriced quality of construction and other services, along with threats to enterprise and an alternative structure of economic 'progression'. There is no credible basis for imputing economic costs to many aspects of these costs.

Homicides connected with organised crime

Violent crimes, particularly homicides, offer another area of evidence from which conclusions about the prevalence and reach of organised crime can be deduced. In southern Italy, homicides and threats by organised criminals are commonplace (though expectations can command acquiescence without the need for specific threats; and as in Colombia, rates can vary greatly in different periods as responses to control efforts). Meanwhile, a British study (Hopkins, Tilley, & Gibson, 2013) concluded that about 6% of criminal homicides in England and Wales in 2005–2006 had some form of link to organised crime. Of the 696 cases reviewed, 54 were attributed by circumstantial evidence to the activities of organised criminal groups, and of these, 17 were directly caused by groups with a distinct organisational structure (corresponding perhaps to Mafia-type associations). Those cases with such links were far more likely than other homicides to remain 'undetected' by police. The aggregate level of criminal homicide has declined significantly in recent years across most European countries, but given that most homicides in most countries are domestic followed by acquaintance killings, it is not possible from this alone to deduce that violence associated with serious organised crime has been declining too.

Among the EU MS, Italy, Belgium and Bulgaria top the figures for per capita homicides by firearm, with Italy also ranked highest in terms of the absolute number. England and Wales have one of the lowest per capita rates of gun-related homicide in Europe, but the absence of studies on organised crime-related gun homicides elsewhere should induce caution: guns are also used in family homicides. Taking its figure of 6% of homicides being linked to organised crime as an average rate for Europe, and using EU homicide data for 2010, this would imply conservatively some 500 organised-crime-related homicides in the EU. However, because such violence is unevenly distributed, the rates in some jurisdictions are significantly higher (and conversely lower in others). The professional consensus is that criminal markets give rise to far less actual violence than people generally believe, and that homicide and other serious violence is normally a result of unstable personalities and market incursions by outsiders. Outside Italy, Mafia-type large-scale organised crime is rare in the EU: looser SME-type affiliations are far more widespread. On the other hand, particular incidents can give rise to 'moral panics' about previously undetected organised crime influences: 6 mobsters were assassinated by Italian gangsters outside a pizzeria in a sleep German town of Duisberg in 2007, and eventually leaders were imprisoned, but meanwhile there have been many stories about the 'Unstoppable' spread of Calabria's 'ndrangheta mafia sees outposts established in UK and Ireland' (*The Independent*, 22 June 2012).

Cost of responses to organised crime

It is important to look at the costs of responding to organised crime, but to keep that separate from the costs of crime themselves. The minimum response costs to organised crime *at an EU level* are €210 million (Europol/Eurojust/EMCDDA/Frontex only): this does *not* include *national* agency budgets. In the UK alone, for example, the 2013/2014 budget for the Serious and Organised Crime Agency was €498 million, and this does not include main UK policing or prosecution costs. A substantial proportion of the Metropolitan Police Specialist Crime Directorate budget of €490 million in 2012–2013 was spent on organised crime (€17 million was budgeted 2013/14 for reducing serious and organised crime by disrupting criminal networks; the budget for the later disbanded Police eCrime Unit was €12 million). The Italian Direzione Investigativa Antimafia's budget has dropped markedly in recent years to around €10 million, but there are significant expenditures on organised crime by other Italian investigative bodies. In addition, there are many other costs, for example, the very substantial ones incurred by the private sector in responding to money laundering and transnational bribery – as required by EU Directives and other legal obligations – and (in their self-interest) frauds and conventional crimes against them. These have not been reliably counted across the EU or even in any individual MS, but they comfortably exceed the cost of EU-level anti-crime expenditures from the EU budget.

EMCDDA (2013) has estimated €34 billion as the cost of responding to illicit drugs in the EU. Some might consider that these are costs of illegal drugs themselves. But health expenditures are only partly a reflection of problem drug use itself, and treatment costs are determined by what governments are prepared to spend on drug treatment, not on its impact on users or society. (See Trautmann, Kimler, & Turnbull, 2013 for some detailed analysis.)

Analysing cost directs our focus to fairly specific and material consequences of serious crimes for gain, but we can fail to assess the benefits to some parts of the population as well as harms. Where state institutions have only a minimal footprint or legitimacy, the activities of some organised crime groups also provide publicly valued protection and dispute settlement services that the state fails to do. If organised crime groups do occasionally act as a 'shadow state' then is it right to see this solely as a cost? Mafia-type Associations may be concentrated in some pockets of the EU, such as Italy and Bulgaria – and might reasonably be viewed as a threat to the state there – but have primarily a local or at most regional effect elsewhere – though their laundering may assist crimes elsewhere. In looser networked terms, some activities of organised criminals do cause severe harm, and criminal capital is a source of criminal reinvestment and enhancing the capability to do further harm, but this occurs *without* the intertwining of criminality with politics that makes organised crime a threat in some MS.

Conclusions

Based upon expert assessment of the current state of our knowledge about the prevalence, distribution and impacts of organised crime across Europe, Levi et al. (2013) concluded that a number of developmental steps are required to advance understanding in this area and consequently the efficacy of interventions. First, without more sophistication underpinning attempts to think about and measure the prevalence and distribution of various forms of organised crime cost, applied in a more consistent way across European States, it will be impossible to be confident in any estimates produced. It was beyond the scope of this small study to undertake such work, but one approach might be based upon profiling countries' risk exposure and situation, and using relatively reliable data collected in one country to derive estimates for countries with similar profiles. Such an approach would incrementally improve the quality of the evidence base for European agencies working in this area, to improve their effectiveness efforts at organised crime reduction. It is also beginning to be needed for the National Risk Assessments that are required when countries are evaluated for their efforts against money laundering, though this author would stress that the costs and impacts of organised crime are far from being the same as the level of money laundering of domestic and foreign crime proceeds and the realisable profits from crime.

Second, accompanying such a manoeuvre, we start to outline how, in thinking about costs and impacts, it can help to differentiate between:

- Private costs: which impact upon individuals directly connected to the victim.
- Parochial costs: that are born through community ties, for example, extortion threats or Ponzi fraud against a particular business community or ethnic group.
- Public costs: are where the impacts are shared between citizens who are not directly connected to each other.

The principal advantage of introducing such an approach is that it steers attention in meaningful ways to those who are exposed to any such costs and could contribute data to fill in our understandings. For example, some forms of fraud tend to predominantly involve private costs – the victims are dispersed individual citizens of the EU. The main targets of other fraud types are small businesses, social enterprises and individuals who are inter-connected, and so involve parochial costs. In addition, as intimated in the headline cost figures listed above, some frauds, against EU institutions for instance, involve public costs. We recommend that detailed attention be given in future to organised crimes against these sectors of society and economy, and how they evolve over time and place. This might be more fruitful in guiding enforcement and prevention interventions than using generic terms like 'the cost of organised crime'.

The case for transnational action against many types of organised crime is overwhelming, whether by prevention or, where this fails as it inevitably will, by criminal prosecution and administrative sanction in a mixed economy of sanctions. Clarity is important in deciding what purposes, beyond this, we want better aggregate evidence for. We need different data for judging culpability, harm and future threat. We would prefer there to be more data. It is tempting to become post-modern alchemists, inventing estimations that are hard to falsify: but this would not contribute to rational decision-making. Some of the issues alluded to in this article may never be capable of resolution without disproportionately costly research and a higher degree of social surveillance than would be considered tolerable in a liberal democracy. However, if organised crime and its component parts are as serious a threat to society as many officials claim, more effort needs to be paid to understanding these dimensions than has occurred to date. The UK, Belgium, Italy (on Mafia proceeds), Netherlands and Sweden have been the only EU MS that have put significant effort into this to date, and even their efforts have been modest. One of the prime requirements is for greater modesty in claims, and more refined attention to which aspects of 'organised crime' are the primary focus of attention for different aspects of control strategies. The 'usual suspects' of drugs and people trafficking are being broadened out by Europol and the European Commission, which acknowledge that 'economic crime' is a growing focus of crime for gain. What now needs to be appreciated is that important economic crimes are also committed by elites who were not delinquents in their youth and have not grown up through the traditional mechanisms of upward criminal mobility. The relative 'harmfulness' as well as 'wrongfulness' will continue to be a matter of debate, but the traditional demarcation between white-collar and organised crime is slowly dissolving.

It is important to understand the implications of the choice to examine the costs of organised crime as a large set of looser networks rather than as 'criminal organisations'. In his work on the character of harms, Sparrow (2008) stresses the importance of capacity and intent as features of harm, and indeed, it is precisely this that (as with terrorist organisations) gives rise to judgements of the specially threatening character of organised crime. Yet are loose networks as threatening as tight organisations and is this verdict true across the board or are there circumstances in which looser networks are *more* threatening, for example, because of their adaptability? if not, how should we adjust our judgements and priorities in the light of this? This needs much more attention in policy development than it has received to date.

Acknowledgements

I am grateful to Rajeev Gundur, Martin Innes and Peter Reuter for their contribution to the research, and to the now disbanded European Parliament's Special Committee on Organised Crime, Corruption and Money Laundering for commissioning it.

References

Anderson, R., Barton, C., Böhme, R., Clayton, R., van Eeten, M., Levi, M., … Savage, S. (2012). *Measuring the cost of cybercrime*. Paper presented at the WEIS. http://weis2012.econinfosec.org/papers/Anderson_WEIS2012.pdf

Antonopoulos, G. A., & Hall, A. (2015). The financial management of the illicit tobacco trade in the United Kingdom. *British Journal of Criminology*. DOI:10.1093/bjc/azv062.

BAE Systems Detica. (2011). *The cost of cyber crime*. London: Detica and Office of Cyber Security and Information Assurance.

CASE. (2013). *Study to quantify and analyse the VAT Gap in the EU-27 member states final report*. Brussels: European Commission.

Dugato, M., Favarin, S., & Giommoni, L. (2015). The risks and rewards of organized crime investments in real estate. *British Journal of Criminology, 55*(5), 944–965.

van Duyne, P., & Levi, M. (2005). *Drugs and money: Managing the drug trade and crime-money in Europe*. London: Routledge.

EMCDDA. (2013). *European drug report 2013*. Lisbon: Author.

Greenfield, V. A., & Paoli, L. (2013). A framework to assess the harms of crimes. *British Journal of Criminology, 53*(5), 864–885.

HM Revenue & Customs. (2012). *Measuring tax gaps 2012*. London: Author.

Hopkins, M., Tilley, N., & Gibson, K. (2013). Homicide and organized crime in England. *Homicide Studies, 17*(3), 291–313.
House of Lords. (2013). *The fight against fraud on the EU's finances*. London: Author.
Hunter, A. (1985). Private, parochial and public social orders: The problem of crime and incivility in urban communities. In G. Suttles & M. Zaid (Eds.), *The challenge of social control: Citizenship and institution building in modern society* (pp. 230–242). Norwodd, NJ: Ablex Publishing Corp.
IFB. (2013). *Crash for cash: Putting the brakes on fraud*. London: Author.
Innes, M. (2014). *Signal crimes*. Oxford, MA: Oxford University Press.
IPSOS MORI Scotland. (2013). *Public attitudes to organised crime in Scotland*. Scottish governmental social research, 2013. Retrieved from January 27, 2014. http://www.ipsos-mori.com/Assets/Docs/Scotland/Scotland_SPOM_Organised_Crime_Report_190913.pdf
Levi, M. (2008). 'Organised fraud': Unpacking research on networks and organisation. *Criminology and Criminal Justice, 8*(4), 389–419.
Levi, M. (2012). The organisation of serious crimes for gain. In M. Maguire, R. Morgan, & R. Reiner (Eds.), *The oxford handbook of criminology* (5th ed., pp. 595–622). Oxford, MA: Oxford University Press.
Levi, M., Burrows, J., Fleming, M. H., Hopkins, M., & Matthews, K. (2007). *The nature, extent and economic impact of fraud in the UK*. London: ACPO. http://www.cardiff.ac.uk/socsi/resources/ACPO%20final%20nature%20extent%20and%20economic%20impact%20of%20fraud.pdf
Levi, M., Innes, M., Reuter, P., & Gundur, R. (2013). *The economic, financial and social impacts of organised crime in the European Union*. PE 493.018. Brussels: European Parliament.
McAfee. (2014). *Net losses: Estimating the global cost of cybercrime*. Washington, DC: McAfee and CSIS.
Mills, H., Skodbo, S., & Blyth, P. (2013). *Understanding organised crime: Estimating the scale and the social and economic costs, home office research report no. 73*. London: Home Office.
National Crime Agency. (2015). *National referral mechanism statistics – End of year summary 2014*. London: Author.
National Fraud Authority. (2013). *Annual fraud indicator*. London: Author.
OLAF. (2013). *Fraud in figures*. http://ec.europa.eu/anti_fraud/investigations/fraud-in-figures/index_en.htm
Paoli, L., & Greenfield, V. A. (2013). Harm: A neglected concept in criminology, a necessary benchmark in crime policy. *European Journal of Crime, Criminal Law and Criminal Justice, 21*, 359–377.
Reckon, L. L. P. (2009). *Study to quantify and analyse the VAT gap in the EU-25 member states*. http://ec.europa.eu/taxation_customs/resources/documents/taxation/tax_cooperation/combating_tax_fraud/reckon_report_sep2009.pdf
Reuter, P. (1984). The (Continued) vitality of mythical numbers. *Public Interest, 75*, 135–147.
Savona, E. (2014). Estimating proceeds of crime and mafia revenues in Italy. *Special Issue of Global Crime, 15*, 1–9.
Sparrow, M. (2008). *The character of harms*. Cambridge, MA: Harvard University Press.
Symantec. (2013). *Internet security threat report 2012 trends* (Vol. 18). Mountain View, CA: Author.
Transcrime. (2013). *Gli investimenti delle mafie*. Milan: Author.
Trautmann, F., Kimler, B., & Turnbull, P. (Eds.). (2013). *Further insights into aspects of the illicit EU drugs market*. Luxembourg: European Commission.

Homelessness among formerly incarcerated African American men: contributors and consequences

Myia C. Egleton, Diari Marcus Banigo, Branden A. McLeod and Halaevalu F.O. Vakalahi

> This article critically analyses the existing literature on the contributors and consequences of homelessness among formerly incarcerated African American men. Offered is a discussion of a conceptual framework that incorporates anti-discrimination/anti-oppression, Afrocentric, social and community development perspectives, as a lens through which to conceptualise this topic. Gaps in the existing literature related specifically to reintegration, stigma, barriers, and perspectives of family members and service providers are identified. Implications are offered for education, research, practice and policy. Urgent attention is needed to identify and reverse the systemic factors contributing to the cycle of poverty, incarceration and homelessness among African American men.

African American males have historically experienced and been subjected to policies and practices that have traditionally discriminated against and perpetuated inequality and inequity in socio-economic status (Smith & Hattery, 2010). Formerly incarcerated African American males are additionally challenged by the implementation of such policies and practices. Housing, employment, health and mental health are but a few important socio-economic indicators that can create stability or instability in the lives of these individuals. For example, despite the United States' rank by Forbes as the seventh richest country in the world, homelessness is a pervasive socio-economic problem that plagues urban communities which are populated by African American men, across the United States. The US Department of Housing and Urban Development (HUD) (2013) found that 610,042 individuals experienced homelessness in the US in 2013; whereas, the resources aimed at preventing homelessness remain disproportionately inadequate and often exclude African American men (National Alliance to End Homelessness, 2014).

An estimated 3.5 million people are homeless at any given time in the United States, yearly. People of colour, particularly African American males are overrepresented in the homeless population with African Americans comprising about 42% of the homeless population (United States

Conference of Mayors, 2006). Not only is homelessness more prevalent among African American men, but they also experience lengthier durations of being homeless. Research has shown that racism and the stigma of homelessness have created obstacles for the formerly incarcerated African American male compared to any other subset of the homeless population which have contributed to the negative perception by the public and media (Burt, Aron, Lee, & Valente, 2001; Ireland, 2003; Lee & Farrell, 2003; Park & Burgess, 1925; Young, 2006). African American males are overrepresented as criminal perpetrators and victims, and consequently in the impoverished, homeless and underclass populations (Donley, 2008; Gans, 1995; Lee & Farrell, 2003; Ponterotto, Utsey, & Pedersen, 2006).

In general, formerly incarcerated African American men are challenged with complex and intertwined consequences including joblessness, homelessness, familial and psychological distress, poor health outcomes and often recidivism. Guided by an integrated conceptual framework, this discussion offers a critical analysis of the limited existing literature pertaining to formerly incarcerated African American men and factors that impact the experiences of these men after incarceration.

Review of relevant literature

Conceptual framework

This discussion is conceptualised by a few select relevant theories and perspectives that attest to the importance of comprehensive and multi-systems transformation and capacity building on the individual, family and community levels. The following theories and perspectives including anti-discrimination/anti-oppression theory, Afrocentric perspective and social and community development perspectives, are offered as a guide for conceptualising the discussion of the existing literature on the experiences of formerly incarcerated African-America men with systems historically embedded with inequality and inequity.

Anti-discrimination/anti-oppression perspective

Hinson and Bradley (2011) stated that people experience discriminatory and oppressive situations because they are a part of a group that is defined on the basis of shared characteristics (e.g. race, class, gender, ethnicity, sexuality, nationality, age, ability, etc.), which are erroneously deemed inferior. In particular, Landis (1998) found that institutional discrimination is more clandestine but intentional than individual discrimination. In terms of racism as a type of individual discrimination, Landis (1998) states that within this social construct, people are divided into distinct hereditary groups. Because of the perceived differences between these groups, they are ranked as superior and inferior by those in power.

In response to discrimination and oppression in systems such as housing and employment, some scholars proposed empowerment strategies which argued that 'power does not need to be equated with control, but can be spread widely in society amongst powerless groups' (Payne, 2005, p. 282). On the contrary, scholars such as Fook (1993) used a structural approach criticising empowerment scholars for not actively opposing structural oppression. Scholars of structural oppression recognised that oppression is embedded in the major economic, political and cultural systems/institutions of society. Evidently, empowerment and equity cannot be balanced without transforming these major societal systems and institutions.

As such, the work on institutional racism began with a focus on inequalities in housing and employment systems (Payne, 2005). Families earning median income are challenged by housing affordability. For the one in 32 American adults transitioning from prison to society access to housing is even a more daunting task (Bradley, Oliver, Richardson, & Slayter, 2001). Bradley et al. (2001) affirmed that housing is one of the most critical barriers to reentry. For returning citizens, not only is private market housing cost-prohibitive due to underemployment or unemployment and low-to-no earnings, but regulations in the public housing market bar many returning citizens from living in government supported units due to criminal convictions. Even if criminal records were not a barrier to publicly subsidised housing, 'deep-subsidy' programmes that predominantly support the poorest households have seen steep decline of over 250,000 housing units between 1995 and 2011 (Schwartz, 2013). Federal funds from the American Recovery and Reinvestment Act of 2009 provided additional funds for physical improvements in public housing, project-based subsidy programmes and tax credit projects, however, funding for such programmes declined with shifts in the political landscape within the 111th Congress. Meanwhile, the US Department of Housing and Urban Development (HUD) reported a shortfall of 5.1 million rental units in adequate physical condition, which would be affordable to low-income renters. Thus, given the shortfall of affordable housing available to most low-income individuals and families, access to housing, job and other resources is much more complex and complicated for individuals reentering society from correctional institutions.

Afrocentric perspective

The 'Africentric' (as referred to by Everett, Chipungu, & Leashore, 2004) or 'Afrocentric' (as referred to by Schiele, 2000) perspective is a worldview that embraces the cultural values, beliefs and practices of individuals with indigenous African heritage. This perspective appears to have emerged from tension within the social sciences, which placed a considerable amount of credibility and attention on Western cultural, political and economic theories and models, without acknowledging the contributions of non-western frameworks. Schiele conveyed (2000) that oppressed groups across the globe constantly struggle for advancement, equal rights and economic liberation. The worldview, humanity, culture and political and economic systems of oppressed groups are consistently invalidated by the dominant group. On the other hand, the Western worldview, paradigms and theories are considered supreme and regarded as preeminent. Schiele called this concept 'Eurocentric cultural universalism'. While Eurocentric cultural universalism, in and of itself, assumes its features are broadly applicable across groups, it places people of colour particularly African Americans at a great disadvantage. Such disadvantage is described and measured in a multitude of ways in Schiller's (2008) book *The Economics of Poverty and Discrimination*. Whether it is the rate of relative or absolute poverty, labour force participation, educational attainment, negative effects of globalisation and other measures of wealth, ethnic minorities, especially African Americans are at the bottom (Schiller, 2008). According to Schiller, 'their money incomes don't buy the same access to housing, schools, jobs, or justice. Money helps but doesn't fully overcome racial barriers' (Schiller, 2008, p. 15).

Social and community development perspective

Social and community development are important aspects of equality and equity particularly for formerly incarcerated African American men. Paiva (1977) stated that social development includes building the capacity of people to work continuously for their own and society's wellbeing. While there is a strong emphasis on individual capacity, social development also includes four additional aspects: structural change, socio-economic integration, institutional development and renewal. The institutional renewal emphasis relates to planned changes that result in a better fit between 'human needs and aspirations on the one hand and social policies and programs on the other' (Payne, 2005, p. 217). Henderson and Thomas (1981) also found four contemporary concepts that guided community work, which includes social capital, civil society, capacity building and social inclusion. Marginalised individuals such as formerly incarcerated African American men must become re-connected to their communities and the wider society for capacity building and social and community development.

In summary, these select theories and perspectives suggest that a comprehensive framework for transformation and capacity building must exist both on the micro and macro-level systems in order for sustainability to occur. As indicated by the anti-discrimination and anti-oppression perspective, solution points to recognising and reforming the intentional yet subtle racial injustices within the housing, employment and criminal justice systems, while building the social and human capital of formerly incarcerated African American men. The Afri/Afrocentric perspective further advocates that legitimising non-western perspectives engaging them on equal grounds will advantage all individuals socially and economically regardless of cultural groups. Likewise, as suggested by the Social and Community development perspective, placing value and validation on the lives of formerly incarcerated African American men will open access to capacity building that positively transforms both individual and systems.

African American males and incarceration

The International Centre for Prison Studies (2014) reported that out of 224 countries, the United States of America has the highest prison population, with China and the Russian Federation ranking second and third, respectively. Similarly, US Congressman Conyers (2013) found that in the United States, the last 40 years has seen a mass of over incarceration, overall – from 300,000 to more than 2 million. Conyers noted (Maher, Pathak, Skinner, Conyers, & Bendor, 2013) that the United States has the highest incarceration rate at approximately 700 per 100,000 people. Within the United States prison population ethnic minorities such as African Americans and Latinos are overrepresented (NAACP, 2013). Darensbourg, Perez, and Blake (2010) also found that in 2006 African Americans comprise 12.5% of the US population, yet they accounted for 35% of all state and federal prisoners. According to the US Department of Justice (2013), 86% of the prison population is comprised of males, and black males are six times more likely to be imprisoned than white males. Also, black males ranging from 18 years to 21 years are more than 9.5 times more likely to be imprisoned than their white counterparts. If the current trend of mass incarceration does not seize, one in every three African American male born is at risk of experiencing incarceration during their lifetime (NAACP, 2013).

The US Department of Justice (2012) confirmed that the highest population of prisoners in the US is African American men. The incarceration rate among African American men is at 3000 per 100,000 citizens which is six times the rate of white men. The NAACP (2013) also indicated that individuals of racial and ethnic minorities make up two-thirds of people in prison and one in every eight African American male is either imprisoned or jailed in any given day. Western's (2007) analysis of the fivefold increase in the US imprisonment rate during the three decades of 1975–2005 also concluded that African Americans in their 30s were seven times more likely than white men to have a prison record. Raphael (2007) references data from the Bureau of Justice Statistics that indicates that more than a third of all young black men are now incarcerated, on parole, or on probation at any point in time.

In examining the linkages between mass incarceration of men by the Prison Industrial Complex (PIC) and adverse outcomes on economic, political, human and social capital, Smith and Hattery (2010) found that US capitalists in the twentieth and twenty-first centuries established a legal process for exploiting the labour of African American men via the PIC. Consequently, racialised wealth gaps continue to exist in educational attainment, home and business ownership, as well as representation in the political system. Western (2007) also found that although college graduation, military service and marriage were important adult life milestones that lead to employment and home purchase, the racial disparities in imprisonment obstructed the path to progress throughout these important developmental milestones. African American males have a greater risk of being incarcerated than graduate from college. In 2010, there were 37% school dropouts among African Americans whereas only 26% of these African American males were engaged in employment. In other words, more African American male school dropouts were jailed than employed in 2010 igniting concerns that the 'deep race and class inequalities in incarceration' reinforces inequality in social and economic status among poor communities. Wage decrease, health and mental health problems, and family instability as a result of incarceration are multiple problems experienced by formerly incarcerated African American males (Western, 2014).

Housing inaccessible

In the United States, 650,000 people are released from incarceration yearly often with no housing plans to facilitate their rehabilitation and reintegration into society (Mayock, Corr, & O'Sullivan, 2008). Many are confronted with the problem of homelessness emanating from multiple barriers including restrictive housing policies preventing people with criminal records from residing in public housing units (Moreno et al., 2012). Homelessness has been viewed as a recurring urban phenomenon as some central cities have 71% of homeless citizens; homelessness in the suburbs is about 21% and 9% in the rural areas. Research findings also revealed that 1 in every 111 released prisoner in the United States becomes homeless as a result of limited access to resources to facilitate reintegration (National law Center for Homelessness and Poverty, 2013). Thus, many formerly incarcerated African American men experience homelessness resulting from lack of adequate rehabilitation plans and limited access to employment and housing resources to facilitate rehabilitation and reintegration. Cooke (2004) attributed the overrepresentation of African American ex-prisoners among the homeless population to such financial constraints and difficulties with securing paid employment. Incarceration and homelessness are often mutually inclusive in relation to the experiences of formerly incarcerated African American males. Cooke (2004) affirmed that the homelessness of formerly incarcerated African American men correlates with difficulties in securing employment post-release from prison as well as systemic barriers and minimal familial/communal resources for successful rehabilitation. Fontaine (2013) further affirmed that formerly incarcerated men including African American males experience homelessness due to personal challenges including employability, family support, substance abuse and mental health histories as well as systematic barriers such as public housing restrictions and landlord discrimination. As poverty continues to be a recurring factor in homelessness, findings by the United States Department of Housing and Urban Development (2007) revealed that about 23% of African Americans lived in poverty. The rate of poverty among blacks is three times higher than the poverty rate of Caucasians which is 7.1%.

Kenemore and Roldan (2006) also found in a study that as African American men are released from incarceration with lack of appropriate rehabilitation plans, they are challenged with lack of money, unemployment, loss of social support and homelessness. African American men released from incarceration are an extremely underserved population needing social work attention (p. 6). This study revealed that spending lengthy periods of time in solitary or isolated housing results in formerly incarcerated men suffering from mental health problems and being ill prepared for life in the community. For this reason, appropriate rehabilitation plan prior to release from incarceration is a key factor for successful reintegration.

Concurring with previous research, The Urban Institute reported that African American men with a history of incarceration are challenged with housing resulting in 'episodic homelessness'. Appropriate post-release housing arrangements with supportive services such as job placement, substance abuse and mental/behavioural health treatment were recommended for positive outcomes and reduction of recidivism. Among the few sustained programs for addressing this issue of homelessness among formerly incarcerated men, is the Frequent User Service Enhancement (FUSE) programme. The Corporation for Supportive Housing introduced this Returning Home Initiative. The FUSE program aims at reducing housing instability/homelessness in order to reduce risk for incarceration which in turn can decrease risk for homelessness. Research findings on the effectiveness of FUSE programme concluded that it successfully decreased homelessness and recidivism among formerly incarcerated men.

Socio-economic insecurity

HUD's (2007) report stated that black poverty runs deeper than the poverty of other racial and ethnic groups. Shinn (2007) described four types of social disparities that serve as important mechanisms linking race to employment, distribution of wealth, access to housing/real estate and imprisonment rates. Cole (2010) argued that race-related experiences are not recognised in the assessments, interventions and work done with minority offenders which has a major impact on the population's reentry into society. Furthermore, low educational achievement compounded with mental illness and substance abuse has been associated with economic insecurities such as joblessness and homelessness among formerly incarcerated individuals (Greenberg & Rosenheck, 2008; Sabol, Couture, & Harrison, 2007). Complicating the difficulty of economic insecurity is the limited expenditures on pre-release preparation, substance abuse treatment, job training, and skill-building programmes in prisons and jails which often decrease the chances of an individual successfully reintegrating into the community upon release (Nelson, Deess, & Allen, 1999). Consequently, formerly incarcerated individuals are released back into their home communities or neighbourhoods of origin with little or no money and without necessary identification needed to access employment opportunities or public assistance. These strains often lead to criminal activity for survival (Hammett, Roberts, & Kennedy, 2001; Nelson et al., 1999; Nelson & Trone, 2000; Travis, Solomon, & Waul, 2001). Likewise, the public's stigmatisation of people with criminal records and individuals on parole leads to disenfranchisement from employment opportunities, housing, and family and community support networks.

Moreover, a study by Holzer (2009) showed that both the employment and labour force activity of young black men have deteriorated since 1980, with a secular decline in employment for young blacks as well as a widening gap between their employment rates and those of less educated whites and Hispanics. In general, research indicates that employment outcomes of young black men continue to deteriorate over time, while their educational and behavioural outcomes lag behind those of all other demographic groups in the United States. However, Holzer (2009) sheds light on the forces that may affect employment opportunities and outcomes for young black men which include: (1) labour demand factors such as employer attitudes and hiring behaviours towards black men and (2) labour supply factors such as family formation and skill development.

Additionally, referenced in Moynihan's report, other factors that affect black male employment opportunities include: employer demand for skills which are increasing over time (through an evolving occupational structure); employer discrimination against black men; the effects of urban segregation on employer demand and employer reliance on informal networks to generate job applicants and trainees (Holzer, 2009). As such, employers are generally more averse to hiring black male applicants than those from any other racial/gender group, especially in jobs requiring social/verbal skills and in service (relative to blue-collar) occupations. The tendency of employers to locate farther away from the central city also generates a 'spatial mismatch' for those blacks who continue to reside in segregated, central-city neighbourhoods and who lack transportation to and information about suburban opportunities. And, employers frequent use of informal methods, especially employee referrals, to fill jobs that require relatively little formal education, often to the detriment of young black men (Holzer, 1996, 2001). Another crucial factor is that employers are extremely reluctant to hire men with criminal records, especially for jobs that require contact with customers, handling cash or other skills requiring employer trust (Holzer, Raphael, & Stoll, 2004; Pager, 2003). Pettit and Lyons (2007) found that initial increases in employment after prison among Washington State ex-inmates were followed by steep declines that eventually fell below pre-incarceration levels. These findings on employment and earnings suggest that the consequences of incarceration tend to persist or even intensify over time.

Analysis and discussion

Review of the limited yet important literature on formerly incarcerated African American males suggested a relationship between incarceration, difficulty in securing employment, housing inaccessibility and socio-economic insecurity. The literature spoke to the increased rates of incarceration among African American men and the lack of pre-release discharge planning for housing, education, employment and other basic necessities. Historical and emerging prejudicial and discriminatory policies and practices compounded with criminal records and low educational attainment amplifies the less likelihood of upward mobility among formerly incarcerated African American males.

The literature showed that formerly incarcerated African American males are a marginalised and underserved population in our communities particularly in terms of accessing housing, employment, mental and physical health services to facilitate their reintegration into society. Furthermore, the existing stigma and the accompanying experiences of discrimination because of a criminal record increase the chances of recidivism. Effective policies and services for this population continue to lag behind the need of this marginalised and underserved population. Anti-discriminatory and anti-oppressive theorists also acknowledged the need for consciousness towards oppression and overcoming misconceptions centred on race and the need for positive systemic reforms to address inequalities, individual and institutional racism across systems. In promoting access, equity, inclusion and reintegration of formerly incarcerated African American men, social and community development perspectives highlighted the concurrent need for individual development, structural change, socio-economic integration and institutional development.

Implications for social policy

First, effective policies and regulations are imperative to examining mass incarceration relative to sentencing guidelines and addressing the problem of the PIC that has incarcerated people of colour en masse. Returning formerly incarcerated African American men to their communities with limited resources and access, depletes human, social and financial capital and ameliorates the chances for these individuals to obtain housing, employment, education and other basic necessities.

Second, policies that offer a college education in prisons in the 1970s–1990s benefitted many individuals in terms of enhancing their own and their family's economic well-being upon release. A reinstatement of this recidivism reduction strategy or Congressional funding of similar programmes would offer great benefits to formerly incarcerated individuals. Third, funding for substance abuse and mental health treatment, alternative or jail diversion programmes for nonviolent offenders are also possible methods for reducing recidivism. Undiagnosed mental health challenges can compound the effect on one's ability to obtain and maintain adequate employment, housing, and access healthcare. Funding that help diagnose and provide treatment during and after release from the criminal justice system may be beneficial.

Fourth, the Affordable Care Act or 'Obamacare' is one viable option to ensure access to healthcare for the formerly incarcerated; however, many states are racing to amend their laws to exclude this population. Studies have shown that access to adequate healthcare is at the core of overall economic sufficiency. Finally, policies are needed to fund programs to ready inmates for life on the outside. These programmes could assist by enrolling inmates into the Affordable Care healthcare prior to release, helping them access legal documents needed for employment, and linking them with programs that provide mentorship, substance abuse and mental health counselling.

Implications for social work practice

First, practice with this underserved population in the US and around the globe requires a basic commitment to the humanity of the client as well as advocacy and collaboration with the client and other service providers in the community. Monitoring existing biases and stereotypes and keeping an open-mind will more likely result in a holistic, non-biased assessment and comprehensive treatment plan. Second, utilisation of strengths-based and empowerment approaches to hear the client's storyline, understand personal, cultural and historical factors (racism, marginalisation) and complete an unbiased biopsychosocial assessment and service plan will benefit the therapeutic relationship. Third, use of relevant code of ethics as the basis for serving this population can be universal in assisting a formerly incarcerated client to reintegrate into society. Finally, family and social supports are imperative in the reintegration process and should be considered prior to release.

Implications for social work education

Across the globe, social work education focusing on training professionals to serve formerly incarcerated individuals can benefit from inclusion of criminal justice content and other disciplinary contents in the curriculum. Connecting the two fields can help students effectively navigate the criminal justice system with and on behalf of clients who may frequent this system. The multidimensional nature of the experiences of formerly incarcerated individuals suggest the need for more in-major and continuing education training on homeless services, health care access, housing, education and employment for formerly incarcerated individuals. Also, cross-disciplinary and cross-cultural education models from countries around the world may help inform effective solutions for reintegration of returning citizens to their communities in the US.

Implications for future research

First, incarceration and reintegration into the community is a global and multidisciplinary issue that may benefit from a global and multidisciplinary conversation in which interactive and cross-country learning can occur. A longitudinal and cross-country study on the barriers experienced by formerly incarcerated black males can shed light on societal solutions to the problem. In the US, a longitudinal study would reveal the long-term readjustment experiences of African American males with prison records including the perspectives of family members, criminal justice staff and service providers who work with this population. Data can also be collected on the impact of stigma, social rejection and resultant fears on the homeless citizens' willingness to seek services and on their overall psychological functioning. Second, there needs to be a more in-depth examination of the systems and dynamics that affect formerly incarcerated African American males. More literature is needed on the effects of linking formerly incarcerated African American males with programmes that can jump-start their economic self-sufficiency. Additional information is also needed on the effectiveness of providing life skills training prior to release.

In summary, unemployment and homelessness are a few serious problems affecting the lives of formerly incarcerated African American men. Social work posits that policies and programs are imperative to reduce poverty and enhance the well-being of these citizens challenged with the consequences of incarceration serving as a barrier to self-actualisation. Multidisciplinary and multicultural solutions may be of some advantage to this underserved yet growing population.

Disclosure statement

No potential conflict of interest was reported by the authors.

References

Bradley, K. H., Oliver, R. B., Richardson, N. C., & Slayter, E. M. (2001). *No place like home: Housing and the ex-prisoner*. Issue brief. Boston, MA: Community Resources for Justice.

Burt, M., Aron, L., Lee, E., & Valente, J. (2001). *Helping America's homeless*. Washington, DC: The Urban Institute Press.

Cole, D. (2010). *No equal justice: Race and class in the American criminal justice system* (10th Anniversary ed.). New York, NY: New Press.

Cooke, C. L. (2004). Joblessness and homelessness as precursors of health problems in formerly incarcerated African American men. *Journal of Nursing Scholarship, 36*(2), 155–160.

Darensbourg, A., Perez, E., & Blake, J. (2010). Overrepresentation of African American males in exclusionary discipline: The role of school-based mental health professionals in dismantling the school to prison pipeline. *Journal of African American Males in Education, 1*(3), 196–211.

Donley, A. M. (2008). *The perception of homeless people: Important factors in determining perceptions of the homeless as dangerous*. Orlando, FL: ProQuest.

Everett, J., Chipungu, S. S., & Leashore, B. R. (Eds.). (2004). *Child welfare revisited: An Africentric perspective*. New Brunswick, NJ: Rutgers University Press.

Fontaine, J. (2013) *Examining housing as a pathway to successful reentry: A demonstration design process* (pp. 1–13). Urban Institute. Retrieved from http://www.urban.org/projects/reentry-portfolio/index.cfm

Fook, J. (1993). *Radical casework: A theory of practice*. St. Leonards: Allen & Unwin.

Gans, H. (1995). *The war against the poor: The underclass and antipoverty policy*. New York, NY: BasicBooks.

Greenberg, G. A., & Rosenheck, R. A. (2008). Jail incarceration, homelessness, and mental health: A national study. *Psychiatric Services, 59*(2), 170–177. [PubMed: 18245159].

Hammett, T., Roberts, C., & Kennedy, S. (2001). Health-related issues in prisoner reentry. *Crime Delinquency, 47*, 390–409.

Henderson, P., & Thomas, D. (Eds.). (1981). *Readings in community work*. Crows Nest: George Allen & Unwin.

Hinson, S., & Bradley, A. (2011). A structural analysis of oppression. The Grassroots Policy Project. Retrieved from http://www.strategicpractice.org/system/files/structural_analysis_oppression.pdf

Holzer, H. (1996). *What employers want: Job prospects for less-educated workers*. New York, NY: Russell Sage Foundation.

Holzer, H. (2001). Racial differences in labor market outcomes among men. In N. Smelser, W. J. Wilson, & F. Mitchell (Eds.), *America becoming: Racial trends and their consequences* (vol. 2, pp. 98–123). Washington, DC: National Academy Press.

Holzer, H. (2009). The labor market and young black men: Updating Moynihan's perspective. *Annals of the American Academy of Political and Social Science, 621*, 47–69. The Moynihan Report Revisited: Lessons and Reflections after Four Decades.

Holzer, H., Raphael, S., & Stoll, M. (2004). Will employers hire former offenders? Employer preferences, background checks and their determinants. In M. Pattillo, D. Weiman, & B. Western (Eds.), *Imprisoning America: The social effects of mass incarceration* (pp. 205–246). New York, NY: Russell Sage Foundation.

International Centre for Prison Studies. (2014). *Highest-to-lowest-prison population total*. Retrieved from http://www.prisonstudies.org/highest-to-lowest/prison-population-total?field_region_taxonomy_tid=All

Ireland, J. (2003). *Poverty in America: A handbook*. Berkley: University of California Press. *15*(5), 22–24.

Kenemore, T., & Roldan, I. (2006). Staying straight: Lessons from ex-offenders. *Clinical Social Work Journal, 34*(1), 5–21. doi:10.1007/s10615-005-0003-7

Landis, J. R. (1998). *Sociology*. Belmont, CA: Wadsworth Publishing Company.

Lee, B., & Farrell, C. (2003). Buddy, can you spare a dime? Homelessness, panhandling, and the public. *Uinrban Affairs Review, 38*(3), 299–324.

Maher, B. S., Pathak, A., Skinner, C. P., Conyers, Jr, C. J., & Bendor, J. (2013). The incarceration explosion. *Yale Law & Policy Review, 31*(2). Retrieved from http://digitalcommons.law.yale.edu/ylpr/vol31/iss2/4

Mayock, P., Corr, M., & O'Sullivan, E. (2008). *Young people's homeless pathways*. Dublin: The Homeless Agency. Retrieved from http://www.tcd.ie/chiodrensresearchcentre/assets/pdf/Publications/Homeless_Pat

Moreno, E., Patterson, P., Peirce, K., Rogers, V., Shryock, E., & Zapata, J. *Best practices for housing former offenders to promote family reunification*. Retrieved from http://www.reentryroundtable.net/wp-content/uploads/2012/08/Housing-Family-Reunification-Paper.pdf

NAACP. (2013). *NAACP supports passage of comprehensive ex-offender re-entry legislation*. Retrieved from http://www.naacp.org/action-alerts/entry/naacp-supports-passage-of-comprehensive-ex-offender-reentry-legislation

National Alliance to End Homelessness. (2014). *The state of homelessness in America*. Washington, DC: Author. Retrieved from http://b.3cdn.net/naeh/d1b106237807ab260f_qam6ydz02.pdf

National Law Center on Homelessness and Poverty. (2013). *Statistics*. Retrieved from http://www.nlchp.org/reports

Nelson, M., Deess, P., & Allen, C. (1999). *The first month out: Post-incarceration experiences in New York City* (pp. 1–31). New York, NY: Vera Institute of Justice.

Nelson, M., & Trone, J. (2000). *Why planning for release matters*. New York, NY: Vera Institute of Justice. Retrieved from http://www.vera.org

Pager, D. (2003). The mark of a criminal record. *American Journal of Sociology, 108*, 937–975.

Paiva, J. F. X. (1977). A conception of social development. *Social Development Issues, 15*(2), 327–336.

Park, R., & Burgess, E. (1925). *The city*. Chicago: University of Chicago Press.

Payne, M. (2005). *Modern social work theory* (3rd ed.). Chicago, IL: Lyceum Books.

Pettit, B., & Lyons, C. (2007). Status and stigma of incarceration: The labor-market effect of incarceration, by race, class, and criminal involvement. In S. Bushway, M. A. Stoll, & D. F. Weiman (Eds.), *Barriers to reentry* (pp. 203–226). New York, NY: Russell Sage.

Ponterotto, J. G., Utsey, S. O., & Pedersen, P. B. (2006). *Preventing prejudice: A guide for counselors, educators, and parents* (2nd ed.). Thousand Oaks, CA: Sage.

Raphael, S. (2007). The impact of incarceration on the employment outcomes of former inmates: Policy options for fostering self-sufficiency and an assessment of the cost-effectiveness of current corrections policy. In *Institute for research on poverty, working conference on pathways to self sufficiency: Getting ahead in an era beyond welfare reform*, September 6–7, 2007, University of Wisconsin, Madison.

Sabol, W., Couture, H., & Harrison, P. (2007). *Prisoners in 2006*. Washington, DC: US Department of Justice, Bureau of Justice Statistics.

Schiele, J. H. (Ed.). (2000). *Human services and the Afrocentric paradigm*. New York: Psychology Press.

Schiller, B. R. (2008). *The economics of poverty and discrimination* (10th ed.). Upper Saddle River, NJ: Prentice Hall.

Schwartz, A. F. (2013). Affordable rental housing in the United States: From financial crisis to fiscal austerity. *Housing Finance International, 27*(3), 17–24.

Shinn, M. (2007). International homelessness: Policy, socio-cultural, and individual perspectives. *Journal of Social Issues, 63*, 657–677.

Smith, E., & Hattery, J. (2010). African American men and the Prison Industrial Complex. *Western Journal of Black Studies, 4*(34), 387–398.

Travis, J., Solomon, A., & Waul, M. (2001). *From prison to home: The dimensions and consequences of prisoner reentry*. Washington, DC: Urban Institute.

United States conference of mayors. (2006). Retrieved from http://www.usmayors.org/.

US Department of Housing and Urban Development. (2007). *The annual homeless assessment report to congress*. Retrieved from http://www.huduser.org/publications/povsoc/annual_assess.html

US Department of Housing and Urban Development. (2013). *Office of community planning and development*. The 2013 Annual Homeless Assessment Report to Congress. Retrieved from: https://www.hudexchange.info/onecpd/assets/File/2013-AHAR-Part-2.pdf

US Department of Justice. (2012). *Labor force statistics*. Washington, DC: Bureau of Justice Statistics.

US Department of Justice. (2013). *Labor force statistics*. Washington, DC: Bureau of Justice Statistics.

Western, B. (2007). The prison boom and the decline of American citizenship. *Society Journal, 34*, 30–36.

Western, B. (2014). Incarceration, inequality, and imagining alternatives. *The ANNALS of the American Academy of Political and Social Science, 651*, 302–306. Retrieved from http://ann.sagepub.com/content/651/1/302

Young, V. (2006). Demythologizing the criminal black man: The carnival mirror. In R. Peterson, L. Krivo, & J. Hagan (Eds.), *The many colors of crime: Inequalities of race, ethnicity, and crime in America* (pp. 54–66). New York, NY: New York University Press.

An inside look at Israeli police critical incident first responders

Brenda Geiger

In this study 11 police first responders revealed during in-depth interviews their experience of managing critical incidents of terrorist attacks. On the way to the site, they reported getting ready, preparing for the worst and freezing all feelings to act as they were trained to do. Once on site they performed, in a robot-like manner, all operations needed to prevent further casualties and make the site safe for rescue vehicles. Once the dead and the wounded were safely evacuated they engaged in site reconstruction and allowed the public to return to their daily activities. On the way home they reported feelings of professional pride and sorrow over the dead and tried to defreeze their feelings by engaging in routine activities. Despite emotional numbing that was an integral part of their training, first responders revealed intense awareness and vivid traumatic memories of the scene which they seldom shared with family members or therapists. In this macho subculture treatment was rarely sought since it would entail stigmatisation and the preferred mode of relieving tension with the use of black humour with other team members. Most importantly, the bond uniting first responders, their feeling of being connected with something greater than themselves and to a calling from above were found essential components in their quest for meaning, coherence and purpose. These components allowed for the transformation of the intense memories of disaster and chaos into a source of resiliency and growth that strengthened their faith in their mission of saving lives.

Background

Critical incident (CI) first responders refers to trained individuals, for example, police officers and firefighters, and, at times, to untrained volunteers, who participate under life-threatening conditions in the rescue, evacuation and recovery operations pre- and post-terrorist attacks (Herbert et al., 2006; Liu, Tarigan, Bromet, & Kim, 2014). Police first responders are usually the first to arrive at the scene of the terrorist attack and manage the CI. Having police CI first responders attend my seminar on law enforcement gave me the unique opportunity to find out more about their experience of managing terrorist attacks and to inquire about the extent they were able to confront and make meaning of what was happening on the scene.

Frequency of terrorist attacks in Israel

The year of 1993 marks for Israel a turning point in the history of Islamic Fundamentalism with the Declaration of Principles signed by the Mufti of the Palestinian Authority. One of its principles sanctions, as part of the holy war-Jihad, the legitimacy of terrorist attacks on innocent civilians (Government Speaker, 2010; Israeli Ministry of Foreign Affairs [IMFA], 2005). In September 2000, year of the second Intifada [uprising], terrorist attacks originally localised in the West Bank and Gaza strip penetrated Israel (Government Speaker, 2010). From September 2000 to November 2015, the number of terrorist attacks, mainly suicide bombings targeting Israeli citizens, reached 697 with a peak of 509 suicide bombings and 1163 casualties between 2000 and 2008 (Johnston, 2015). Years 2014–2015 mark the Intifada of individuals with 136 lone wolf Jihadists stabbing, running over or stoning 311 innocent civilians and soldiers at bus stops or in their cars.

Terrorist attacks by Jihadist organisations such as Al Qaeda, and the Islamic State of Iraq and Syria (ISIS) have spread beyond the Middle East, to Iran, Pakistan and Afghanistan, and thereafter to Western countries. Al Qaeda has called upon Muslims in Iraq and Afghanistan to fight for freedom and avenge the humiliation and shame of living under occupation (Atran, 2003; Hassan, 2009). The first terrorist attack by Al Qaeda on US grounds in 11 September 2001 has resulted in the atrocities and destruction of the Twin Towers of the World Trade Center in New York. In 2013, another terrorist attack by Al Qaeda targeted the Boston marathon. Since 2013, the ISIS has used a Jihadists' ideology and state-of-the art technology to recruit and train Muslims worldwide to re-establish the Islamic Caliphate by conducting terrorist attacks (Brown, 2015; Guitta, 2015). Among such attacks were the bombing of the satirical magazine Charlie Hebdo office in Paris (2011), and a lone wolf Jihadist shooting in a Jewish school in Toulouse (2012), and in the Jewish museum in Brussels (2014). After Russia, France and other allies' 2015–2016 air attacks against ISIS in Iraq and Syria, the ISIS' more recent call is upon all Muslims in Western countries to avenge the blood of ISIS Jihadists by conducting terrorist attacks in European and US grounds. In the Fall of 2015, French and Belgium Islamic Jihadists coordinated a massive terrorist attacks in Paris shooting people in several restaurants and in the Bataclan club then crowded with people. Similarly a fervent lone wolf Jihadist in California decided to shoot disabled civilians in San Bernardino, California (Dassanayake, 2015; Onyanga-omary, 2015).

Counter-terrorist models

Up until the end of the twentieth century, counter-terrorist models were predominantly offensive and aimed at destroying the physical, economic and organisational infrastructure of terrorist organisations in the countries from which they were operating (Chalk, 1995, 1998). For this purpose, the Israeli Defense Forces launched two defensive operations: Operation Defensive Shield (2012) in the West Bank and Operation Protective Edge in the Gaza strip (2014) to destroy the infrastructure of Hamas and other Palestinian organisations and neutralise the tunnel system built in Gaza (2014).

Increasingly, however, experts in counter-terrorism strategic models recognise that the infrastructure of the Jihadist terrorist organisations Al Qaeda and ISIS is fluid and network based with more than 35 nodules of tribal organisations often likened to metastases (cancer) that spread all over the world. These characteristics increase the flexibility and operational capabilities of terrorist organisations while simultaneously limiting the impact of offensive strategies and attacks on one specific terrorist location (Crelinsten & Schmid, 1992; Pape, 2006). More recently individuals espousing ISIS Jihadist ideology have declared in a 'selfy' video their faith to ISIS before shooting innocent civilians and being themselves shot (Yaheslely, 2016); hence the eminent need to expand counter-terrorist models to include intelligence gathering and proactive strategies besides offensive ones (Avery, 2004; Perliger & Pedahzur, 2006; Sharkansky, 2003; Waugh, 2003, Yaheslely, 2016).

The proactive counter-terrorist models currently adopted in the US and Israel include the following stages: Prevention, Crisis Management and Site Reconstruction. Prevention, the first stage of this model, focuses on intelligence gathering, tightening of the borders and conducting reconnaissance activities within the country's borders to prevent the infiltration of members of terrorist organisations (Avery, 2004; Waugh, 2003). The flow of information/intelligence thanks to cooperation between local and national agencies and between the police and alert by-standers is essential in situational prevention and target hardening. By-standers are instructed to call the police anytime they identify a suspicious object, individual or activity and the police take these calls seriously and respond to them immediately. Intelligence gathering on suspected activists, activities or planned terrorist attacks gives police first responders the time to arrive at the scene and detonate bombs and/or arrest suspects before they explode themselves and shoot others (Perliger & Pedahzur, 2006; Sharkansky, 2003).

Crisis Management, the second stage of the model, focuses on the actions and operations performed by first responders when managing CIs such as terrorist/suicide bombing attacks. Police CI first responders are usually the first to enter the site of terror, to verify that the attack is over and address concerns of follow-up attacks to secure the area for safe approach of emergency medical personnel. These operations require a high level of coordination and free-flow of information between the police, and emergency personnel who will provide on-site treatment and quick evacuation of the wounded to nearby hospitals (Davis, Treverton, Byman, Daly, & Roseanu, 2004; Wise & Nader, 2002).

Site reconstruction is the last stage in the counter-terrorism model during which first responders will remove debris and repair damage to allow civilians to resume their daily routine activities. These tasks performed in proximity of the attack are to minimise the impact of terror and panic produced by terrorist attacks on civilians.

Post-traumatic stress and post-traumatic growth

CI first responders are constantly placed in situations in which they will have to confront the threat of or the actual death and injury to self or others (Karlsson & Christianson, 2003; Liberman, Best, Metzler, Fagan, Weiss, & Marmar, 2002; Tedeschi & Calhoun, 1996). The possibility of death and personal injury and the sight of the dead and of dismembered body parts and other visual, tactile and olfactory sensations are acute stressors likely to put CI first responders at risk of experiencing symptoms related to post-traumatic stress disorder (PTSD). Symptoms of PTSD may include dissociation, emotional numbing, alienation and loss of connection with others, hopelessness and lack of purpose in life. To be diagnosed with PTSD these symptoms must last more than one month and be severe enough to interfere with personal relationships, work and normal functioning (American Psychiatric Association, 2013; Chopko, 2008).

The PTSD symptoms that first responders may experience were found related to the type of life threat they had confronted. First responders who experience a direct threat to their lives are more likely to experience symptoms of dissociation and distress, nightmares, headache, faintness/dizziness and/or chest or heart pain (Marmar et al., 2006; Neylan et al., 2002). In contrast, those who experienced the loss or the threat of life of significant others, coworkers, family members, friends and especially children, are more likely to experience symptoms of depression, fear and bereavement that are often accompanied with feelings of shame and self-blame for not having saved the lives of these people (Karlsson & Christianson, 2003; Liu et al., 2014; Perrin et al., 2007).

Some research indicated that the frequency, intensity and duration of PTSD symptoms reported by first responders in the police, medical emergency care and combat units who operate under life-threatening conditions were related to the intensity of the training of these forces. Components found in common in the training of these forces were mental preparedness, numbing of feelings and task performance in a robot-like manner. These essential components of training aim at increasing the resiliency and efficient functioning of first responders under the threat of death, destruction and other forms of disaster (Grinker & Spiegel, 1963; McCauley, 2003; Reissman & Howard, 2008; Stouffer, 1965). One of the consequences of this training was reduced incidence of PTSD symptoms found among trained police, firefighters and paramedics as opposed to untrained CI volunteers. The percentage of trained CI responders meeting the diagnostic criteria of PTSD ranged between 6% and 7% and that for untrained CI volunteers ranged between 21% and 23% (Luft et al., 2012; Marmar et al., 2006; Perrin et al., 2007; Pietrzak et al., 2014, Wisnivesky et al., 2011).

Aside from the professional training, other efficient strategies were counselling and debriefing post-CI. These treatment methods were mentioned as enabling first responders reintegrate their traumatic experience and thus mitigate the PTSD symptoms that they may experience (APA, 2014; Bloom & Reichert, 1998). Nevertheless and despite the availability of treatment, CI first responders surveyed in Israel and worldwide reported seldom seeking and/or undergoing psychological treatment (Chopko, 2010; Grinker & Spiegel, 1963; Malach-Penis & Kinan, 2003; McCauley, 2003). One-fourth of the Israeli police first responders included in Malach-Penis and Kinan (2003) survey were found to exhibit symptoms of PTSD as they reported anger, indifference, fatigue and no longer being able to find a sense of satisfaction on the job. However, only 12% of the sample reported seeking professional counselling following a terrorist confrontation. These findings led Malach-Penis and Kinan (2003) to conclude that Israeli police first responders preferred to live in denial, rather than confront the debilitating effects of their traumatic experiences.

Several studies conducted with combat soldiers, police and firefighters first responders in the US have reported similar findings concerning CI first responders' reluctance to seek professional treatment. However, rather than attributing the paucity of first responders seeking treatment to denial, this finding was explained by the machismo culture to which first responders belonged. In this culture anyone undergoing treatment was condemned and stigmatised for not being a 'real man', that is, not strong enough to confront alone his traumatic experiences (Chopko, 2010; Grinker & Spiegel, 1963; McCauley, 2003; Stouffer, 1965).

More current approaches are strength based and look for the positive outcomes, and changes that may occur following traumatic events during which one is confronted with death and other life-threatening situations. Post-traumatic growth (PTG) resulting from traumatic events that have shattered one's view of the world was exhibited by a greater appreciation for life, more meaningful interpersonal relationships, and an increased sense of purpose and personal strength (Chopko, 2010; Helgeson, Reynolds, & Tomich, 2006; Hobfoll et al., 2008; Laufer & Soloman, 2006; Schorr, 2006; Tedeschi & Calhoun, 2004). Indicators of PTG have been reported by cancer patients (Schorr, 2006), combat soldiers (Benetato, 2011), CI first responders (Chopko, 2010; Freedman, 2004) and disaster survivors (Tang, 2006).

The process of PTG finds an explanation within Frankl's (1946/2006) and Antonovsky's (1987) existential framework. For these authors reality is constantly constructed, appraised and given meaning to. Individuals who face the chaos created by loss, suffering and distress are nevertheless free to create meaning, purpose (Frankl, 1946/2006) and coherence (Antonovsky, 1987) out of this chaos. Frankl (1946/2006) argued that even under the worst and dehumanising life conditions of the concentration camps man was able to detach himself from the situation, and from himself, and become responsible for himself and for the meaning he had created. Similarly, for Antonovsky (1987) the extent to which stressful and/or traumatic events will cause harm is related to whether they hurt our sense of coherence. To the extent that we can comprehend, manage and give meaning or purpose to stressful events such as death and suffering, these events will not harm us. In congruence with Frankl (1946/2006) and Antonovsky (1987), research shows that individuals who put an active effort in observing or describing a tragic event and in reflecting on its consequences were not harmed by it (Baer, Smith, & Allen, 2004; Chopko, 2010). This deliberate cognitive processing was found crucial to the quest of meaning and coherence and to revision of our schemas, allowing for the transformation of these chaotic events into sources of personal, social or spiritual growth (Calhoun & Tedeschi, 1998; Tedeschi & Calhoun, 2004).

Some of the positive or strength factors that were found to promote resiliency and growth among first responders were the support, cohesion and unity among peers on the team, their dedication to a cause and the use of humour. These components enabled first responders to collectively confront and reintegrate traumatic experiences (Jackson, 2007; Malach-Penis & Kinan, 2003; Marmar et al., 2006; Pietrzak et al., 2014; Walsh, 2007).

Additional components found to promote PTG among individuals who faced death, disasters and other life-threatening situations belong to the realm of the spiritual. They include openness to religion and to religious activities (Laufer & Soloman, 2006), and intrinsic religiousness (Linley & Joseph, 2004) and/or religious changes that do not necessarily entail the search for God or any other supernatural being (Chopko, 2010). The spiritual experience most commonly reported by first responders following a CI was a sense of connectedness to a universal presence, to something greater than oneself they had not experienced before the traumatic event (Calhoun, Cann, Tedeschi, & McMillan, 2000; Chopko, 2010; Linley & Joseph, 2004). Freedman (2004) who conducted qualitative interviews with CI firefighters in the aftermath of the 9/11 Twin Towers terrorist attack emphasised the importance of spiritual components of meaning-making of disasters. The solidarity, brotherly unity and belief in a God-given mission was found to unite 9/11 first responders in a Ground-Zero 'religion' with its own rituals. One of these rituals first responders reported engaging in is silent prayers with all those present and in communion with those who no longer were (Freedman, 2004). These components enabled CI responders to engage individually and collectively in an active quest for meaning and purpose (Frankl, 1946/2006) and to regain a sense of coherence (Antonovsky, 1987) out of the chaos created by terrorist attacks, death and suffering. Several other studies on first responders reported similar spiritual components of meaning-making that allowed to mitigate post-traumatic symptoms and were conducive to post-traumatic growth following CIs (Calhoun et al., 2000; Chopko, 2010; Linley & Joseph, 2004).

Goal of this research

The primary goal of this research was to examine the inside world of Israeli police CI first responders, their feelings, thoughts and experiences of CIs as they drove to the emergency site, managed the terrorist incident and after they left the site to resume their daily routine. Also examined was the way and extent to which the memories of traumatic incidents had transformed their world view and meaning in life, and had impacted on their relationships with coworkers, family and friends and on their mission of saving lives.

Methods

Sample

Having three police CI first responders in my seminars on law enforcement on campus gave me the unique opportunity to recruit through an informant snowball method eight additional police first responders for this study. The 11 research participants recruited were males aged between 27 and 42 years with a mean age of 34 years. They had 7–15 years of experience on the job and had responded to three or more bombing/terrorist attacks. Eight of the responders were married and had between two and five children.

Instruments

The semi-structured in-depth individual interview was chosen as the most appropriate research tool to find more about the inside world, feelings and thoughts of the research participants who were sharing the common experiences of responding to CIs. The interviews started as an informal conversation with the opening question 'Tell me about your feelings, thoughts and reactions from the moment you receive intelligence concerning a bombing/terrorist attack until the moment you manage the CI and return home?' As the conversation progressed the interview became more structured and followed an interview guide with open-ended questions to guarantee that all the interviewers would address the same topics. Aside from demographic information, topics included in the interview guide related to the feelings, thoughts and reactions of the research participants on their way to the scene, when managing the CI and on their way back home. Additional questions inquired about the skills needed to function in the midst of the disaster. The research participants were also asked about their memories of the events, the people with whom they shared these memories and the impact of these memories on their worldview, perception of life and desire to continue their mission of saving lives.

Procedure

Prior to obtaining consent, the purpose of the study was explained to the research participants, and anonymity was guaranteed. All the interviews were privately conducted by a police first responder who had previously been trained by the researcher in the art of interviewing. Being himself a first responder who had managed six bombing/terrorist attacks increased the rapport and eased the conversation between interviewer and interviewee. To allow the research participants to express themselves freely and in their own words, the sequence of the questions in the interview guide was not strictly followed. Permission to tape the interviews was obtained under the provision that the tapes would be destroyed once the interview data were transcribed and all names and identifying information were replaced by pseudonyms.

Content analysis

The analysis of the transcripts was solely based on the subjective meaning and interpretation that the CI police first responders attributed to the shared experience of responding to terrorist/bombing attacks (Denzin, 1989; Holsti, 1969). Although questions of 'objectivity' and fact validation are not objectives in a qualitative study (Bruner, 2004; Denzin, 1989; Holsti, 1969), the common themes and examples provided by the police first responders interviewed increased the reliability of the findings concerning their inner world and joint experience. Additionally, to reduce any potential bias that may emerge from having one researcher analyse the narratives, triangularity was achieved by adding an additional researcher besides the main investigator who analysed one-third of the interview narratives. Any disagreement on a topic, theme and/or category emerging from the narratives was discussed until inter-analyst agreement was reached. Finally, by including direct quotes from the narratives, the author allows the reader to comprehend the experience of CI police first responders in their own words and from their own perspective (Bruner, 1990; Lincoln & Guba, 1985; Patton, 2002).

Results

The interviewees often characterised being called to respond to a bombing/terrorist attack as a sudden transition from the on-the-job routine activities they were engaged in. In Mani's words,

> The first step is getting intelligence about the scene of terror from your commanding officers who continue to instruct you when driving to the scene of the event. (Mani)

In a split second, following the information obtained, the interviewees reported an adrenaline flow rushing throughout their body, sharpening their senses and increasing their alertness prior to switching to an automaton robot-like mode of functioning. In the words of one of the interviewees,

> The adrenaline goes up from the minute we get information from above. You feel that your pulse is beating higher, and you are excited. From then on you must proceed by the book as a robot performing all steps and procedures you have been trained to do. (Yosi)

On the way to the scene they reported getting mentally prepared by imagining the worst. In their own words,

> I prepared myself for the worst. I felt that I will see the most horrible things that I could imagine and then I prepared myself so I could function in the best possible manner. (Dany)

> We do not talk to each other. We concentrate on being prepared for the worst. (Mani)

> I prepared myself for the worst. As we were driving to the site, my only thoughts were about how to act in the best possible manner when confronting the scene. (Rami)

To the interviewees, numbing their feelings and distancing themselves from all emotions were part of becoming mentally prepared to act professionally. In such a manner they could use all their thoughts and concentrate on how to manage the CI in the most efficient and productive manner. In their own words,

> My main concerns related to my job: what I will have to do and how good I will be at performing all my tasks. At this point, the horrible sights were not of concern to me. (Rami)

> All that I was thinking about was how to help people on the site without being hurt by screws and bolts flying everywhere. (Roni)

The interviewees explained that they had been trained to perform as an automaton, in an orderly and technically efficient manner, all the operations and procedures to manage the CI. The short answers provided by the interviewees show their focus on task performance and goal achievement.

> At this point I do not feel anything. I do my job. That's it. (Moti)

> When you are on the scene of a bombing attack there really is no place for feelings. You work in a state of an automaton and concentrate only on your work. (Erez)

> The minute you arrive to the scene you start working based on what you have been trained to do, step by step, following a specific order of procedures and activities. (Dany)

Sensation of time

The interviewees emphasised the variability in their sensation of time based on the stage of the CI they had been called to manage. On the way to the site no matter how short the distance was in kilometres, time did not go by, and the minutes and seconds that it took to arrive at the site felt to them like an eternity. In their own words,

> Before you arrive time goes by like an eternity. (Yosi)

On the way to the site even when you drive with a siren and speed the feeling is that you are crawling and not moving. (Dany)

In contrast, time stopped once on the site when performing all the emergency operations. The interviewees no longer counted the minutes and seconds and no longer could estimate the time period that had elapsed on the scene. It is only when they completed all the tasks needed to manage the CI and reconstruct the site that their sensation of time returned to normal. Reuven and Rami recount,

When you are on site and you are taking care of the incident, and watch for each other, time flies without you feeling it. Afterwards, when you are finished, time comes back as normal. (Reuven)

During the evacuation time flies and afterwards time come back to routine. (Rami)

Once the CI was managed and the scene reconstructed, first responders had completed their duty. While driving back home they reported experiencing a sense of professional satisfaction mixed with guilt and sorrow over the deaths that could have been prevented had they received intelligence and/or arrived at the scene earlier. In their own words,

My feelings are satisfaction mixed with pain that the terrorist was not caught before he had succeeded to explode himself. (Yosi)

Job satisfaction, and sorrow over the dead. (Erez)

An additional feeling experienced was that of contamination. The interviewees invariably reported feeling filthy and needing decontamination or sterilisation after they left the scene. Their most intense desire was now to take a shower to remove filth. The sensations of filth and foulness remained with them for several days before they disappeared. In their own words,

Before I enter into my house I take off my clothes and throw them in the garbage. I take a long, long shower and go to sleep. (Yosi)

I go back to my routine. I think about my performance on the scene. I scrub myself and despite all the scrubbing and sterilization I continue to feel contaminated at least for several days. (Dany)

Defreezing

Once at home some of the respondents reported trying to regain a feeling of normalcy by engaging in daily routine activities and interacting with family members. Playing with their children, helping them shower and/or preparing dinner were some of these activities. In their own words,

I engage in routine tasks. I do the same things I usually do: shower, dinner and play games with the children. (Nir)

Other interviewees reported preferring to go to sleep:

I take a long, long shower and go to sleep. (Ofer)

Others reported becoming restless or withdrawn before they could start to defreeze. In their own words,

I remember one event when my girlfriend mentioned that I was behaving a little weird. (Erez)

I usually want to be left alone and withdraw into myself for a short time period. (David)

Memories of the scene: A two-layered state of consciousness

Despite the shutting of feelings and robot-like performance, first responders reported intense sensory memories of what was happening outside and inside of them, when on the site of terror. The sights, sounds and smells of the scene remained vivid for a long period of time. One of the first responders interviewed recalled the sounds of bullets exploding, of people screaming when going on fire and of him, standing there, unable to rescue them. In his own words,

> I was the first to arrive at the scene. The bus was still on fire and I could hear sounds of gunshots. Many of the soldiers who were in the bus were carrying weapons and their bullets were exploding because of the fire. This made it impossible for me to come close to the survivors in the bus who were screaming as the bus was going on fire. (Yosi)

The sight of dismembered bodies and body parts all over the scene and the unique odour of burnt bodies and blood mixed with gasoline were imprinted in their memories. Some of the first responders interviewed had tried to wear surgical masks to avoid the strong odour of burnt flesh, but soon realised that the smell was inescapable. They simply could not wipe out of their memory the smells of burnt flesh and blood mixed with gasoline. The interviewees recounted,

> Blood, a strong smell of gasoline mixed with the smell of blood, soot and ashes, the bus had totally burnt down and crashed. Dismembered body parts were scattered on the site and the remains of a baby carriage was lying there upside down. (Dany)

> I was very close to the site. I arrived first. The dead bodies were lining up on the ground and body parts were scattered everywhere. You are torn inside. The blood mixes with the water of fire extinguishers. And the smell, the unbearable smell of burnt flesh. (Nir)

While the odours of the site were inescapable, first responders reported that they often tried to avoid looking at the face of the dead and dismantled bodies lying around. By not looking at the faces, the bodies became de-personified with flesh losing its human significance. In their own words,

> I try not to look at the faces of the dead bodies. (Erez)

> I do my job and try not to look at the faces of the dismantled bodies. In so doing I avoid forming a picture of the human body of a person on the site of the bomb attack. (Moti)

To the first responders interviewed the hardest sights were those in which children were among the casualties. In their own words,

> Every event in which there are many injured and dead, especially dead children. Basically, I would erase all my memories of bombing events and give up the privilege and honor of being a first responder on the scene of terror. (Yosi)

Traumatic memories

Every single one of the first responders interviewed could describe in minute detail the vivid olfactory and visual sensory memories of the specific incident that was throwing them back to the site of horror, this time without preparedness or emotional numbing. The memories of specific incidents were reported to haunt them for days and months, if not permanently. In their own words,

> The events stay engraved in your head. If anyone says that he is used to this type of event he is not speaking the truth. These incidents stay with you. You go to sleep with them and you wake up with them. They stay with you for a long time, for days, months. It is not easy to be in them. (Yahel)
>
> The terrorist attack during which I was injured was for me a traumatic experience. It keeps on coming back. It somehow permanently affected me. (Dany)
>
> The feeling of disgust from what I saw on site and the unbearable smell of burnt flesh and blood at the scene; they stay with you for days and months. (Erez)
>
> Days and months these memories stuck to me, and would not let go of me. (Moti)

The interviewees reported that these memories would haunt them and pop in and out of their awareness for months until they started to fade out. They nevertheless reported that time heals their wounds and nightmares, and that with time their memories became fainter. In their own words,

> The vividness of the memories changes over time, but I am sure that these sights are permanently stored somewhere in my memory. (Moti)
>
> Close by to the event I could still visualize the scene of terror and the event that had occurred. After a period of time my memories got fainter and stopped haunting me. (Erez)

First responders also reported that the memories from these events had permanently changed their view of the world and the way they felt and behaved. In their own words,

> It is an experience that changes your outlook on life and leads you to behave in a different manner for the good and for the bad. (Dany)
>
> It is an experience that pushes you to remember and leads you to feel for years the feelings you felt during and after the event. (Yosi)
>
> These events make you see life from another perspective. I tell myself that these people were standing at the bus stop a minute ago. Suddenly, the terrorist who blew himself up there took their life away, simply like that. This makes you think. (Yahel)

Confronting trauma and psychological treatment

First responders reported that debriefing for post-CIs, psychological counselling and medication were available to them free of charge. In their own words,

> Anyone who wants treatment can get it. I do not know if it helps. I never went to a psychologist. (Guy)
>
> You can talk about what happened during the attack with your officer, go to the psychologist to tell what disturbs you and even obtain medication. (Erez)
>
> You can be referred to professional care and undergo treatment, if need be, so that you can continue your daily functioning. (Moti)

Despite the availability of treatment, the first responders who were interviewed seldom requested it. They often viewed psychological treatment as tinted with stigma and something to be avoided. Aware of the Machismo culture to which they belonged, the interviewees reported that going to the psychologist was a sign of weakness in their subculture and would entail gossip and a change in status among their peers. In their own words,

I would not go as far as saying that seeking treatment would result in negative labeling. But I am sure that anyone seeking treatment would become the topic of gossip among the members of the team. (Yosi)

I do not have any problem going to treatment. But, I know that any first responder who goes to a shrink is stigmatized and that the peers on his work team will change their behavior and attitude toward him. (Dany)

I do not know how much treatment helps and it is better not to know. Who goes to the psychologist! We are part of machoistic group and fulfill manly roles. If you show a drop of weakness all the snakes will be on your head and all the vampires will suck your blood. (Yahel)

Sparing family members from the details of the terror incident

Most of the first responders reported rarely sharing with family members any details of the CIs or operations they had been involved in. They wanted to spare them from the sensations and memories of the horrors they had themselves experienced. Additionally, nothing would be gained by increasing the fear, anxiety and constant worries of their dear ones as would be the case if they became aware of the risks and dangers they had been facing while on duty. In their own words,

I do not tell them anything! What will they gain from it? It is totally unnecessary. (Erez)

I avoid giving my parents any information related to my job or what is going on at the site of terror. I do not want my parents to worry about me. (Yosi)

I share with them very technical and general information such as 'I participated in the evacuation and it was interesting.' I never get into real descriptions and never go into details. I do not want them to worry. (Rami)

In some cases the interviewee reported the total support of his spouse, her readiness to listen, while in others interviewees' cases the spouse was reported to live in denial and to refuse to hear anything about the incidents.

My wife is a social worker so she knows how to listen. She supports me and tries not to ask too many details to make it easier on me. (Mani)

My wife lives in denial. She does not think, speak or ask me questions about it. She does not want to hear any description of what happened. And to my parents I do not reveal any information. (Moti)

Every first responder in this research reported feeling more at ease to share their experiences with other members on the team. The terms 'team members' and 'friends' were often used interchangeably which indicates that the members of the team were also the close friends with whom the interviewees could share their feelings and memories. In their own words,

I speak with my friends about what we did. (Dany)

I try to disconnect. I only speak about the events with those who are in the same job. (Moti)

Yes! I tell my friends on the team much more than I tell my wife. (Yosi)

Humour and cynicism

Some of the first responders interviewed reported that humour and cynicism were favourite modes of relieving tension as they reflected with other members of the team specific details of their traumatic experiences.

> I believe you must speak about what is bothering you and not keep it inside. So I speak with friends from my team who were with me in the incidents or with my commanding officer and tell them about the incidents. We do not speak with anyone who is not in the same job; they cannot relate to what we saw or experienced. (Mani)

> We usually address the events in our meeting with a lot of black humor, indirectly and tensely. (Dany)

Other first responders added that the anguish and fear that had coloured their memories of the events were seldom shared with their peers. In their own words,

> Anxiety and fear are topics that we avoid talking about because of their possible repercussions. (Yosi)

The first responders interviewed reported feeling connected to a force greater than themselves and shared the belief in a God-given mission. To them it is this force they called 'God' who regulates the course of events and decides what will happen and when. In the words of Yosi,

> He is the one who directs me to perform the right things at the right time.
> Being a person who believes in God, I know he has a central role in directing what will happen in the world.

All the first responders I interviewed regarded their work as a mission and a calling from above. It was God who guided them to do the right things when fulfilling their mission. Despite the risks, dangers, anxiety and trauma that were an integral part of their work reality, the belief that they were part of God's plan and mission gave them the strength to carry on with their calling. In their words,

> Yes, the belief in God gives power and strength. Many first responders in the police have served more than 20 years. It is their calling. (Erez)

> The belief in God helps in all life confrontations, especially during my work. (Dany)

The first responders interviewed mentioned that members of the work team who did not feel such a connection with the universe often broke down and left,

> Some of my friends broke down and were not capable of confronting the scene of horror during a terrorist attack. (Moti)

> I saw a friend who simply froze during the event and could no longer perform his job. I heard about many others who left, but I did not know them personally. (Yosi)

It was the force greater than themselves to which they felt connected that helped deal with their existential anguish in the aftermath of terror attacks. The only member of the team who did not believe in God explained,

> Yes, belief in God helps because there is always someone you may blame for what is happening in the world. (Israel)

Being called by God or something more powerful that themselves to fulfil their mission of saving lives, none of the responders felt they were a hero for performing their job. Their mission was nevertheless a source of meaning and pride.

> I feel very proud, but not a hero. (Dany)

I see my job as a mission with all the risks and dangers there are on the job. I feel as we say 'to save a soul is to save a whole world'. (Yahel)

Guy: I do not feel like a hero, it is my mission.

Interviewer: Do you feel that your friends are heroes?

Guy: Each one of us is doing his job.

I am far from being a hero, just a human being fulfilling my calling. (Yosi)

When looking at the future, most of the first responders were optimistic and had faith in a better future. Pessimism, if espoused, was short lived. The first responders interviewed believed that in the long run things would change and get better. In the words of the interviewees,

I believe that in the near future there will be a global war and afterwards we will have peace. In the long run things will get better in the Middle East. (Erez)

I believe that things will get worse before they get better. (Moti)

Discussion

This study examined the inside world of 11 police CI first responders who in their professional career had managed at least three bombing/terrorist incidents. During semi-structured in-depth individual interviews, police first responders revealed their experiences, feelings and thoughts about the terrorist attack until when they reached the scene, (2) on the scene when managing the CI and (3) on their way back home to resume their daily routine activities. In the first stage first responders mentioned the adrenaline flow they felt running throughout their body when obtaining intelligence on the terrorist attack and preparing themselves to encounter the worst as they drove to the site. At this stage, the sensation of time changed and minutes became eternity until they reached the scene. During the second stage, when managing the CI, time was reported to stop and first responders entered a numb state during which they froze their feelings to perform all operations and tasks they were trained to perform step-by-step in a robot-like automatic manner. Despite their distancing, the first responders remained intensely aware of what was happening on the scene. This intense observing and processing were particularly evident in first responders' effort to avoid looking at the faces in order to objectify the dead bodies around them.

Mental health professionals often regard numbing, splitting of affect and robot-like functioning as debilitating symptoms of PTSD that reduce lucidity and impair normal daily functioning (Malach-Penis & Kinan, 2003). In contrast, the findings of the present study show that numbing of feelings and robot-like performance were found to be an integral part of police first responders' training, allowing them to perform step-by-step the multitude of operations they were trained to perform to manage the CI despite the threat to their lives and the sight of disaster. Similar findings have been reported in research conducted with firemen responding to the 9/11 terrorist attack, paramedics, police officers and combat unit soldiers. The shared conclusion of these studies was that numbing of feelings and robot-like performance were essential tools for these units to efficiently complete the tasks and procedures they were called on to perform under life-threatening situations (Freedman, 2004; Grinker & Spiegel, 1963; McCauley, 2003; Stouffer, 1965).

The findings of this study also indicate that while police CI responders could intentionally shut off their feelings and impressions to perform their job in a robot-like manner, they nevertheless remained intensely aware of what was happening inside themselves and outside of themselves when operating in the site. Awareness of the details and dangers on the scene has been reported to be an essential component of CI management. It allowed first responders to address concerns about follow-up attacks and to secure the site and guarantee the safe passage of emergency and rescue personnel.

First responders' awareness of their feelings and thoughts and of all that was happening inside of them during the CI was evidenced by the intensity of their sensory memories reported after defreezing. A similar phenomenon has been exhibited by firefighters in the aftermath of the 9/11 bombing (Freedman, 2004). Based on interviews with 9/11 firefighters, Freedman (2004) inferred that these responders exhibited a two-layered state of consciousness. At one layer firefighters numbed their feelings and performed in a robot-like manner, and at another they remained intensely aware of what has happened internally and externally of them (Freedman, 2004).

Defreezing was another phenomenon that started to occur on the way back home from the scene. After completing their mission, CI police responders moved back from a numb, robot-like condition to a defreezing mode during which their feelings and sensory memories started to emerge. The police CI responders who were interviewed in the present study felt proud of completing their job. Yet this feeling was also mixed with regret and sorrow over the dead they had not saved. In the process of defreezing, first responders reported feelings of exhaustion and the need to sleep. Also reported were vivid olfactory and visual sensory memories, in particular the smell of burnt flesh, of blood mixed with gasoline and the sight of dismembered bodies. These memories invariably made them feel contaminated, thus the ardent wish to wash up and sterilise. Similar sensory memories have been reported by firefighters in the aftermath of the 9/11 attacks on the Twin Towers (Freedman, 2004).

Despite the attempt to resume routine activities by playing with their children, cooking or going to sleep, CI first responders reported vivid memories of the events that remained with them long after the CI had terminated. The sight of atrocities, the smell of burnt flesh and blood, children's shoes and baby carriages and people screaming while the bus was going on fire came to haunt them in their sleep and while awake. Similar nightmares were reported in the literature as symptoms of PTSD experienced by CI first responders following an imminent threat to their life and/or personal injury (Marmar et al., 2006; Neylan et al., 2002). Also reported in our findings, as in previous literature on PTSD, were the feelings of shame and guilt when children were among the casualties (Karlsson & Christianson, 2003; Liu et al., 2014; Perrin et al., 2007; Wilson, Drozdek, & Turkovic, 2006).

Congruent with past research, the first responders interviewed in the present study rarely sought professional treatment and seldom shared memories of the scene with family members, for whom they wanted to spare anxiety and worries. (Chopko, 2010; Grinker & Spiegel, 1963; McCauley, 2003; Stouffer, 1965). The low incidence of counselling may be attributed, as in previous studies, to the macho culture to which first responders belonged and to the potential threat of stigma and loss of status among coworkers as reported in previous studies (Chopko, 2010; Freedman, 2004; McCauley, 2003; Stouffer, 1965). Nevertheless and as in previous studies the support, cohesion and special bond experienced by the police CI responders with other peers on the team, the common dedication to a cause and the use of black humour allowed them to collectively confront traumatic experiences and probably mitigate the severity and duration of PTSD symptoms (Jackson, 2007; Malach-Penis & Kinan, 2003; Marmar et al., 2006; Pietrzak et al., 2014; Walsh, 2007).

Another explanation that may mitigate the traumas and the debilitating symptoms of PTSD may be related to two states of consciousness reported by Freedman (2004). Despite detachment and numbing of feelings, the police first responders in the present study, just as the firefighters in the aftermath of the 9/11 disaster, were intensely aware of what was happening inside and outside of themselves during the CIs. As reported in previous research (Chopko & Schwartz, 2009; Freedman, 2004) police first responders' intense awareness of internal and external stimuli- emotions, sights, and sounds experienced when on site of the terrorist attack and the active reflection on them were crucial components of meaning-making that allow for the transformation of their schemas and world views. This process coincides with humans' quest for meaning, purpose (Frankl, 1946/2006) and coherence (Antonovsky, 1987) out of the chaos created by loss, suffering and distress. This findings of the present study lead to the conclusion that the active reflection and meaning-making of traumatic events engaged in by police first responders allowed them to transform traumatic events and the harm they may cause into a source of personal, social or spiritual growth (Calhoun & Tedeschi, 1998; Chopko, 2010; Tedeschi & Calhoun, 2004).

Openness to religion and religious activities (Laufer & Soloman, 2006), or to intrinsic religiousness and religious changes (Linley & Joseph, 2004) and religious changes that do not necessarily entail the search for God or any supernatural being have been reported as an essential spiritual component in the quest for meaning of traumatic life events. In several studies, first responders and combat soldiers confronted with death and disaster reported a feeling of being connected to something greater than themselves and to a universal presence they never had experienced prior to the traumatic event (Calhoun et al., 2000; Chopko, 2010; Linley & Joseph, 2004). Freedman (2004) concluded based on interviews with 9/11 firefighters that the brotherly unity and the belief in a God-given mission united these responders in a Ground-Zero 'religion' that enabled them to engage individually and/or collectively in meaning-making in the aftermath of terror and disasters. Similar spiritual components were indicated by combat soldiers and cancer patients who exhibited increased resiliency and post-traumatic growth (Chopko, 2010; Helgeson et al., 2006; Hobfoll et al., 2008; Laufer & Soloman, 2006; Tedeschi & Calhoun, 2004; Zoellner & Maercker, 2006).

As in previous research the findings of this study show that religion and religiosity were additional spiritual components of meaning-making that mitigated symptoms of primary and secondary trauma, while promoting resiliency and growth (Calhoun et al., 2000; Chopko, 2010; Freedman, 2004; Linley & Joseph, 2004). Police CI first responders' belief in God and in a God-given mission allowed them to actively reflect and give meaning and coherence to the horrors they had confronted during terrorist attacks. It was God who was ordering the events and was calling on them to fulfil their mission. The spiritual connectedness of first responders with the universe strengthened their faith in a better world and gave them the strength to continue their mission of saving lives. The author of this study therefore concludes that the sense of connectedness to something greater than oneself that united first responders engaged in their mission of saving lives during terrorist attacks had the restorative power of promoting post-traumatic resiliency and growth.

Disclosure statement

No potential conflict of interest was reported by the author.

References

American Psychiatric Association. (2013). *Diagnostic and statistical manual of mental disorders* (5th ed.). Washington, DC: Author.

Antonovsky, A. (1987). *Unraveling the mystery of health: How people manage stress and stay well.* San Francisco, CA: Jossey-Bass Pu.

Atran, S. (2003). Genesis of suicide terrorism. *Science, 299,* 1534–1539.

Avery, G. (2004). Bioterrorism, fear, and public health reform: Matching a policy solution to the wrong window. *Public Administration Review, 64*(3), 275–288.

Baer, R. A., Smith, G. T., & Allen, K. B. (2004). Assessment of mindfulness by self-report. *Assessment, 11,* 191–206.

Benetato, B. B. (2011). Posttraumatic growth among operation enduring freedom and operation Iraqi freedom amputees. *Journal of Nursing Scholarship 43*(4), 412–20. doi:10.1111/j.1547-5069.2011.01421.x.

Bloom, S. L., & Reichert, M. (1998). *Bearing witness: Violence and collective responsibility.* New York, NY: The Haworth Maltreatment and Trauma Press.

Brown, A. (2015, November 18). An operative working for Islamic State has revealed the terror group has successfully smuggled thousands of covert jihadists into Europe. ***Express.*** Retrieved from http://www.express.co.uk/news/world/555434/Islamic-State-ISIS-Smuggler-THOUSANDS-Extremists-into-Europe-Refugees

Bruner, J. (1990). *Acts of meaning.* Cambridge, MA: Harvard University Press.

Bruner, J. (2004). Life as narrative. *Social Research, 71*(3), 691–711.

Calhoun, L. G., Cann, A., Tedeschi, R. G., & McMillan, J. (2000). A correlational test of the relationship between posttraumatic growth, religion, and cognitive processing. *Journal of Traumatic Stress, 13,* 521–527.

Calhoun, L. G., & Tedeschi, R. G. (1998). Beyond recovery from trauma: Implications for clinical practice and research. *Journal of Social Issues, 54,* 357–371.

Chalk, P. (1995). The liberal democratic response to terrorism. *Terrorism and Political Violence, 7*(4), 10–44.

Chalk, P. (1998). The response to terrorism as a threat to liberal democracy. *Australian Journal of Politics and History, 44*(3), 373–388.

Chopko, B. A. (2008). The relation between mindfulness and posttraumatic growth in law enforcement officers. *Dissertation Abstracts International: Section A: Humanities and Social Sciences, 68*(12A).

Chopko, B. A. (2010). Posttraumatic distress and growth: An empirical study of police officers. *American Journal of Psychotherapy, 64*(1), 55–72. Retrieved from http://search.proquest.com/docview/748828758?accountid=41977

Chopko, B. A., & Schwartz, R. C. (2009). The relation between mindfulness and posttraumatic growth: A study of first responders to trauma-inducing incidents. *Journal of Mental Health Counseling, 31*(4), 363–376.

Crelinsten, R. D., & Schmid, A. (1992). Western responses to terrorism: A 25 year balance sheet. *Terrorism and Political Violence, 4*(4), 307–340.

Dassanayake, D. (2015, January 26). Islamic State calls on Muslims in the West to carry out terror attacks and 'Shed Blood'. *Home of the daily and Sunday Express.* Retrieved May 12, 2015, from http://www.express.co.uk/news/world/554370/Islamic-State-IS-Muslim-West-terror-attacks-Abu-Mohammed-al-Adnani

Davis, L. E., Treverton, G. F., Byman, D., Daly, S., & Roseanu, W. (2004). Co-ordinating the War on Terrorism Rand Publications: see www.rand.org

Denzin, N. K. (1989). *Interpretive interactionism.* Newbury Park, CA: Sage.

Frankl, V. (1946/2006). *Man's search for meaning.* Boston, MA: Beacon press Ilse Lasch (Translator).

Freedman, T. G. (2004). Voices of 9/11 first responders: Pattern of collective resilience. *Clinical Social Work Journal, 32*(4), 377–393.

Government Speaker. (14.4. 2010). Terrorist attacks on Israel. List of terrorist attacks. Prime minister office (in Hebrew). Retrieved from http://www.pmo.gov.il/pmo

Grinker, R. R., & Spiegel, J. (1963). *Men under stress.* New York, NY: McGraw Hill.

Guitta, O. (2015, December). ISIS Jihadists returning to Europe. *World affairs.* Retrieved from http://www.worldaffairsjournal.org/article/isis-jihadists-returning-europe

Hassan, R. (2009, September 3). What motivates the bombers? Study of a comprehensive database gives a surprising answer. *Yale Global.* Yale Center for the Study of Globalization. Retrieved November 2, 2012, from http://yaleglobal.yale.edu/content/what-motivates-bombers-0

Helgeson, V. S., Reynolds, K. A., & Tomich, P. L. (2006). A meta-analytic review of benefit finding and growth. *Journal of Consulting and Clinical Psychology, 74,* 797–816.

Herbert, R., Moline, J., Skloot, G., Metzger, K., Baron, S., Luft, B., ... Levin, S. M. (2006). The World Trade Center disaster and the health of workers: Five-year assessment of a unique medical screening program. *Environmental Health*. Retrieved July 27, 2016, from http://www.ncbi.nlm.nih.gov/pmc/articles/PMC1764159/

Hobfoll, S. E., Canetti-Nisim, D., Johnson, R. J., Palmieri, P. A., Varley, J. D., & Galea, S. (2008). The association of exposure, risk, and resiliency factors with PTSD among Jews and Arabs exposed to repeated acts of terrorism in Israel. *Journal of Traumatic Stress*, 21, 9–21. doi:10.1002/jts.20307

Holsti, O. (1969). *Content analysis for social science and humanistics*. Reading, MA: Addison Wesley.

Israeli Ministry of Foreign Affairs Statistics. (2005) and other bombing/terrorist attacks in Israel since the 1993 Declaration of Principles. Retrieved from http://www.mfa.gov.il/mfa/foreignpolicy/terrorism/palestinian/pages/

Jackson, C. A. (2007). Posttraumatic growth: Is there evidence for changing our practice? *The Australian Journal of Disaster and Trauma Studies*, (Electronic Version). Retrieved from http://www.massey.ac.nz/%7Etrauma/issues/2007-l/jackson.htm

Johnston, R. (2015, October 12). *Chronology of terrorist attacks in Israel*. http://www.johnstonsarchive.net/terrorism/terrisrael.html

Karlsson, I., & Christianson, S. (2003). The phenomenology of traumatic experience in police work. *Phenomenology of Traumatic Experience*, 26, 419–438.

Laufer, A., & Soloman, Z. (2006). Posttraumatic symptoms and posttraumatic growth among Israeli youth exposed to terror incidents. *Journal of Social and Clinical Psychology*, 25, 429–447.

Liberman, A. M., Best, Z., Metzler, T., Fagan, J. A., Weiss, D. S., & Marmar, C. R. (2002). Routine occupational stress and psychological distress in police. *Policing: An International Journal of Police Strategies & Management*, 25(2), 421–441. doi.org/10.1108/13639510210429446

Lincoln, Y. S., & Guba, E. G. (1985). *Naturalist inquiry*. Beverly Hills: Sage.

Linley, P. A., & Joseph, S. (2004). Positive change following trauma and adversity: A review. *Journal of Traumatic Stress*, 17, 11–21.

Liu, B., Tarigan, L. H., Bromet, E. J., & Kim, H. (2014). World Trade Center disaster exposure-related probable posttraumatic stress disorder among responders and civilians: A meta-analysis. *PLoS One*, 9(7), e101491. Retrieved from doi:10.1371/journal.pone.0101491

Malach-Penis, A, & Kinan, G. (2003). Stress and burnout among Israel police. Ministry of Internal Security Report (in Hebrew). Retrieved from http://mops.gov.il/Documents/Publications/RD/BehaviourSocialeReaserches/StressandFatigueinworkoftheIsraeliPoliceOfficers2003.pdf

Marmar, C. R., McCaslin, S. E., Mettzler, T. J., Best, S., Weiss, D. S., Fagan, J., ... Neylan, T. (2006). Predictors of posttraumatic stress in police and other first responders. *Annals of the New York Academy of Sciences*, 1071, 1–18. doi:10.1196/annals.1364.001

McCauley, C. (2003). *Men in Combat*. Retrieved from www.psych.upenn.edu/sacsec/online/bib-agg.htm

Neylan, T. C., Metzler, T. J., Best, S. R., Weiss, D. S., Fagan, J. A., Liberman, A., ... Marmar, C. R. (2002). Critical incident exposure and sleep quality in police officers. *Psychosomatic Medicine*, 64, 345–352.

Onyanga-omary, J. (2015, January 7). Timeline: Terror attacks in Europe over the years. *USA TODAY*. Retrieved from http://www.usatoday.com/story/news/world/2015/01/07/terror-attacks-europe/21384069/

Pape, R. (2006). *Dying to win: The strategic logic of terrorism*. London: Gibson Square.

Patton, M. Q. (2002). *Qualitative research and evaluation methods* (3rd ed.). Thousand Oak, CA: Sage Publication.

Perliger, A., & Pedahzur, A. (2006). Coping with suicide attacks: Lessons from Israel. *Public Money & Management*, 26(5), 281–281.

Perrin, M. A., DiGrande, L., Wheeler, K., Thorpe, L., Farfel, M., & Brackbill, R. (2007). Differences in PTSD prevalence and associated risk factors among World Trade Center disaster rescue and recovery workers. *American Journal of Psychiatry*, 164, 1385–1394. doi:10.1176/appi.ajp.2007.06101645 17728424

Pietrzak, R. H., Feder, A., Singh, R., Schechter, C. B., Bromet, E. J., Katz, C. L., & Southwick, S. M. (2014). Trajectories of PTSD risk and resilience in world trade center responders: An 8-year prospective cohort study. *Psychological Medicine*, 44(1), 205–219. doi:10.1017/S0033291713000597

Reissman, D. B., & Howard, J. (2008, January 28). Responder safety and health: Preparing for future disasters. *Mount Sinai Journal of Medicine: A Journal of Translational and Personalized Medicine*, 75, 135–141. SecurityInfoWatch.com

Schorr, Y. H. (2006). Quality of life after exposure to trauma: Moving beyond symptom assessment and exploring resilience factors. *Dissertation Abstracts International: Section B: The Sciences and Engineering, 67*(2-B).

Sharkansky, I. (2003). *Coping with terrorism: An Israeli perspective*. Lanham: Lexington Books.

Stouffer, S. A. (1965). *The American soldier*. New York: John Wiley & Sons.

Tang, C. S. (2006). Positive and negative postdisaster psychological adjustment among adult survivors of the Southeast Asian earthquake-tsunami. *Journal of Psychometric Research, 61*(5), 699–705.

Tedeschi, R. G., & Calhoun, L. G. (1996). The posttraumatic growth inventory: Measuring the positive legacy of growth. *Journal of Traumatic Stress, 9*, 455–471.

Tedeschi, R. G., & Calhoun, L. G. (2004). Target article: "Posttraumatic growth: Conceptual foundations and empirical evidence". *Psychological Inquiry, 15*, 1–18.

Walsh, F. (2007). Traumatic loss and major disasters: Strengthening family and community resilience. *Family Process, 46*, 207–227. doi:10.1111/j.1545-5300.2007.00205.x17593886

Waugh, W. L. (2003). Terrorism, homeland security and the national emergency management network. *Public Organization Review, 3*, 373–385.

Wilson, J. P., Drozdek, B., & Turkovic, S. (2006). Posttraumatic shame and guilt. *Trauma, Violence and Abuse, 7*, 122–141. doi:10.1177/1524838005285914

Wise, C. R., & Nader, R. (2002). Organizing the federal system for homeland security: Problems, issues, and dilemmas. *Public Administration Review, 62*(Special Issue), 44–57.

Wisnivesky, J. P., Teitelbaum, S. L., Todd, A. C., Boffetta, P., Crane, M., Crowley, L., ... Herbert, R. (2011). Persistence of multiple illnesses in World Trade Center rescue and recovery workers: A cohort study. *Lancet 378*(9794), 888–897.

Yaheslely, Z. (August, 2016). ISIS the next Gereration: Vengance against the West. (2nd Episode). *Nana10 News*. Retrieved from https://www.youtube.com/watch?v=bJMHwFnv7RU

Zoellner, T., & Maercker, A. (2006). Posttraumatic growth in clinical psychology – A critical review and introduction of a two component model. *Clinical Psychology Review, 26*, 626–653.

Tackling sexual violence at UK universities: a case study

Graham Towl

There has been international and national concern about the prevalence rates and impacts of sexual violence [Towl, G. J., and Crighton, D. A. (2016). The Emperor's new clothes? *The Psychologist, 29*(3)]. In recent years this area has been brought into sharper focus in Higher Education. The film 'The Hunting Ground' shone a light on this area and particularly the inadequate responses of North American university administrations to the problem. The film has recently been shown widely at Australian universities and the same is the case in the UK. There have been concerns reported that university leaders are fearful of the perceived repetitional (and potentially financial) damage associated with high report rates of sexual violence. At Durham University the starting premise was a recognition that the problem of sexual violence is a societal problem and one that universities have an important role to play in addressing. In this paper I contest the premise that high levels of sexual violence reporting at universities will necessarily result in reputation damage. Indeed on the contrary this case study account makes a compelling case that the contrary is true. I argue that both the civic and educational responsibilities of universities are such that it is essential that such matters are addressed. This, ethically, is especially so in view of what we know about the under reporting of sexual violence and also the potential physical and mental health impacts. Much of the focus is on prevention. Contributions can be made to prevention, it is argued, through increased reporting and also potentially through bystander intervention initiatives and consent workshops. A key benefit of increased reporting is that if universities know there is a problem there is the opportunity to help. An underlying principle to policy and practice development in this challenging area is the empowerment of those with trust in us to make such reports.

Nationally and internationally there are growing concerns about sexual violence (Abrahams, et al., 2014) and this extends into Higher Education Institutions too where there has been a focus upon student perspectives (Vidu, Schubert, Munoz, & Duque, 2014). The film 'The Hunting Ground' has been shown at a number of UK universities and is currently being

---

The views expressed are those of the author and may not necessarily reflect the views of Durham University. Members of the Durham University Sexual Violence Task Force: Professor Tom Allen, Courtney Caton, Sam Dale, Sophie Daniels (from janauary, 2016) Caroline Dower (from April, 2016) Hannah Francis (until December, 2015) Esther Green, Professor Clare McGlynn, Professor Graham Towl (Chair) and Professor Nicole Westmarland.

shown at universities across Australia having been made in the US highlighting the financial interests associated with, for example, university sports teams and culture (McCray, 2014). The film highlights a number of cases, which serve to illustrate poor university responses to individual reports from students of sexual violence. The poor responses are presented as being driven by the institutional need to protect the financial and reputational interests of the universities included. The North American literature is better developed than in the UK with a number of reviews having been undertaken in this challenging area (e.g. McCaskill, 2014). Universities UK are due to report on this area to the sector and government in Autumn, 2016 (Home Office, 2016). In 2015 at Durham University, a Task Force on Sexual Violence was set up with the former Chief Psychologist at the Ministry of Justice, and PVC for Student Experience, as the Chair. This case study of the work of the Task Force is set in the broader context of the Higher Education sector and Criminal Justice System. Our starting premise was that sexual violence is a problem across society and that there would be no reason why we would expect this not to be the case at universities.

Educational and civic responsibilities of university communities

Universities have a range of civic responsibilities as well as some specific educational responsibilities to their students. The former is sometimes contested whereas the latter seems axiomatic. In terms of some of the civic responsibilities, these include contributing to community safety, rights and responsibilities. Young women do not always feel safe in UK society and institutions in receipt of public funding, in particular, each have a role in tackling such inequalities (End Violence Against Women Coalition [EVAWC], 2015; Home Office, 2016). Below, I begin by addressing the importance and practical implications of some of the educational responsibilities of universities in relation to sexual violence. I then move onto the importance of civic responsibilities. After making the case for universities tackling this challenging area I go on to describe some of the work of the Task Force, to include issues of implementation and future directions for research, policy and practice.

The aftermath of sexual violence can involve the experience of a range of adverse health effects, both physical and psychological. Unmet mental health needs can, in turn, result in our students being unable to reach their full potential whilst at university. Student support services have increasingly experienced increases in requests for support in response to reports of mental health related problems (Universities UK, 2015). Student mental health needs have perhaps not had the profile they should have in terms of a wider recognition of prevalence rates in the past (Towl, 2013a, 2013b). There is a clear duty on universities to ensure that their students are able to achieve their full educational potential. Those mental health needs which are as a direct, or indirect, result of sexual violence, may very well not come to the attention of higher educational institutions in view of the well documented under reporting of sexual violence. The evidence for under reporting is largely based upon the results of confidential surveys of rates of victimisation. These show marked differences in the numbers of cases reported to the police compared with those reported anonymously as part of, for example, the Crime Survey for England and Wales, which uses an anonymous self-report measure of experiences of sexual violence (MoJ, HO, & ONS, 2013).

Such evidence of high rates of unreported sexual violence, along with the serious harms caused is of fundamental importance in contributing to the argument for the need for university communities to enact their civic duties in both improving the prevention of sexual violence and also ensuring that those reporting sexual violence get the appropriate support along with respondents. We know that sexual offences are very significantly under reported as indicated above. Universities are uniquely well placed in some key ways to help address this issue of the under reporting of sexual violence. The level of risk of being the victim of sexual violence appears to differ markedly by gender and age. Young women appear to be at the highest level of risk. A growing and significant number of our students are young women and they are at greater risk of being victims of sexual violence. Perpetrators of sexual violence also appear to be disproportionately young men. University student populations tend to be characterised by both the 'high risk' victim and perpetrators. There may also be additional environmental factors impacting upon behaviour. For example, for many young adults university is the first time that they have been away from their parents in their own accommodation with new sets of responsibilities for themselves. We may hypothesise that adaptation to such a transition may add some additional vulnerability to a risk of sexual violence. In terms of our civic responsibilities if we know, as we do, that there is a higher risk of sexual violence taking place in university communities then it is surely incumbent upon us to address this, especially in view of the problem of reported cases representing only a small percentage of actual cases. And these considerations serve to further strengthen the argument for the civic responsibilities of university communities to take actions to address sexual crime.

If university communities are able to increase reporting rates there are two clear benefits. First, this gives the potential to ensure that the educational support needs of victims may be met along with, subject to agreement by the victim, the possibility of reporting the incident to the police with a view to criminal prosecution and subsequent potential imprisonment of perpetrators. Second, if report rates rise, such that potential offenders know that the chances of being reported whilst at university are appreciably higher than they would be in society in general then this may have, in some cases, a deterrence impact and hence contribute to prevention. Recent reviews of the evidence about the efficacy, or otherwise, of sex offender 'treatment' on reoffending show disappointing results regarding the efficacy of such interventions (e.g. Towl & Crighton, 2016). Given the generally low levels of prosecution and conviction for sexual crime, there is an arguably disproportionately high level of additional societal benefit from a robust targeting upon prevention.

Much of what is sometimes claimed that we know about sex offenders is derived from research with imprisoned convicted sex offenders (Towl & Crighton, 2016). It may be that this group is a sub sample of the population of sexual offenders in that there may well be some systematic differences between those individuals who get caught, prosecuted and convicted and those who do not. Given that one of the purposes of universities is to contribute to our knowledge, this is an area of wider interest too. One research question may be what are the differences and commonalities in these groups of offenders? Such potential differences may be dispositional or situational or indeed both. It was outside the remit of the work of the Task Force to examine this area further but nonetheless the work in this respect has helped to raise some interesting and broader questions for the forensic psychology field. We know from various studies that abuse may be more likely to happen in the case of particularly steep differences in the gradient of power relationships both for individuals and organisations. University graduates will disproportionately go on to positions of power and responsibility. In view of that it is arguably all the more important that their time at university includes a culture, which has absolute clarity around the unacceptability of sexual violence. And, as outlined below graduates need to have the confidence and skills to intervene as bystanders if they see a third party being victimised.

Sexual Violence Task Force (SVTF)

Consistent with the above the Task Force sought to focus upon the prevention of sexual crimes whilst also ensuring improved services and support for those reporting sexual violence to members of the university community. One key underlying operating principle that we found useful, was that of victim empowerment. Empowerment in coming forward and reporting to our university community and empowerment in terms of how, as an institution, we worked with students reporting sexual violence to ensure appropriate emotional support and to address any relevant educational needs. The principle of victim empowerment provided a key test of our procedures and processes whilst also being a useful check against which proposals for improvements could be judged.

We undertook consultation over a period of around 12 months, which informed the iterative development of our recommendations and some implementation of changes over this period, for example, improved resources such as more sessions from Rape Crisis. Colleagues from the police, County Council, Sexual Assault Referral Centres (SARCs) and student activist groups were all consulted along with staff and students more broadly. We also ensured that we heard the voices of those who had reported sexual violence to the institution and in particular what had worked well and what had not. We commissioned a rapid evidence review undertaken by colleagues in our School of Applied Social Sciences. We also ensured that the work of the SVTF was included and updated on the university website.

We quickly identified a number of areas of work for investigation and development; policy and procedures, support and publicity of services, generating culture change and disclosure training, reporting and resourcing.

Our major conclusion in relation to the assessment of our policies and procedures to address sexual violence, those of other universities and the feedback from our consultation processes, indicated strongly the need for a separate and specialist sexual violence and misconduct set of procedures as part of our new policy. Whilst this is an innovation to some degree it simply serves to codify our emergent practices over the year. Two key further innovative elements of the emergent policy are; First, a clear message that we will undertake an internal assessment through a case management-based approach in each case which is individually reviewed to investigate a breach of our policies and also address any safeguarding issues. This would still be so even if the criminal justice process has concluded with a not guilty verdict or made a decision of no further action. This is partly in recognition of the differing levels of evidence required in terms of our internal assessments as a civil level of proof on the balance of probability rather than the criminal level of proof, which is beyond all reasonable doubt. It is also because we recognise our duty of care to students who have trusted us enough to make such reports. So, at a case management meeting we would assess what actions we need may need to take and this would include potential restrictions upon the respondent (or alleged perpetrator in Criminal Justice terms). Second, that we will undertake internal assessments when the reporting party does not wish to report matters to the police but does want something done to reduce the risk of further assault or intimidation by the perpetrator, in order to establish if there has been a breach of our internal policies. Both of these aspects of our approach reflect the underlying principle of empowering the reporting party. This is a challenging area where we are conscious that in a number of respects this is breaking with the previously received policies and practices in this challenging area. Additionally, we do not lose sight of our responsibilities, and in particular, duty of care, towards respondents, those who stand accused of sexual violence. We ensure that there is access to counselling (and educational) support for those going through the challenging process of being a respondent in such cases.

Another feature of our approach involves working with specialist providers of relevant services. Upon review we increased our contract with our local Rape Crisis service to facilitate improved support for those students reporting sexual violence to us as a university community. Additionally we are seeking further specialist training for our counselling staff in working with students who report experiences of sexual violence either whilst they are at university or in terms of their experiences prior to attending university. The recommendation for a full time member of staff with a remit solely around sexual violence has been another service innovation, which has been implemented for our students with the recruitment of a new member of staff to work solely in this challenging area. This will be especially helpful with regard to the extensive training and educational programmes that are rolling out across the institution. In particular consent training, bystander awareness and disclosures training will be the three areas of focus working with the Students' Union. This combination of educational programmes is intended to impact upon the university community culture as well as address the specific issues reflected in the module titles. It is recognised that there is a compelling need to work closely alongside the Student Union in acknowledgement of their expertise, the power of peer persuasion and the responsibility of the university to both the educational and civic. Additionally, we have raised awareness amongst students and staff about how to access services.

Improving reporting processes and encouraging victims to report at the university remains a critical element of the approach. As indicated above, increased reporting means potential opportunities for support and, subject to this being what the respondent wants to pursue, the possibility of the perpetrator being sentenced and imprisoned. But it is important to stress that the approach is predicated on the empowerment of those making reports hence the decision to proceed to the police remains with them. Individuals making such decisions can withdraw their consent at any time. There are different levels of potential reporting. For example, an anonymous reporting facility may very well illicit higher prevalence rates. Student listening services such as Nightline and university counselling services may well hear of more cases than are formally reported to universities. But such rates need, if possible, to be tracked to further inform institutional responses.

One core theme from the consultations undertaken was the importance of transparency of process. For example, the need for universities to record the number of cases of sexual violence reported with an outline of actions taken. Reporting levels can be used as one measure of institutional success in tackling sexual violence. In particular higher reporting levels demonstrate an increase in student trust in the institution. For prospective students it demonstrates that student safety and support is taken very seriously. And this is not just from the perspective of the institution. For example, the 'End Violence Against Women' group recommends that universities and colleges address violence against women students by monitoring levels of violence, linking in with specialist support services, staff training, developing policies with staff and students with clear response procedures and a commitment to bystander intervention training (EVAW, 2015). We have welcomed and are implementing such guidance as reported above and below.

One key challenge has been appropriate resourcing. Ethically this becomes even more pertinent as the work of the Task Force has become more widely known. In other words the increased transparency of services may very well (and we would hope that it would) lead to greater demands upon service provision. Resource allocation speaks loudly to the level of institutional commitment perceived across the culture of the organisation. Our response to the challenge of sexual violence has been to recognise that it is a societal problem usually left largely to Criminal Justice agencies to address. We recognise that Higher Education as a sector is uniquely well placed to contribute to addressing, working alongside our partners at the police, Sexual Assault Referral Clinics, Rape Crisis, It Happens Here, Nightline, Student Union and Feminist societies. Together we have begun to make a difference.

Disclosure statement

No potential conflict of interest was reported by the author.

References

Abrahams, N., Devries, K., Watts, C., Pallitto, C., Petzold, M., Shamu, S., & Garcia-Moreno, C. (2014). Worldwide prevalence of non-partner sexual violence: A systematic review. *The Lancet, 383*(9929), 1648–1654.

End Violence Against Women Coalition. (2015). *Spotted: Obligations to protect women students safety & equality*. London: Bahá'í International Community.

Home Office. (2016). *Ending violence against women and girls, strategy 2016–2020*. London: HM Government.

McCaskill, C. (2014). *Sexual violence on campus*. Columbia: U.S. Senate Subcommittee.

McCray, K. L. (2014). Intercollegiate athletes and sexual violence; a review of literature and recommendations for future study. *Trauma, Violence & Abuse, 16*(4), 438–443. doi:10.1177/1524838014537907

Ministry of Justice, Home Office & the Office for National Statistics. (2013). *An overview of sexual offending in England and Wales*. London: Statistics Bulletin.

Towl, G. J. (2013a). Student mental health; Below the radar? *Evidence Based Mental Health, 16*, 1.

Towl, G. J. (2013b). Student mental health: A cause for concern? *Evidence Based Mental Health, 16*, 29.

Towl, G. J., and Crighton, D. A. (2016). The emperor's new clothes? *The Psychologist, 29*(3), 188–192.

Universities UK. (2015). *Student mental wellbeing in higher education: Good practice guide*. Available from http://www.universitiesuk.ac.uk/policy-and-analysis/reports/Pages/student-mental-wellbeing-in-higher-education.aspx

Vidu, A., Schubert, T., Munoz, B., & Duque, E. (2014). What students say about gender violence within universities: Rising voices from the communicative methodology of research. *Qualitative Inquiry, 20*(7), 883–888.

Index

Entries in **bold** denote tables; entries in *italics* denote figures.

9/11 terrorist attacks 2, 22–3, 43, 133, 136, 144–6

abortion, reckless 68
active shootings 8, 18n2
ADF (Augmented Dickey–Fuller) 53, 55–8
adolescent sexting 101–2
adolescent sex workers: drug use by 67–8, 77; in Lagos 71–3, **72**, 78; motivation of 69–71, **74**, **75**; in Sub-Saharan Africa 66–7, 73; worldwide research on 65–6
adrenaline flow 138, 144
Affordable Care Act 128
African-Americans: and criminal justice system 3, 80–4, 87–8; dehumanization of 11; employment of 126–7; ex-prisoners 4, 121–9; masculinity of *see* Black masculinity; Rodger on 14–15
Afrocentric paradigm 121–4, 130
AI (anticipatory injustice) 80–1
AKP (Adalet ve Kalkinma Partisi) 40
alcohol: Islamic prohibition on 3, 33, 36–7, 41–3; and sex workers 67–8, 77; in Turkey 38–9
al Qaeda 133
American Indians *see* Native Americans
American way of life 2, 22–9
anomie theory 68–71
anti-ascetic theory 34, 43
anxiety, for first responders 142–3
Atatürk, Mustafa Kemal 35
augmented reality 92
authority: and cybercrime 93, 99; masculine claims to 10, 13

Belgium 116, 118, 133
bitcoin 98
black market 94, 97–8
Black masculinity 14
Bor, Turkey 38, 41–2
BPI (British Phonographic Institute) 98, 100
Breivik, Anders 19n5
brothels, in Nigeria 3, 71–2, 75, 77
Bulgaria, organised crime in 112–13, 116–17
Bundy, Ted 19n8

burglary 52–5, 58, 61, 113
bystander intervention 5, 150, 154
bystanders, and counter-terrorism 134

CAM (Child Abuse Material) 94, 97, 100–3
CBT (criminal breach of trust) 53, 55, 58, 61
CDA (critical discourse analysis) 7–8, 12
cheating: as crime in India 52–3, 55, 57, 61–2; in exams 38
child labour 74
child pornography *see* CAM (Child Abuse Material)
children: dead 140; sexual abuse of 94, 100
CHNM (culpable homicide not amounting to murder) 55, 61
CHP (Republican People's Party) 35, 40
Christianity 33, 37, 44, 72
CIs (critical incidents) 132, 134–9, 142, 144–6; *see also* first responders; terrorism
cognitive distortions 10–11
Columbine shootings 11, 19n5
consciousness, two-layered 140, 145
consent training 5, 150, 154
contamination 139
copyright infringement 91, 94, 97–8, 100, 102–3, 116
corporate social responsibility 97
counterfeiting 52–3, 55, 57–8, 61, 114
counter-terrorist models 133–4
Crash-for-Cash rackets 114
credit cards, stolen 98
crime: rational utility approach to 54; social implications of 1–5
crime rates: definition of 55; economic theory of 68–9; natural 3, 5, 52–4, 58, 61
criminal records, social consequences of 123, 125–7
Crisis Management 134
curiosity, and cybercrime 95–6
cybercrime 4; categories of 95–6; organised 116; policy and policing 102–3; reactions to 93, 96–7; social impact of 91–2, 98–9, 103; use of term 94

INDEX

cyberpsychology 92, 102–3
cyber security 92–4, 96–7
cyberspace 5; human interaction in 92–3; as lawless 96; policing of 103
cycles of offending 5
cynicism 88, 142

dacoity 52–3, 55, 58, 61, 62n2
DarkMarket 98
dark net 94
data matching 112, 114
DDoS (Distributed Denial of Service) 94–5
Deep Web 97–8
defreezing 132, 139, 145
dehumanisation 11, 135
deprivation, relative 68–9
deterrent measures: and case clearance 81; effectiveness of 3, 52, 54; religion as 37, 41–2; and sexual violence 152
deviance: anomie theory of 70; life-time 37–8, 41–3; sociological theories of 34
disclosures training 153–4
discrimination 81, 122–3, 125–7
disenfranchised communities 4
dissociative imagination 93
DP (Democrat Party, Turkey) 35
drugs: buying on deep web 97–8; EU response to 117; and organised crime 112–15; in Turkey 38
drug use: and criminality 74, 75, 77; and religion 34, 36; by sex workers 3, 65–9, 67, 75–6
Durham University 150–1

École Polytechnique de Montréal 13, 19n10
economic crimes 61, 119
emotive language 15–16
empowerment 122, 128, 150, 153–4
End Violence Against Women 154
ethnic minorities, in United States 2, 80–2, 123–4
EU (European Union): and cybercrime 103; homicides in 116–17; organised crime in 110–14, 115, 118
Eurasian ethnicity 8, 15
Eurocentrism 123
Europol 97, 102, 111, 117, 119
exhaustion 145
ex-prisoners, and housing 122–3

family members: of adolescent sex workers 73; of ex-prisoners 121, 128; of first responders 132, 139, 142
fate, belief in 39
FBI (Federal Bureau of Investigation): on cybercrime 96; and homicide investigations 81, 88; on mass shootings 8, 18n2, 19n7
fear, for first responders 134, 142–3
feelings, numbing of 135, 138, 144–5
feminist linguistics 7, 12
file-sharing 98–100

first responders, impact of experiences on 4–5, 132, 134–7, 139–46
framing 7–8, 11–12, 18
Frankfurt School 12
Frankl, Viktor 135
fraud: as cybercrime 91, 94; and organised crime 4, 111–14
Freud, Sigmund 5
friends: deviant 40; of different sects 40, 42
frontier justice 93–4
FUSE (Frequent User Service Enhancement) 126

G7 countries, natural rate of crime in 54–5
'Game of Thrones' 100
gender, and homicide victims 10, 82–3, 88
Ghana 65
globalisation, of criminality 4
God-given mission 136, 143–4, 146
Gülen movement 36, 46
gun-related homicide 82, 86, 116
guns: and masculinity 9; in Turkey 38–9
Gun Violence Archive 8, 18n4

hacking 38, 91, 93–7
harbouring of criminals 65, 68, 76–7
harms, character of 119
Hausa/Fulani ethnic group 73
headscarves 23
hegemonic masculinity 7, 9–11, 13, 17–18
herd immunity 93
heterosexuality, and masculinity 9, 13–14, 16–18
HIV/AIDS 68, 77
homelessness 4, 121–2, 125–6, 128–9
homicide: case clearance 3, 80–3, 85, 86–8; and organised crime 116–17
housing, and ex-prisoners 122–3, 125–7
HUD (US Department of Housing and Urban Development) 121, 123, 125–6
human trafficking 113–16
humiliation 15, 133
humour, black 132, 136, 142–3, 145
'The Hunting Ground' 150
hysteresis 53

identity theft 94, 98
Igbo ethnicity 71–3
impulsive crime 34, 43
incarceration, consequences of 4, 121–2, 124–9
India, crime rates in 3, 52–3, 55, 58–62
inequality: and crime 52–4, 61; and discrimination 122; and incarceration 125; and mass shootings 2, 9, 12, 17–18; structural 69–70
insecurity 72, 113, 126–7
institutional development 123, 127
institutional trust 81
instrumental crimes 3
intelligence gathering 133–4, 144
intergroup contact, and prejudice 24–30

INDEX

Internet, as public space 4
ISIS (Islamic State of Iraq and Syria) 133; *see also* terrorism
Islam: and crime 2–3, 33–4, 36–7, 42–4; in Turkey 35–6; US attitudes to 22–3, 30; *see also* Muslims
Isla Vista, California 7, 12, 16
Israel: counter-terrorism in 134; first responders in 4, 135–6; terrorist attacks in 132–3
Italy, organised crime in 112–13, 116–18, 120

J-CAT (Joint Cybercrime Action Taskforce) 102
jihadist organisations 43, 133
JSTOR 95

KA (kidnapping and abduction) 53, 55, 57, 61–2

labelling theory 95
Lagos, sex workers in 3, 65, 68–9, 71–2
Latinos 23, 124
law enforcement: African-American attitudes to 3, 82, 88; and cybercrime 94, 96, 102
Lee-Strazicich test 53–4, 56–7, **59–60**
LM (Lagrange Multiplier) 53, 56–7

macho subculture 132, 135, 141–2, 145
Mafia-type associations 111–13, 116–18
malware 91, 94–6, 103
marijuana 37, 67–8, 75, 96
masculinity: fragile 9; and mass shootings 7–8, 11; in "My twisted world" 13–17; and positioning theory 10; *see also* hegemonic masculinity
mass shootings 2, 7–8, 10, 13, 18n2, 19n5
meaning-making 135, 137, 146
medication, psychoactive 141
mental health: and ex-prisoners 121, 125–8; impact of sexual abuse on 150–1; and mass shootings 10–11
Merton, Robert K. 70
metamessages 12, 18
MHP (Milliyetçi Hareket Partisi) 40
migration, illegal 115
Mitnick, Kevin 93, 95
money laundering 110, 113–14, 117–18
moral community theory 34, 37, 43
moral panics 117
murder: and authority 10; in India 55; by sex workers of clients 68; *see also* homicide
Muslims, prejudice against 2, 22–30, **27–8**, 95; *see also* Islam
"My twisted world" *see* Rodger, Elliot

Napster 98–9
narratives, discursive approach to 11–12, 15
Native Americans 81
nativism 22–30
Netherlands 102, 118
newspapers, in Turkey 35, 39–40, 42–3

Nigde, Turkey 37–8, 41–3
Nigeria: and anomie theory 70; poverty and unemployment in 69; sex workers in 3, 65, 67–9, 73, 77–8; *see also* Lagos
normlessness *see* anomie
NRC *see* crimes rates, natural
NRH (natural rate hypothesis) 53

online disinhibition 92–3, 99, 101
organised crime: cost of responses to 117; costs of 110–16, **115**, 118–19; exposure to 4; measurement of 110; perceptions of 113–14; and sex work 77; as shadow state 117; transnational action against 118–19; use of term 111–12
Oyingbo community 71–2

Palestinian territories, occupied 133
parochial costs 113, 118
payment card fraud 113–14
peer group influence 34, 69, 73, 99
Peltzman effect 93
PESTLE (Political, Economic, Social, Technological, Legal and Environmental) framework 112
PIC (Prison Industrial Complex) 124, 127
piracy *see* copyright infringement
The Pirate Bay 98, 101
police expenditure 52, 54
political identity 40–1, 43
Ponzi fraud 113, 118
positioning 7–11, 13
poverty: and African-Americans 125–6; and case clearance 86–8; and crime 52–4, 68–9; and ex-prisoners 129; and homicide victims 80; in India 61, 62n7
pride, professional 132
privacy paradox 102
private costs 113, 118
procedural justice 81
proof, civil and criminal levels of 153
property-related crime 3, 54–5, 61, 94
prostitution *see* sex workers
psychological treatment 135, 141–2, 145, 153
PTG (post-traumatic growth) 134–6, 146
PTSD (post-traumatic stress disorder) 134–5, 144–5
public costs 113, 118

Qur'an 36, 39–40

racial hierarchy 13–17
racism 18, 122, 127–8
rage 11, 14–15, 17
Ramadan 44
ransomware 96, 112
rape: and human trafficking 115; in India 55; and murder 10
recidivism 122, 126–8

INDEX

religion: and crime 2–3, 34–7, 39, 41–3; and first responders 136, 146
Religion and Diversity Survey 23–4, 30
religious symbols 40–1
resiliency 132, 135–6, 146
RIAA (Recording Industry Association of America) 99
risk homeostasis 93
ritual perpetrations 68, 75, 77
robbery: in India 54–5, 58, 62n2; by sex workers 65
Rodger, Elliot 7–8, 12–17, 18n1, 19n9
rootkits 96
Russia: cybercrime in 96; Middle Eastern interventions of 133; religion and crime in 36

SARCs (Sexual Assault Referral Centres) 153
schizophrenia 11
school dropouts 125
Scotland, organised crime in 113
secular social disorganisation theory 34
security, false sense of 93
self-positioning 10, 12, 14
September 11, 2001 terrorist attacks *see* 9/11
sex offenders 101, 152
sexting 101–2
sexual abuse: of children 94, 100; on university campuses 5, 150–4
sex workers 3, 65–6, 72, 75, 77, 79; categories of 66; and criminality 3, 5, 65, 75, **76–7**; income of **73**; motivations of 69–70; and organised crime 114; risk behaviours by 67; *see also* adolescent sex workers
Silk Road website 98
site reconstruction 132, 134
slavery 13–14, 113, 115–16
social and community development 123–4
social control 34, 70
social engineering 95
social impact, use of term 91–2
social integration 34–5
social justice 80, 82, 87–8, 102
social learning theory 34, 99
social networking, and child pornography 101
social work, and ex-prisoners 128
sociocultural ways of telling 12
spyware 96
stalking 94
stigma: and ex-prisoners 121–2, 126–8; and mental health 11, 141, 145; and sex workers 67, 72
street fighting 68, 77
structural breaks 52–8, 61–2, 62n3
substance abuse, and ex-prisoners 125–6, 128
suicide bombing 133–4
SurfWatch 94
SVTF (Sexual Violence Task Force) 152–3
Swartz, Aaron 95
Sweden 99, 118

tagging 95
terrorism: fear of 2, 22–8, 30; impact on first responders 4, 134, 136–43, 146; Islamic extremist 132–3
theft: in India 52–5, 58, 61; and religiousness 34; by sex workers 77
thematic analysis 7–8, 12–13
time, sensation of 138–9, 144
Tor browser 97–8
traditional American values *see* American way of life
trans-disciplinarity 92
traumatic memories 132, 135–6, 140–3, 145–6
Trojans 95–6
Turkey: Islam and crime in 2–3, 41–4, **46–51**; religion and secularism in 33–6, 39–40

UAVs (Unmanned Aerial Vehicles) 103
UCR (Uniform Crime Reporting) 82–3, 88
UK (United Kingdom): CAM in 101; file-sharing in 98, 100; natural rate of crime in 54; organised crime in 111, 114, 117–18; people smuggling to 115–16; policing cybercrime in 102–3; sexual violence at universities 150–4
Ulukisla 38, 41
underenforcement, urban 81–2, 87
unemployment: and African-Americans 122; and crime 53, 61, 68–9; and ex-prisoners 123, 126, 129; natural rate of 52, 54, 62n1
United States: criminal justice in 81–2, 87; first responders in 135; homelessness in 121; homicide victims in 3, 80–2, 88; immigrants to 22–3, 25–7, 29; prison population 124–5; religion and crime in 36; sexual violence at universities 151; terrorism and counter-terrorism in 133–4; *see also* African-Americans; American way of life
unit root tests 52–7, **58**, 61, 62n3
universities, sexual violence in 5, 150–4
unknown offenders 82–4, 86–7

value consensus 70
violence: and masculinity 18; and mental health 10–11; and religiousness 34, 36–7, 41–3; by sex workers 65, 68, 77
violent crime 3, 11, 54, 58, 61, 116

wealth gaps, racialised 124–5
weapons, keeping for criminals 65, 68, 77
whiteness: definition of 19 n6; and mass shootings 8–11, 13–17
women: and hegemonic masculinity 9; as homicide victims 87–8; mass shootings of 7–8; Rodgers on 13–18
World Value Survey 35, 37

Yaba community 71–2
Yoruba ethnic group 71, 73